Aeroscouts in Vietnam
Combat Chronicles®

Written by Wayne Mutza

Squadron Signal®
Publications

Cover Art by Don Greer

Don Greer 2012

(Front Cover) In 1971, OH-6A S/N 68-17198 was assigned to B Troop, 1st Squadron, 9th Cavalry and named *Little Caesar.* One of the Aeroscout pilots that flew the Loach was Capt. Jon E. Swanson, Scout Platoon Leader, who was killed in a sister aircraft and, years later, awarded the Medal of Honor.

(Back Cover) *War Wagon* OH-6A S/N 68-17222 was one of two Loaches of D Troop, 3rd Squadron, 5th Cavalry shot down on 10 September 1969. Number 222 went down trying to rescue the pilot and observer of Loach number 68-17224. Under Covering fire of supporting helicopters, both crews were rescued by the Command & Control Huey, although two were wounded.

Don Greer 2012

About the Combat Chronicle Series

Volumes in the *Combat Chronicles* series bring you action-packed, eye-witness war stories, interviews, and first-hand reminiscences from the front lines. The wartime history of a particular type of aircraft, vehicle, or vessel is recounted systematically from the factory to the field of battle, through the reports and recollections of the former crewmen.

Hard cover ISBN 978-0-89747-675-1
Soft cover ISBN 978-0-89747-674-4

Proudly printed in the U.S.A.
Copyright 2012 Squadron/Signal Publications
1115 Crowley Drive, Carrollton, TX 75006-1312 U.S.A.

Military/Combat Photographs and Snapshots

If you have any photos of aircraft, armor, soldiers, or ships of any nation, particularly wartime snapshots, why not share them with us and help make Squadron/Signal's books all the more interesting and complete in the future? Any photograph sent to us will be copied and returned. Electronic images are preferred. The donor will be fully credited for any photos used. Please send them to:

Squadron/Signal Publications
1115 Crowley Drive
Carrollton, TX 75006-1312 U.S.A.
www.SquadronSignalPublications.com

(Title Page) A familiar sight in Vietnam's unfriendly skies was OH-6A "Loaches." This pair, called a "White Team," hailed from the 1st Aviation Brigade's Apache Troop, 7th Squadron, 1st Cavalry, known in Army parlance simply as A/7/1. The Loach in the foreground is S/N 66-14380. Apache Aeroscout crews comprised right-seat pilot, and next to him, his observer/gunner, or crew chief. (Bill Staffa)

Acknowledgments

My heartfelt thanks to Bill Pool, Paul Pelland, Jim Preston, John DePerro, Randy Bresnik, Tom Pearcy, Bob Hoffman, Curt Knapp, W.M. Sullivan, John B. Whitehead III, Sandee Swanson, Tom Genetti, Kent D. Converse, Rick Waite, Bill Hanegmon, Doug Smith, Don Langlois, Lou Rochat, Ed Sweeney, Joe Crockett, Danny Aiken, Ed Gallagher, John Lindgren, Henry Leigh Ballance, Rick Roll, Walker Jones, Robert Clark, Don Callison, Steve Nagle, Peter Bales, Kurt Schatz, Larry Brown, Jim Howard, Graham Stevens and Lad Vaughan.

Dedication

Dedicated to the Aeroscouts of Vietnam -- those who came home, and those who didn't.

Contents

Bill Staffa poses with a Hiller OH-23G "Raven" during his tour as Section Leader "Skeeter Leader" of B Company (Aeroscouts), 123rd Aviation Battalion in Vietnam. (Bill Staffa Collection)

Bill Staffa and his wife, Pat, who, along with Bill's mother, on 24 October 1967 pinned on his Army aviator wings at Flight School graduation. Staffa logged more than 2,400 flight hours during two tours in Vietnam in armed reconnaissance units. He logged over 700 flight hours flying Scouts during both tours. His awards include two Silver Stars, three Distinguished Flying Crosses and two Purple Hearts. During his 30-year career, he commanded a number of units. His favorite two jobs, he says, "were being an Aeroscout and commanding a light field artillery cannon battery."

Some 40 years past, my major contribution to the United States was played out in service as an Army helicopter pilot during the war in Vietnam.

I emphasize the term "helicopter pilot" instead of the more officious and impressive title "Army Aviator." I was, literally, a driver of helicopters, and was trained in much the same way the Army would train the driver of a dump truck. I never thought of myself as a "warrior" or as an "aviator," especially in the sense of the over-dramatic and self-aggrandizing manner in which those labels are currently bandied about by many who wore a uniform during the period. I was a soldier, and a Reserve Officer of the Army. In Vietnam I was afforded the chance to pay my dues to this great nation.

Of course, as a junior commissioned officer, I did things other than piloting a helicopter.

My greatest sense of accomplishment and fondest memories reside in my recollection of commanding air cavalry soldiers in combat. Commanding American soldiers in combat is, without argument, the greatest honor a serving officer can hope to achieve. It is a sacred trust of the rarest sort. Living up to that trust, for most of us, was a difficult path, strewn with the landmines of pressure and expectation, and ever enfiladed by second-guessing and doubt.

The world has turned many times since I left Vietnam and the memories have certainly dimmed, the edges softened by the passage of time. The memories that remain tend to be of the most pleasant sort, and highlight the best face of my comrades.

Heroes? Another word that gets thrown about a bit much these days, but these fellows surely exhibited some heroic qualities, especially loyalty to their comrades and a sense of duty while standing in fire.

There's a bit of hero in all of us, just as there's a bit of the cad, or the boor. Sometimes there is even the metallic-tasting sweat born of cowardice. We all have our moments.

Some are never given the opportunity to test their mettle; some are caught unaware, at their worst, when the moment arrives. Most, however, dig down and find whatever it takes when a spotlight of chance isolates them on a crowded battlefield or some other chaotic situation. The folks you will read of here attracted that spotlight like moths circling an open flame, and they performed in the harsh glare of its reality.

And how they performed!

The Aeroscouts, those swashbuckling kids in their tiny little helicopters, they were positively bristling with attitude, and little else. Protective armor, heavy weapons, the element of surprise; for the most part these were all advantages others enjoyed . . . at least until after contact was initiated. A concealed enemy knew they were coming and almost always got in the first shot. Only then were the Aeroscouts able to summon the terrible and violent firepower resident the modern-day cavalry unit.

The Scouts were a different kind of soldier. These were young men who could trace the heritage of their units and unique mission back through the history of the U.S. Cavalry and the U.S. Scouts. Their task was simply stated, and their march order was clear, if not slightly lacking in a clear declaration of the end game. "Go out and find the enemy. When you find him, grab him somewhere that gets his attention, and hold on. We'll think of something."

What was an Aeroscout? These were the young airmen who crewed the reconnaissance helicopters assigned to the Air Cavalry

Hughes Aircraft Company concept art shows the OH-6A "Cayuse" in spirited company with its namesake, the sturdy Cayuse horse bred by the Native American tribe of the same name. The official title fell into disuse in favor of the name "Loach," for LOH, which stood for Light Observation Helicopter. (Hughes)

Troops in Vietnam. There was one additional non-cavalry unit in Vietnam that was officially assigned the Aeroscout mission, and acted as an additional cavalry troop. That was a company designated, fittingly, The Aeroscout Company, assigned to an infantry division in I Corps.

How young were the soldiers in these stalwart bands? Well, crew chiefs and observers were usually in their teens and early twenties. Warrant Officer pilots in these units were also in the 19-to-23 range, and even the lieutenants and captains were as young as 20 and rarely exceeded 24 or 25. They did not comprise a large number at any given time, but their effect on combat operations was quite disproportionate to their actual numbers.

Tactics gave the appearance of being deceptively simple. The Scout helicopters dropped down to very low altitude, usually within 10 to 15 feet above the highest obstruction within a couple of yards of the rotor blades, and just started looking around. It was almost as if they intended stirring up trouble by their mere presence. In most cases, it was, and they did. The crews had their heads "outside the cockpit" looking for indicators of their quarry, and generally heard, or even smelled, fluctuations in operating parameters as opposed to reading the instruments. The entire crew was, literally, flying by the "seat of their pants."

Whenever someone took offense at the impertinence of the Scouts, and exposed their own position in some manner, the game was afoot. This brought in the gunship helicopters or an introduction to field artillery within a few seconds, sometimes resulting in an air assault by a large number of soldiers. At the very least, it yielded intelligence that pinpointed, temporarily at best, the locations of a clever and elusive enemy. I'd like to point out that the crew of a Scout helicopter wasn't exactly helpless. Actually, I'd venture to say, they were usually the most heavily armed two or three people you'd ever want to meet. The variety of weapons on board these aircraft and the ingenuity with which they were employed is the stuff of legend, and I'm sure you'll read more on that score in the tales that follow.

Of course, it was not really as simplistic as it appeared. The Scouts were fairly well informed as to where they were and what they were looking at or looking for. They were trained in the most exacting of crucibles. They learned on-the-job how to find the enemy.

Very little real training prepared these young soldiers. Many died or were injured before they ever had the opportunity to reach their potential. The ones that survived did things most people have not dreamed of doing, and probably wouldn't believe.

Contributors to this book will bear that out.

The tenth-built OH-6A, S/N 65-12925, exhibits the features that identify initial production models. They include blade cuffs, nose-mounted landing light, cockpit glass antenna, pilot door strengthening ribs and early M-27 minigun system. (U.S. Army)

There's a question that might have been posed by The Sundance Kid: "Who are those guys?" They, like the World War II bomber crews we've come to love in old war movies, came from everywhere. In my two full tours, my Scout Platoons were made up of princes and fools, careful plodders and impulsive gamblers, teachers, stock-brokers and stock clerks, dropouts, and college graduates, gas station attendants, and farm boys. Their flying and mechanical skills were superb. To a man, their combat skills were eventually honed to a sort of indescribable perfection, meaning that at some times it was hard to tell how they survived or killed the enemy, but they had. Some of them died looking the man that killed them right in the eye. The war, for these men, was as up-close-and-personal as any airman has ever experienced. They grew into the role, and in many of their battles, due to the nature of the conflict, they hardened beyond belief. The role of an Aeroscout was not one where you could expect quarter, and in many cases there was no way to grant quarter.

What these men had in common was that they wanted to fly and fight from the air.

Nobody was forced into a Scout platoon. They were all assigned to a cavalry troop in a squadron of one of the U.S. Cavalry regiments, all of which had regimental colors with a history of many years, some 100 or more. That's a lineage that required some living up to.

These were men who performed the mission of the cavalry:

reconnaissance, security, and economy of force.

As an individual, my ability to weave the drama and interest into a "war story" has always been lacking. I'm sure I was involved in some action that would or could cause you to shake your head, but I never have been able to tell a tale with the sort of élan and passion that holds interest and leaves an audience wanting for more.

Therefore, I leave it to my comrades. Some of the things you will read may seem a bit hard to believe, but I assure you . . . these things happened, to someone, just the way they are related in this book.

It is to the credit of Wayne Mutza that he has made the effort to get the recollections of these soldiers recorded before they have passed the stage or aged beyond caring. The Aeroscouts, as I think of them, operated within a very narrow window in time, maybe eight or nine years. Much like the fabled Pony Express, the Aeroscout star burned extraordinarily bright for a short period of time, only to consume itself in the shadows of tactical progress.

No quote better describes the OH-6A scout helicopter or the scout mission than that spoken by Captain John Paul Jones: "I wish to have no connection with any ship that does not sail fast, for I intend to go in harm's way."

Bill Staffa
Springfield, Virginia

Author Wayne Mutza served first as a Huey crew chief in Vietnam in 1971, and then worked with Loaches, ending his tour as a UH-1 maintenance/gunnery advisor to the Vietnamese Air Force at Biên Hòa Air Base. Prior to Vietnam, he served with the 82nd Airborne Division as a Paratrooper/Recondo. (Author's Collection)

Wayne Mutza poses for a portrait next to an aircraft in more peaceful times, having moved on indulging a variety of passions including family, college, and occupations such as the fire service, writing and teaching. As of this writing, Mutza has authored more than two dozen books and penned numerous articles for a variety of publications. (Debra Mutza)

January 1972, Lai Khe, South Vietnam – I'm grateful for the long walk from the operations shack to the flight line. Although encumbered with gear – flight helmet, body armor, weapons, and tool box – the long walk gives me time to run through a mental pre-mission checklist and shake any apprehension about the day ahead. Few novices make this walk, since Aeroscouts are on at least their second tour, have seen helicopter combat, or served as "grunts." They are the cutting edge of Army Aviation.

I begged my way into the Scout section of F Troop of the 4th Cavalry at Lai Khe, having been a Huey crew chief in an assault helicopter company during much of the previous year. The words emblazoned on F Troop's patch make the point: "Hunter Killer."

Nearing the flight line, dark oval shapes emerge through the fog as the sun burns away morning's gray veil. The shapes become more recognizable, Light Observation Helicopters, or "Loaches," sprouting spindly rotors – the hunters. Even more ominous are the larger, angular shapes topped by broad, drooping rotors – the killers. The rising sun does nothing for the Cobra gunship's olive drab paint, but it spotlights the sinister red and white shark's mouth leering on every "Snake." Fiendish eyes painted above the mouths watch my every move.

Satisfied that I'm mentally prepared for whatever this day brings,

my thoughts drift to a time not so long ago . . . *I can't wait for the bell to end this boring English class. Renee, sitting at the desk next to mine, sure has great legs . . . I wonder if she . . .* voices, a hoarse nervous laugh, metallic clatter, cursing, movement among the dark shapes . . . *Renee will have to wait. It's time to go to work. Gooood Mornin' Vietnam!*

The quickly rising sun splashes its fiery glow across the horizon, glaring, intensifying the damp odors of smoke and rotting jungle. I'm sweating already. My Nomex flight clothing itches my neck and shoulders. *It's fire retardant, Wayne; careful what you complain about.* I reach my Loach, drop my gear, and strip off my shirt, tossing it onto the thin stretch of sage green nylon that serves as a seat. One of these days I'll stop wearing this "WAR" medallion around my neck; it feels heavy, and its novelty has worn off. My pilot approaches, equally encumbered. His head bobs rhythmically with his lanky frame draped with everything he'll need for a day at work. I wonder why flyboy didn't stay in college.

"Good mornin', Mister B." I'm not showing disrespect; many Army pilots are warrant officers, who are officially addressed "Mister." Besides, we have flown together, having found common ground and gained mutual respect, and we are keenly aware that our lives are in each other's hands. Being uncertain of how the other will act when all hell breaks loose, we rely on what we know; I know how he operates and he knows my capabilities.

We're both 20 years old. Although he's built smaller than me, his athletic background allows me to push aside any worry about his ability to carry me if I become wounded, or to get my carcass out of "Indian Country." He told me the first time we flew together that he puts a lot of stock in the jump wings and the Recondo patch that I wear. And I'm humbled by his mention of a tale that shadows me; a tale about a balls-to-the-wall night mission that had a happy outcome for a SEAL team my Huey crew pulled out of the Rung Sat.

The bond is strong. It has to be. Unlike with Hueys, there are only two of us, in a much smaller aircraft, often meeting the enemy face-to-face, and in his own back yard to boot.

Clear, concise communication is vital, as is coordination and perception, to the extent of knowing each other's next move. Speed, instinct, reflexes, determination, skill, a cool head, sheer guts – all are key elements necessary to play this game – and survive. Although my youth, in its foolishly innocent way, inhibits the cold fear I should be feeling, I accept fear, but keep it in check, even harnessing its bizarre power to stimulate thinking. It helps to recall the image of a former platoon sergeant, combat seasoned, yet paralyzed with fear in the doorway of our Huey as we wallowed from terra firma in a hail of bullets during a combat assault. He was quietly transferred out, shamelessly, I'd hoped, but not likely. *Not me. No, you won't get that grip on me.*

Soon the shirtless flyboy is clambering about in the tiny cockpit, wrestling with a huge map. We exchange small talk about the dumbass who got loaded last night and then picked a fight with an Army Ranger. He won't be flying today, and probably not tomorrow either. The map loses and is pummeled down to a manageable size, showing today's hunting ground. Then shop talk – today's AO (area of operations), the mission, enemy situation, radio pushes (frequencies), quirks about the aircraft, and a review of our weapons and ammo.

The certainty of playing dodgeball with the enemy sends a ripple through my gut. I shake off a peculiar chill, which scatters the cowardly gremlins perched upon my shoulders.

The enemy comes in two basic varieties: the black pajama-clad peasant farmer turned guerilla fighter, and the khaki-uniformed, pith-helmeted NVA (North Vietnamese Army) soldier, who is better trained, better equipped, and usually more aggressive. And where there is one, there seem to be hordes of them.

The startling CLUNK of my hard-to-come-by, foot-long screwdriver being chucked into my toolbox signals that my preflight is nearly complete. I've scrutinized, wriggled, pulled, pushed, and thumped everything on my Loach,. I shout to Mister B, who's running a checklist of his own in the cockpit, "Bird's ready to fly, sir." Looking out the windshield, above his regulation "Joe Cool" aviator sunglasses perched on the tip of his bony nose, enthusiastically he answers, "Then let's get it on!" The psyche, the confidence building, continues. "Amen Bro," I drawl, "Let's do it." I make final checks of "Muttering Death," my modified infantry-style M60 machine gun; I learned from the old heads in my previous unit how to make it lighter and fire faster. Ammo belt – check; M-16 with banana clips taped together – check; .38 cal. revolver – check; official USMC survival knife – check; pen flares – check. And grenades. Lots of grenades; concussion, fragmentation (frag), tear gas (CS), white phosphorous (Willie Pete), smokes in a variety of pretty colors, and

a single thermate incendiary that can melt through an engine block. Nerve agent grenades, called CN, were sometimes available, but nobody likes to talk about those and their nasty debilitating effects. Although some pilots made it known that they did not want "those things" on their ship, they were easy enough to hide. We strap on body armor, and then the aircraft. Mister B scans the instruments, caressing the controls. He knows that this is my dark green '69 Ford Mustang Mach 1, and I'm just letting him use it. Staring out his open doorway, he says to no one, "Let's go fuck up Charlie's day."

I'll be sitting up front, in the copilot's seat, the left doorway my lofty portal. I love sitting up front, sharing the glorious view with the pilot, feeling more in control of the aircraft than in the back, where some units position the crew chief. Having been taught how to fly this thing makes me think even more about trying out for flight school when this is over. *Down boy, one war at a time.*

Already, the heat and humidity are oppressive. A rare, quick brush of wind chills my sweaty back, teasing, playfully swirling into a tiny dust devil as it cavorts in the heat waves shimmering atop the PSP. It'll feel good to get into the air, hang out the doorway, build up speed and let the violent slipstream claw at my clothes and make me gasp for air.

Our helmets are on and we're plugged into the radio net, listening to the pilots of other choppers on the pad checking in, makin' small talk. Among the chatter, our "radio ears" pick out the key words, "Crank 'em." I'm outside, yet connected by long cord to the commo system, to watch for fire at engine start. Mister B and I lock eyes, his thin eyebrows raised questioningly. I nod. Start the war. His sure hand throws switches. A spark, hidden deeply somewhere, gives life to the machine. Slight clicking noises, a hum, cold JP-4 courses through its arteries, and then a whine as the turbine spools up, a hollow WHOOSH when the burner can lights. The noise intensifies as the splinter shadows of the rotor blades pass through the cockpit. Like a roused hound, the damp machine shakes the dew from its cool metal skin. That's my cue to crawl into the left seat and get situated. Feeling the Loach come alive is always exhilarating. We both watch the instruments as the bird begins to vibrate, the rotors now a blurred disc overhead, the dizzying effect making me squint. The turbine gets its voice, becoming a whistling roar. We're awash in the heady, pungent odor of jet fuel exhaust. The pulses of man and machine are in equilibrium. Pure sex, man. Pure sex.

Final checks. Sleeves rolled down. Helmet visors down. Chin straps fastened. With a gloved hand I pat the worn, smooth metal side of my M60 hanging from a strap in my doorway. *Be good to me, Baby.* The bird is humming now, eager to fly. As engines are run up along the flight line, sending their power to thundering rotors, I imagine our 5,000 plus combined horsepower making the ground vibrate. Even through the thickly padded earphones inside my helmet, I hear the machines bellow, like penned bulls.

Twelve sets of eyes, now energized, dart across the flight line, and all lock on the loose flight jacket whipped into the vortex, mesmerizing us as it waltzes with the powerful rotor wash, dipping and then sailing abruptly upward, somehow evading the perilous kiss with a spinning rotor. "One-Three, you tryin' to kill us before we get into the AO?" someone quips. It humbly reminds us that we're fallible and that death can come just as easily from carelessness as from a Chicom bullet. The guilty crew chief does a wild dance of his own and the sailing wisp of sage is captured. He ignores the shaking fists and raised middle fingers as he trots back to his bird. I keep my hands in my lap. It could'a been me. *Christ, what's he* need a jacket for, anyway? He stuffs the jacket into a tool box, and clambers back aboard his Loach. I hope he makes it back for the ass-chewing that's sure to come. All is quiet as crews go through systems checks, and sink into a contemplative moment. Our half dozen choppers are turning and burning and ready to fly, and we're ready to go to work. The eerie silence in our helmet earphones is broken by a confident voice from the deep South: "Lai Khe, we're a flight of four snakes and two Loaches ready for departure to the south." The controller responds, "Roger Hotel Kilo, cleared for departure, winds seven knots from the west…good hunting."

My pilot eases us to a hover, nudging the nimble Loach clear of the short revetment walls. I see our teammates doing the same, like angry insects stirred by an intruder. In loose formation we float and bounce in a hover-taxi to the main strip. Black puffs periodically belch from stovepipe exhausts, signaling changes in throttle settings. The gaggle settles into a loose trail formation; we're all over weight limits and stagger as we build speed. Tails high, we lift. Being surrounded by so much glass magnifies the sensation of separating from terra firma. Leaving our red dust blanket behind, we cross the outer wire. There, I glimpse shirtless tankers perched atop their tracks, lost in the early morning sun, probably enjoying a smoke and a cup of Joe. Some wave and some just stare, their weary, upturned faces telegraphing their thoughts: *I wonder what those crazy bastards will get into today; how many of you jokers won't come back across the wire at day's end?* No Matter. A chill of excitement tingles the back of my neck as I watch the other choppers, noses down, pulling skyward. Man, what a rush!

The breeze feels good. I take in the warm metal smell of the chopper blended with the damp Asian air. I'm transfixed, staring ahead at the blurring green landscape sliding beneath our chin bubble. The curtains open wide, revealing a panoramic horizon as we take the stage. We ride the brilliant yellow rays stabbing through distant blotches of pewter. I gasp at the beauty. Smiling, I put the war on hold to bask in such magnificence, such serenity and peace; it is spiritual enough to make me feel, briefly, that I'm safe.

Snapping back to reality, I'm conscious of my pilot beside me. *I wonder if he heard my thoughts.* My mood lightens. I press the intercom button: "Make it go fast Mister B."

Glancing over, I see his head tilt backward with a broad grin. I look at him again. Damn, he's confident and comfortable on those controls. I wish I knew what he's thinking. I need reassurance because soon we'll be knocking on "Charlie's" door, and the little bastard will not be glad to see us.

We'll be snooping around the Cambodian border, and we'll blame inaccurate maps if we get caught slipping "across the fence" in violation of the façade named "Geneva." Our search will be for supplies the North Vietnamese have brought down "The Trail."

Hunting for the hard-core soldiers protecting those goods won't be necessary since they'll see us first, allowing them to lead in our dance of death. On a recent mission into the same AO, amazingly, we found pallets of supplies suspended under the heavy jungle canopy, high in the treetops. I admire the enemy's determination and ingenuity. But that's the limit of my admiration. We're here to lay waste his efforts to use that material against our troops. He has become bolder knowing that our numbers in Vietnam are decreasing.

For us the drawdown means less support and even more danger. *More danger. Can it get any more dangerous? Push the thought aside. Keep the fear in check. Continue the lie . . . Dear Mom and Dad . . .*

still waiting for an assignment and hoping to get some 'blade time.'

Cruising at 4,000 feet, out of range of most small arms fire, we exchange small talk on the intercom. Attached to an invisible 100-foot tether to our right, and slightly ahead, our partner Loach cruises along, bobbing gently on air currents. The two guys in the front seat look so exposed in the open doorway, surrounded by glass. What a ludicrous thought…we're a mirror image! Our poisonous snakes cruise farther out to our right, flashing rows of sunlit white teeth in blood-red mouths. Will those sharp points sink into flesh today? I toy with the knobs on my radio panel, happy to have tuned in a Johnny Rivers song on AFVN. While marveling at the lush green scenery being slowly reeled beneath our skids, I sing along . . . *so welcome back baby, to the poor side of t . . .* "Wake up troops," lead interrupts, "We're comin' up on the AO." Damn! Already?

Lead talks to us, "Comin' left." We, and our sister Loach, start an erratic descending turn into the blinding sun, through the "dead-man zone." It's time for "sloppy flying" to make us a harder target. Thankfully, my iron gut easily tolerates the erratic, often violent, maneuvers. The snakes stay on top. Tension mounts. Pucker factors increase. Undoing my safety belts I reach down into a battered wooden box and pull up the end of the heavy ammo belt, tilt down my M60, open the feed tray cover, and carefully clamp the belt in place. *Serious shit, war.* After halting conversation between the Loach pilots about how to best approach the target area, lead caps it with, "I'm in." Down on the deck, the nimble Loach melts into the thick green carpet. Despite its white-painted visibility marks, we watch intently to keep the little helicopter in view. All of our senses are piqued; anything that happens now will be instinctive and triggered by reflex.

All the players allow lead to dominate the radio now. He and his gunner are center stage, and their asses are hanging out farther than anyone's. They nose around under the canopy, reading sign, relying on their sense of what's not right, hopeful – and not – that khaki-uniformed or black pajama-clad bad guys will reveal themselves. Their heads move on swivels to prevent their eyes from tiring. The pilot tries to keep a light touch on the controls, and his gunner the same on his '60, its dull black barrel moving in synch with his head. *C'mon dink, make a mistake. Who has more balls than brains today? Show yourself. Frenchy won't mind having to clean his gun at day's end and neither will I.*

Tense. Coiled. Ready. Quiet. "There! I got movement," Frenchy blurts. "Come around left." A flush of heat passes through me. Needles prick my temples. I lean out farther, my eyes burning holes into the green mass below them, searching for what he sees. Doesn't seem right. Shouldn't I be leaning inward as we get the hell out of here? The gremlins are in a frenzy. Where's his red smoke? Goddammit Frenchy, pop that smoke! There it is, finally, his clipped message breaking the rush of static in our earphones: "Smoke's out."

After what seems like agonizing minutes, but are mere seconds, I jab a pointing finger into the slipstream. There! A swirling lick of smoke turns bright red as it escapes to the sunlight beyond the canopy. Atta boy French.

The whole world explodes. Thunk, thunk . . . you little bastards! We, both Loaches, are taking fire. The radios come alive. Lead's shooting, duking it out under the trees, refusing to stand that bird on its nose so the Snakes can roll in with heavy stuff. Red and green tracers arc in front of us . . . oooh Christmas, how pretty! They seem to move slowly. I know better. I first sense, and then spot, movement among the trees; tan against green;

North Vietnamese Army; an extra dose of caution is instantly factored in. I press my mike button, "They're running, 10 o'clock." He doesn't answer. He doesn't need to.

Instantly, the horizon tilts crazily as Mister B lets the bird slide down and sideways to line me up, his head cranked upward watching intently for lead to come out of his green rabbit hole. I snap on the intercom, "NVA." Again he doesn't answer but I know he heard it – I can see it in the creases around his mouth. As we close the distance I can pick out details of the khaki-clad figures; legs pumping, clothes flapping, equipment flying. A head turns. He slows and swings a long rifle around in my direction. I see his brown face. Defiant. You want me? It's high noon at the OK Corral and the gunfighters are staring down the barrels of their six-shooters, narrowed eyes locked in the highest of stakes.

Squeeze.

Bye Chuck. I win. I'm conscious of every bullet leaving my weapon, confident in my skill to put the slugs on their mark. Unspeakable power. My sight picture looms. Time slows. I'm barely conscious of the metallic bark of my '60, or the anxious radio calls of the Cobra pilots, who are worried about us and want to get into the fight. I have target fixation. My tracers – pink fingers of death –

The flight line shack of the 240th AHC at Camp Bearcat in 1971 candidly advertised the unit's skill at conducting warfare. Aircrew used the shack to store flight gear, tools and various ordnance. (Author)

burn, glow, dance across the landscape. I wonder what those feel like slicing through flesh. Conflicting doses of wonderment and remorse. *Listen to me, killer boy. When did I grow a fuckin' conscience?*

Light brown clouds of dirt magically appear around the hustlin' little bastards. I wonder if they're scared. Tip the gun up a fraction of an inch and the clouds turn pink; my stream of seven-point-six-two-millimeter copper-jacketed a murderous extension of my reach for their throats. Die, Mother Fucker!

Our job is done but now we have to get out of this hell. Our tail snaps up. I brace myself, pinned into my seat by the giant hand of G forces, staring straight down at the green blurry mass as we gain speed and claw for lift – the turbine screams and the rotor blades loudly slap air. I visualize the snakes already dipping their noses toward where we just were, thundering down an invisible roller coaster, building speed, and raining death on the tough little brown people. Bouncing through my helmet earphones are tinny voices a million miles away: 'Bout time lead shares . . . I got nails . . . comin' hot . . . takin' fire, takin' fire! . . . . Jeesuzz. . . break left One-Four, break left!

Pulse racing and ears ringing, I'm locked into a dizzying state that blends euphoria, adrenaline rush, and relief, which will not quickly dissipate. Slowly my senses stagger back into balance.

On the way out of Dodge, we pull alongside lead. *Shit! Frenchy's doubled over. Never mind. He's just adjusting the ammo belt at his feet.* I glance at my pilot. Jesus, am I sweating like that? Soaked flight suits are fair trade for no gaping holes in our soft flesh.

We face each other – big grins beneath dark visors of bulbous helmets, like two insane giant bugs. Lots of radio chatter now, or I'm becoming more aware of it. And I hear the muffled explosions of rockets spit from the Cobras, and the echoic rip of their miniguns.

We hang around to see if we need to go back in. We don't . . . at least not for a while.

Mister B gets his voice back: "Lead saw so much shit in there . . . Tac Air is inbound." I'm mum. We'll go in later to report on the damage, blood trails, bunkers, and equipment, and maybe even take fire from survivors. There are always survivors. Cruising back to base, we rant like teenagers on the intercom. And livin' is good.

As Lai Khe grows larger in the windshield, we line up for a traditional victory flyby.

Wedging a red smoke grenade in the doorway with my boot, I pull the pin. Frenchy in the lead Loach to our right front does the same. Seeing the red smoke blossom from his doorway, I let the spoon fly. A small pop and we're announcing our only means of determining victory. In the red smoke I see a brown face. Fuck tradition. *Had you been quicker on the trigger, how would you have announced my death?*

Our GI banter back at base will not only be laced with animated replays of today's battle, but talk of our prowess, and what we'll do when we get back to "The World;" as though all we'll have to do is simply discard our memories of the past year on the tarmac before boarding our "Freedom Bird;" as though whatever we did, and whatever we've become, would have no effect on the rest of our lives. How wrong we would be. Closure is a myth. Images diminish only with time, and not all of them go away.

Those watching us buzz the field as we trail the telltale red smoke will want to hear the gory details. I won't share much. Seldom do. Some died today, and we lived . . . today. I'll worry about tomorrow when I take that long walk in the morning. *Now, I wonder if Renee . . . ?*

Introduction

Tradition dies hard, as evidenced by the mounted officer in cavalry dress at the ceremony converting the 11th Air Assault Division to the famed 1st Cavalry Division (Airmobile). The ceremony, held at Fort Benning, Georgia in July 1965, heralded the transition of the trial Airmobile concept to operational status and subsequent deployment to Vietnam. (Ed Lemp)

During the late 1950s and early 1960s, when U.S. Army planners sought to increase the Army's helicopter force, they could not have imagined that their efforts would lead to the creation of the most unique brand of aviator in the history of aerial warfare. Nor could they have realized that the helicopter they selected to replace aging types would become as legendary as those who took it into battle. Never in the history of the Army would a team of aviators place such implicit trust in their skills, their aircraft, and each other.

The Army's development of tactical doctrine using helicopters gave rise to the airmobile concept, which was based largely on air cavalry units. Such units were descendants of the U.S. Cavalry, which had operated as light, horse-mounted infantry. When the cavalry was mated with armor in 1951, the change was met with fierce resistance by ironclad soldiers with ironclad mindsets, who were loyal to the horse and embraced the "why change" adage. Army pioneers, who later proposed that helicopters give the infantry mobility, met the same level of resistance. Air cavalry troopers were, in essence, horse soldiers, and helicopters were their steed. True to their proud and colorful heritage, the Air Cavalry not only employed tactics used by their forefathers of the Indian wars, they embraced their culture.

That they breathed life into the original U.S. Cavalry was evident by the Stetsons and scarves they wore, and even sabers and riding gloves. Units and call signs bore names such as "Darkhorse,"

"Lighthorse," "Apache," "Scalphunter," "War Wagon," "Comanche," and "Silver Spur." Colorful names and emblems of crossed gold sabers and caricatures of American Indians adorned their thin skins and frail glass noses.

These symbols were incorporated into patches and metal insignia, both official and unofficial, and proudly worn on Aeroscouts' uniforms.

Scout aircraft reflected the U.S. Army tradition of naming its aircraft after Native American tribes and woodland animals: "Raven," "Sioux," "Cayuse," and "Kiowa." All were classified as light observation helicopters. While not considered the Army's primary observation helicopter, the Korean War vintage Hiller OH-23G Raven, the last model of the "Killer Hiller," served admirably in the Scout role in Vietnam. It shared the role of armed scout with Bell's more popular OH-13, easily recognizable by its lattice tail boom and fishbowl canopy. The hit TV series *M*A*S*H* gave the Sioux immortality in popular culture. The H-13S model Sioux, along with the Raven, shouldered the load until the most eminent of Scout helicopters arrived: the Hughes OH-6A Cayuse, better known as the "Loach," a nickname derived from its abbreviation LOH, for Light Observation Helicopter.

Weighing only 1,100 pounds empty, the nimble and highly responsive Loach challenged Army pilots who were accustomed to

An early model OH-6A (S/N 65-12935) in November 1967 is prepared at California's Sharpe Depot for shipment to the OH-6A NETT in Vietnam. Number 935 later served the 7th Squadron, 17th Cavalry, which was one of the first Loach units in country. At least half of the OH-6As of the initial production run are known to have been shipped to the war zone in Southeast Asia. The remainder of the aircraft were used for training in the United States and for filling out both U.S. and global assignments. That actual situation was contrary to popular belief among those who felt the war unnecessarily drained U.S. Army aviation assets on a global scale. The transfer of considerable numbers of OH-23s and OH-13s from global bases to the war zone proved that aircraft inventories by type were solvent. (Ken Loveless)

The full-up position of this Loach's collective control lever indicates that the pilot "pulled in" max pitch before a hard landing to slow descent. Such landings caused the main rotor blades to over-flex downward, often severing the tail boom. The crew often was spared serious injury in hard landings and crashes by a high-energy absorbing box structure beneath the floor decks. Huey pilots, who had become accustomed to landing tail low, quickly learned that the OH-6A had to be landed relatively level. This Loach, S/N 65-12960, was repaired and later served the 1st Cavalry Division's 1st Brigade Scout unit called "Flying Circus" in Vietnam. Loaches damaged in Vietnam underwent repair at various levels of maintenance facilities, dependent upon the extent of their damage. Those that appeared beyond repair were shipped to Corpus Christi Army Depot, Texas, to undergo miraculous recovery, which contributed to the confusion over OH-6A production totals. (U.S. Army)

A pair of Loaches, S/N 67-16289 and 67-16262, believed to be of the 5th Aviation Detachment at Vũng Tàu, are parked in high-wall revetments. Seldom did Scout aircraft benefit from such superior protection familiar to Air Force bases. Pilot and cabin doors, which were easily removable, were optional, depending largely upon unit policy, mission, and pilot preference. These two aircraft are wearing the standard color scheme for OH-6As: overall Olive Drab and International Orange tail surfaces. Only a unit emblem is worn on the aft fuselage. Despite the relative safety and security afforded at major bases, tenant units did not give in to complacency since all were susceptible to various methods of attack. (U.S. Army)

A pair of Hunter-Killer "Pink Teams" of D Troop, 3rd Squadron, 5th Cavalry of the 9th Infantry Division head for trouble. The lead Loach is S/N 67-16579, which went on to serve the 17th Cavalry in Vietnam. (Sgt. Mike Galvin, D Troop, 3/5th Cav)

flying heavier and slower choppers. The sturdy truss framework built into its egg-shaped fuselage gave it incredible crash survivability, prompting the adage, "If you have to crash, do it in a Loach." Often, during a crash, it shed parts and rolled like a ball while protecting its occupants, who emerged relatively unscathed after the wild ride. The Loach was the lightest, simplest, fastest, safest helicopter that could be built around a 250-horsepower turbine engine.

Last among the four Scout helicopter types was Bell's OH-58A Kiowa, which appeared later in the war. Since the Kiowa was born of political turmoil and proved underpowered in Vietnam, Aeroscouts did not accept that this was the OH-6A Loach's replacement.

Many, in fact, felt that they had been sold out by politicians, and labeled the OH-58 the 5.8, explaining that it was less than a 6.

Since the Loach and its piston-powered stable-mates were pressed into the worsening situation in Vietnam, there was no time to develop the air cavalry concept. Man and machine were born in battle, with air cavalry troopers writing the book, chapter by bloody chapter. Although a number of units soldiered with the Raven, Sioux, and Kiowa helicopters in Vietnam, the Cayuse, or Loach, was king. More than 170 units flew the Loach in Vietnam, many of which were air cavalry, whose parent units were the 1st Cavalry Division, the 101st Airborne Division, the 1st Aviation Brigade, and the 11th Armored Cavalry Regiment. Prominent among cavalry organizations was the 1st Cavalry Division (Airmobile), which began life in 1921 as horse-mounted cavalry. Known as "The First Team," the division was pulled out of Korea to replace the 11th Air Assault Division at Fort Benning, Georgia, on 1 July 1965. The

11th AAD was the result of studies done by the Army's Tactical Mobility Requirements Board formed in 1962. The success of air mobility forced the enemy to increase his effort, and so it went until the protracted chain of events expanded Army aviation to the extent the conflict was called "The Helicopter War."

Air cavalry units typically comprised an aeroscout platoon, an aeroweapons platoon flying Huey or Cobra gunships, a lift platoon flying "Slick" Hueys, and an aerorifle platoon – called "ARPS" or "Blues" – made up of quick-reaction infantry soldiers.

As hard lessons were learned, tactics changed, and they varied according to geography, enemy situation, unit policy, and sometimes, pilot preference. Air cavalry flight elements were identified by the colors red and white, borrowed from guidons borne by horse soldiers of the original cavalry. Flight elements that comprised scout helicopters were called White teams, while those formed with gunships were called Red teams. Any combination of the two was called Pink teams. Employing the latter became the favored basic tactic, which had one scout helicopter prowling down low, while a high bird watched, provided navigation, and relayed radio messages. The number and types of aircraft used to form Pink teams varied from one unit to another. When contact was made, the low bird instantly marked the target with red smoke, traded blows with the enemy, and then went "tail high" clearing the area, allowing gunships to break from their motherly orbit and roll in hot.

The teamwork displayed by pilots was superb. Their lives depended upon nothing less.

The same mutual reliance existed in the scout aircraft between

SP4 Jack Harah is at the controls of this OH-23G "Raven" of 3rd Brigade "Aloha Airlines," which supported both the 25th and 4th Infantry Divisions in Vietnam. Ravens, along with OH-13 Sioux, shouldered the Scout load pending the arrival of the OH-6A. The observer/crew chief's infantry style M60A hangs from a bungee cord, while smoke and thermate grenades are carried outside the cockpit. (via Dale Wischkaemper and Aloha Airlines)

pilot and observer, and crew chief. Early scout helicopters – the OH-23 Raven and OH-13 Sioux – flew with an observer/gunner and pilot. Use of a minigun system on a Loach restricted the crew to two. Often, the minigun was removed in favor of a third crewman, who had more latitude with an M60 machine gun, and whose eyes and ears were more valued. Scouts went looking for the enemy, which often meant not only flying along the tops of trees, but among, and even under, them. When they found the enemy, the armed red smoke grenade in the gunner's hand was tossed, and the pilot radioed, "Taking fire, smoke's out," and the fight was on. Despite their firepower and aggressive nature, Aeroscouts were not mini-gunships, but would stay in the fight as long as they could match or exceed the enemy's firepower. Beyond that, heavier firepower was summoned.

Unlike the crews of most combat aircraft, Scout crews saw the enemy up close. The Aeroscouts paid a heavy price for engaging in close-quarter battle. Losses of crewmen and aircraft were extremely high. The numbers say it all. Sobering data from the Office of the Secretary of Defense shows that 4,867 helicopters were lost by the Army in Southeast Asia from January 1962 to March 1973. The majority were Hueys, while the most losses of a single type, proportionately, were OH-6As – 842 of a total of 1,419 produced were lost during the war, along with 28 of its successor, the OH-58. Of the early types of scout helicopter, more than 90 OH-23Gs and nearly 150 OH-13Ss were lost.

Like their ancestral scouts, crewmen became expert at reading sign; spotting and interpreting signs of the enemy. How many are there? What is their direction of travel? How heavy? How long ago? Is the water in that footprint clear or muddy? If it's clear, it's old; but how old? Is anything out of place? They noticed how villagers and peasant farmers acted, even developing a sense of a situation. They came to know their cunning and elusive enemy – some of the old hands professed an ability to smell the enemy. Flying low and slow in the enemy's backyard, trolling for fire, required junkyard dog tenacity, exceptional skill, and it took unimaginable courage. I recall how during stateside helicopter training a combat-seasoned instructor tried to describe the mettle of Aeroscouts – he could only shake his head and cup his hands widely and say, "They've got big brass balls." The gunslingers had to think fast, and get wise fast, or, before long, died.

Typical among the Aeroscout force was A Troop, 3rd Squadron, 17th Cavalry "Silver Spurs" of the 1st Aviation Brigade. The Scout platoon adopted the motto, "I have flown among the trees and seen the face of the enemy." More than a motto, it was how those boys put in a day's work. The troop's commanding officer, Major John D. Jenks, made clear his allegiance to his scouts when he had this to say in an interview for the brigade's *Hawk* magazine in 1969:

"What is a Scout? I'll tell you what I demand from my scouts and get. I demand that my scouts have the eyes of Kit Carson. They can tell the difference between a 30-minute old footprint and a day-old footprint. They can track a man, via his footprints, through the nippa palm until they find him and kill him. My scouts find caches, hidden, that the ground troops have missed even though they walked over the same ground. My scouts can draw out a VC. These scout ships are fighting vehicles . . . this entire troop is organized around its scouts. The scouts are the troop. The guns are here only to kill what the scouts find, and to cover the scouts. The lift is here to put infantry on the ground in those cases where it's needed to develop the situation and to protect the scout should he go down.

"The entire troop is here as a scout vehicle to find, fix, and to destroy, if possible, and to recommend the insertion of higher elements. My scouts are my reason for existence. My boys take risks and that's what it takes to do an outstanding job."

So, enter the world of the Aeroscouts and be amazed, impressed, or just downright entertained. These boys let it all hang out. They pulled no punches. They were a fierce, closely-knit lot of which the enemy grew wary. Theirs was a sense of dedication that knew no boundaries. Aeroscouts didn't preach the brotherhood of man; they lived it.

Here, in their own words, they freeze the hands of time, telling what they did during that brief but impacting segment of their lives. Don't merely read their words; listen to them.

Feel the adrenaline rush of battle, the anguish of loss, which is our loss. Let the heady smell of jet fuel and gunpowder, and the stench of rotting jungle, burned flesh, and blood permeate your nostrils. Hear the beat of the rotors, the anxious radio calls, the metallic hammering of guns, and the chilling echo of Taps.

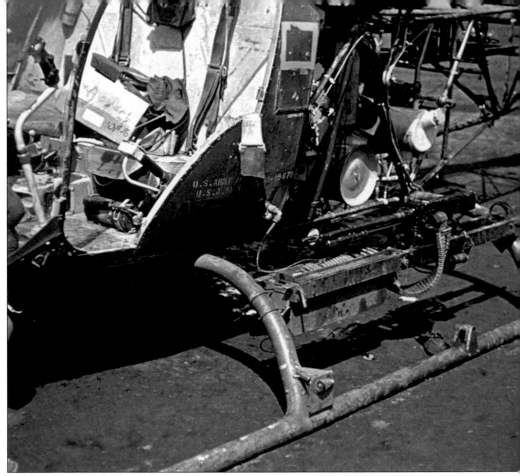

While Bell's OH-13S, along with Hiller's OH-23G, bore the brunt of the Scout role in Vietnam, it was given standoff capability with skid-mounted M60C machine guns. The rudimentary M2 system was one of countless weapon systems tested by the Army for arming its helicopters. This weary Sioux, S/N 63-13678, wears the yellow square identifying B Troop, 1st Squadron, 9th Cavalry, 1st Cavalry Division. (U.S. Army)

Aeroscout pilot Hugh Mills shows the position for flying the OH-6A; both feet are on tail rotor pedals for directional control, right hand on the cyclic for turning the aircraft by tilting the main rotor disc, and left hand on the collective lever, which controlled pitch of the rotor blades and subsequent lift. This lever incorporated the throttle. The Loach is S/N 66-7927 of D Troop. 1st Squadron, 4th Cav of the 1st Infantry Division at Phú Lợi in 1969. (Hugh Mills Collection)

A "White Team," which identified a pair of OH-6As of A Troop, 7th Cavalry, 1st Squadron, heads for its mission area during the Cambodian Incursion in late 1970. Each Loach is manned by a pilot in the right seat and an observer to his left, a common crew arrangement when the minigun was mounted. The OH-6A's capabilities and the skill of Aeroscout crews were fully exploited during the heightened activity of the invasion. Aeroscout crews who had seen plenty of action in Vietnam were impressed with the intensity and level of combat "across the fence" not only in Cambodia but in Laos where America waged "The Secret War." (Bill Staffa)

Installation of the famed 7.62mm minigun on the OH-6A gave Aeroscouts tremendous punch when engaging in close encounters with the enemy. The pilot could control elevation of the weapon but traverse was accomplished only through movement of the aircraft. The complete system, which was designated the M-27 system, was mounted to the aircraft's left side only. The tapered fairing that protected the M134 gun unit was easily removable for gun maintenance. Atop the fairing was a cooling intake scoop, while spent cartridge and link chutes projected below the unit. Mounting of the minigun necessitated not only a shift in tactics, but in crew arrangement. Since the system's weight ruled out a gunner, the crew chief flew as gunner up front next to the pilot. Use of the minigun normally was dictated by unit policy. There were only a few cases in which unit leaders preferred that their Scout crews stick to observation only and not engage. (Robert N. Steinbrunn)

Loaches, like many aircraft, were shipped to Vietnam aboard ships. Alternatively, eight OH-6As could be carried aboard most Air Force cargo transport aircraft. This OH-6A, S/N 66-17798, is being readied for departure from USS *Tripoli* in 1968. After assignment to Headquarters Co., 1st Bde., 1st Cavalry Div., better known as the "Flying Circus," the Loach would be painted with high-visibility markings and unit identifier symbols. Blade cuffs seen on Number 798 would be done away with. The overall Olive Drab finish seen on this Loach quickly succumbed to the elements, not to mention to battle damage and the scarcity of replacement parts in some areas. Unit symbols and personal markings would also dramatically change the drab finish of the Loach. (Frank Vanatta)

In his position as observer aboard an OH-13S of the 1st Cavalry Division's 1st Squadron, 9th Cavalry in 1967, Bill Pool cradles a modified M60A machine gun. (Bill Pool Collection)

Sioux Scouts
by William H. Pool

Prior to the arrival of the OH-6A, the Bell OH-13S, along with Hiller's OH-23G, observation helicopters pioneered the scout mission in Vietnam. Although underpowered in the hot, humid climate, in the hands of Scout pilots, they performed admirably. In December 1967, Bill Pool and three of his fellow Aeroscouts of the 1st Brigade of the 1st Cavalry Division, in their OH-13s, was pressed into the Battle of Tam Quan, near Dai Dong in the Central Highlands Province of Binh Dinh. The battle had begun when scout choppers of the division's 1st Squadron, 9th Cavalry had spotted an antenna protruding from a hut. Infantrymen of the 1st of the 9th were inserted and met stiff resistance from a well dug-in enemy. From his OH-13, Pool threw several grenades onto bunkers and repeatedly strafed the enemy with his machine gun, being credited with five enemy dead. Pool recounts the action:

It began with what was surely an end to some. I remember well the last flight on 5 December 1967. It was almost completely dark as we headed into LZ English in our OH-13.

We were watching a tremendous ground-to-air battle off to our left. Tracers from miniguns were striking the ground in Tam Quan, while tracers from the village were going into the air. Knowing full well that people were dying, the color of battle in the night darkness still was beautiful.

We changed our radio channel until we found their push and listened. A voice filled with terror was screaming on the radio for help. A major was admonishing him over the airways to be calm, or to put someone on the radio who could talk. The terrified soldier replied that there was no one else. The commander asked him where the sergeant or lieutenant was. The troop replied, "They are all dead."

I never found out what happened to that soldier, never saw his face, never knew his name. I never knew if our guys got to him in time, nor do I know if his name is now on The Wall. I feel that few of us who were ever in his position lived to tell the story. I hope, somehow, that he did.

Back at LZ English, we prepared for the morning. Two of our scout ships would go to Tam Quan to assist our infantry, and we knew the battle would be significant. The night would soon be quiet. Tam Quan had been surrounded and we waited.

On the morning of 6 December, four of us began our day with excitement. My pilot, Lt. William Hinson, warmed up our OH-13. WO1 Arthur Essenpreis warmed and checked his. His gunner, Harold Chappell, checked his M60, ammo, and grenades. I did the same. I was somewhat nervous that morning and usually was before a big battle.

At 9:30, our troops, of the 1st Battalion, 8th Cavalry, and 1st Squadron, 9th Cavalry, began the assault of Tam Quan. There was movement in the village but all I could hear was the sound of our helicopter. We four, in our two OH-13s, flew in front of the troops at treetop level. We looked for bunkers, trenches, or any other danger to report back to our guys on the ground.

I saw an NVA soldier running in one of the deep trenches and shot him. It was the first shot fired that morning and thus began The Battle of Tam Quan. After a pause following my shots, it was as though the whole village exploded at once. An armored track

Despite the high-density altitude that plagued helicopters operating in Vietnam's tropical climate, Bell's OH-13S, along with the OH-23G "Raven," pioneered the Aeroscout role. This 1st Cavalry Division Sioux was based at the division's An Khê base in the Central Highlands in 1967. (Robert N. Steinbrunn)

vehicle was hit, probably with a 75mm recoilless rifle, and it seemed to suddenly stop and slide backwards. A giant tree was cut down by gunfire and fell across the backs of two crawling soldiers. It became so intense that we were forced to pull out of the village. Our Phantoms moved in with 750-pound bombs and we watched as craters began to appear and grass hootches disappeared.

The Phantoms moved away and our troops went back in. Again the village erupted. A soldier went down off to my right when an NVA popped out of a hole and shot him.

Three or four Americans were lying flat on their stomachs within a few feet of the hole, trying to keep from being shot. I opened fire on the hole, with my rounds hitting a few feet from our guys' heads. After firing about a hundred rounds into the hole, one of the soldiers raised his hand for me to stop. He then rolled a grenade into the opening. He looked inside and gave me the thumbs up, and we moved on. It had not been pleasant shooting that close to our guys, but I'm glad that I was there to do it. I wonder if some of those guys still remember the incident. None of us would ever know each others' names, but we were soldiers together.

The NVA had built a perfect fortress in Tam Quan. The whole village was a squared system of trenches. As our guys moved forward and took an area, the NVA would run down the trenches or come out of holes in the sides of trenches and suddenly be behind them. We were losing too many troops and it was also very hot for us.

A radio operator on the ground asked Lt. Hinson if one of our choppers had a hole in the gas tank. Since we didn't know which one of us did, we flew a short distance away and set down. It was easy to see who had the leak. Essenpreis had a bullet hole through the left side of his gas tank. I got out, wrapped my chamois around a stick and went over and jammed it through the hole. He flew back to the LZ and got another OH-13.

Hinson and I went back to the battle. Ground troops asked us for assistance as they were pinned down by an automatic weapon in a trench. We could not see the NVA but knew a trench ran under a hedgeline where the gunfire was coming from. The troops directed us to where they felt we were directly over the soldier firing at them. I dropped a couple of grenades out the door and the firing stopped. The radio operator called and said we got the NVA.

The battle again was so intense that our soldiers could not remain in the village. We moved out and again bombed the village and used CS gas. My gas mask would not seal properly and tears were running from my eyes so badly that I couldn't see. A bomb hit so close to us that it blew us straight up in the air. We moved a little farther away.

Heavy equipment was moved in and we got ready to move into the village again. This time, as our troops advanced, the heavy equipment covered the trenches. By then our day was almost over. My M60 was worn out and I was experiencing a runaway machine gun. It would not fire very fast and would not stop firing when I took my finger off the trigger. We headed back to the LZ for fuel and a new M60. However, we had finally broken the NVA's back in Tam Quan, and shortly were relieved by two other helicopter crews. Our battle was over.

Essenpreis and Chappell stayed at the battle a little longer as they had been shot down and had to remain with the ground troops. We didn't know how many NVA we were fighting, but later learned that it was at least two battalions. Soon after we got back to the LZ, we were met by General John J. Tolson, commander of the 1st Cavalry. He presented the four of us Distinguished Flying Crosses. The award is something I am proud today to tell people I have. We were a team, the four of us, and at that time and place, we made a difference.

On a landing zone near the Cambodian border, a Việt Cộng suspect awaits transportation in an OH-13S of the 1st Cavalry Division in 1966. (Ed Lemp)

Scary Night
by Paul Pelland

Before technology changed the face of helicopter combat operations, night missions were avoided, only to be flown of dire necessity. Pelland flew more than his share, earning the nickname, "Night Hawk Papa." With stark candor, he summarizes flying at night in an OH-13.

We HATED flying at night. Just for the hell of it, I checked my flight records and see that I flew 1,005 combat assault hours in Vietnam; of those, 382 were at night. Just like in flight school, I heard all kinds of strange noises, felt weird vibrations, and experienced every kind of vertigo-induced feeling while flying at night. Come to think of it, until I got to Vietnam, I never flew solo, or without another pilot, at night. It was, simply put, scary.

Keep in mind that we didn't have any attitude instruments – except an altimeter, airspeed indicator, and mag compass – you really had to be on your toes keeping the right side up when flying

on those pitch dark, no-horizon nights. They all seemed that way.

I really hated three things: flying out to a hole in the jungle and hovering down without using my landing light, avoiding trees, aiming stakes, antennas, or some grunt's tent; flying at night in thunderstorms and heavy rain; and trying to land at night during the dry season when the Vietnamese burned the stubble from their rice fields.

We hated it!

You never got used to it. You never felt safe. One nice thing was that "Charles" had a very hard time trying to shoot at an H-13 when we didn't show any lights. We learned to dim down or turn off the instrument lights so Charlie didn't have anything to shoot at. The other trick was to always try to keep low power settings so as to reduce the amount of flame that came out of the exhaust stacks. No hot-dogging at low level.

Nope, I'd take flying in daylight and getting shot at all the time over flying at night. Too scary.

First Impressions
by Jim Preston

Having worked with vintage 1950s Sikorsky CH-37 "Mojave" helicopters, Preston made the dramatic transition to the Loach, laying claim to having served as crew chief of the first OH-6A issued to the Army. He later worked for Hughes aircraft crash damage overhaul. Jim describes his introduction to the Loach.

My first view of the OH-6A was at the Paris Air Show in 1965 and this aircraft won 23 world records. I crewed the first OH-6A that was issued to the Army. In 1966, we were forming the 3rd Squadron, 17th Air Cav at Fort Knox. I was Headquarters Troop Technical Inspector. I can't remember them all, but when we transitioned new pilots into the Loach, I flew along as crew chief. The most impressive thing about it was flying at 120 knots about 12 feet off the runway and chopping power, then giving it aft cyclic to go up to 2,000 feet, then auto-rotating down to a soft landing. We didn't chop off any tail booms, but other units were getting good at it.

We took that first ship to Fort Bragg for a firepower demonstration with the minigun mounted; my pilot was CW3 Arnold F. Baily. We had to spend one night at Chattanooga and I took the minigun to the local cop station to secure it for the night. I had to give the cops a lesson on how a minigun worked so they called all the other cops off patrol for me to give them the class. They had never seen anything like that. The firepower demonstration at Bragg went off without a hitch. People were really impressed with the Loach and what it could do. The 3rd of the 17th was the first unit in Vietnam with the Loach, and right behind us was the 7th of the 17th. They went up north and we stayed around Tay Ninh and Di An.

Jim Preston came in on the ground floor of the OH-6A's introduction to the Army, having served as crew chief of the Army's first operational Loach at Ft. Knox, Kentucky. Here, Jim poses with a UH-1B gunship. (Sherry Preston Collection)

Seldom were more than two or three OH-6As seen in one operating location. Here, massed at Ban Mê Thuột in the Central Highlands in March 1968, are five Loaches of A/7/17. Also visible are UH-1C gunships of the squadron's gun platoon. (Robert N. Steinbrunn)

Drawing from his vast experience with Army aviation, John DePerro went on to indulge his passion for Army aviation history. (John DePerro Collection)

If You Have to Crash . . .
by John DePerro

Like any new aircraft introduced to the Army, the OH-6A was subjected to endless testing to work out the bugs and maximize its operational performance. Having been involved with the tests, John DePerro provides insight to early deployment of the Loach, and the beginning of its reputation for crash survivability. Despite the safety features built into the Loach, the aircraft often succumbed to intense enemy fire, and they rarely made it to their required 300-hour maintenance inspection.

I graduated from flight school with class 67-14 in September 1967 at Ft. Rucker in Alabama. As a Transportation Corps officer, I was assigned to the 507th Transportation Company at Ft. Knox, Kentucky. The 507th was supporting the 1/7 Cav, the 3/7 Cav and the 7/17 Cav, which were training to deploy to Vietnam with OH-6A helicopters. In July 1968 I was assigned to the 15th Transportation Battalion of the 1st Air Cavalry Division. I was told I was the first OH-6A qualified maintenance officer of the division to arrive in Vietnam. I managed the direct support for all OH-6As, and some OH-13s and AH-1Gs, assigned to B/1/9 Cav and later A/1/9 Cav. I inspected all damage, often spoke with pilots about damage, evaluated all work needed, supervised mechanics, and test flew all repaired aircraft. The Hughes Aircraft tech representative lived with me.

The data show that the UH-1 Huey fleet required about seven maintenance hours for every flying hour. The number of man-hours to flying hours required by the OH-6A was a whole lot less.

In the 1960s and 1970s, Army publication AR-470-2 listed in detail the Army experience of the man-hours required by most all Army aircraft, but the OH-6A was not listed.

When I arrived in the 1st Cav in July 1968, I was assigned as the section leader of the 20-man light-helicopter section in Company B, 15th Transportation Battalion at Red Beach, just north of Da Nang. I was promoted to Captain, and became the platoon leader of the 125-man shop platoon. Of course I was not replaced in the light helicopters section. Since I was going to continue test flying the aircraft they repaired, I elected to continue as the section leader part-time. By Christmas the section was providing direct support to 28 to 35 OH-6As, and was down to three or four mechanics and myself on a part-time basis.

One of the reasons the ship was so easy to maintain was the 300-hour periodic inspection (PE). While the UH-1 sections were busy every day with 100-hour periodic inspections, the OH-6A rarely saw one. In fact, the first periodic inspection of an OH-6A did not occur until February 1969. At that point we discovered we did not know how to do a periodic inspection, as none of us had ever seen a ship make it to periodic. We had to pull out the manual and read up on them. As I recall the inspection took several days, only because we first had to figure out how to do it.

In early 1969 I was asked to help an accident investigation board. At Tay Ninh a unit maintenance officer had crashed an OH-6A. After a pilot and a mechanic had done some engine adjustments, the aircraft needed to be flown, so the pilot shut down, allowing the mechanic to safety-wire the engine doors shut. The door clamps were a poor design, and frequently would not hold the doors shut.

Capt. John DePerro, Maintenance Officer of the 1st Cavalry Division's B Company, 15th Transportation Battalion, in 1968 signs off the log book of an OH-6A. The log book entry is one of the most serious actions taken by an aircraft maintenance officer. His signature, which often converts non-flyable status to flyable, is a personal pledge to operational pilots that the aircraft is airworthy. The log book dictates operation of the aircraft and entries are taken seriously. (John DePerro Collection)

WO1 William Jones with OH-6A S/N 67-16080, both of D troop (Air), 1st Squadron, 4th Cavalry, nicknamed "Quarter Cav," at Lai Khê in 1969. Jones later was severely burned in a Loach crash, which killed his observer. The unit's "Darkhorse" emblem was worn on the OH-6A's engine access door. (Hugh Mills)

The mechanic used a heavy wire that was often used for this kind of job. When the pilot asked the mechanic to check the barrier filter, the mechanic placed the roll of wire on the control linkage and reached in to clean debris out of the filter. The mechanic and pilot climbed in, and they cranked and took off.

About 15 minutes into the flight, at 120 knots and at treetop level, the roll of safety wire blew back into the linkage. The spool was caught between the rotating and non-rotating swash plates, pulling off the spool and jamming between the two plates. In an instant the two plates were fused, ripping the three control linkages from the cyclic and collective.

The only controls working were the pedals and throttle. The pilot later said the aircraft flew straight and level for 15 to 30 seconds until a skid caught a tree branch. The aircraft flipped and rolled end over end seven times. The rotor system, skids, and tail boom broke off, and the egg-shaped body rolled. Photos showed that the aircraft made a gouge in the ground each time it came around. The aircraft stopped upside down. The pilot and mechanic unhooked their seat belts and fell to the ground, dusted themselves off, and walked into the compound. No fire. No injuries. No kidding.

Another incident in early 1969 illustrates the OH-6A's resistance to fire. A 1/9 Cavalry OH-6A was flown into the maintenance company. Its entire sheet metal bottom had burned away. The pilot said he was in a dive when a .50 caliber incendiary round hit his aircraft. The round pierced the aircraft where the left front strut attached to the fuselage.

It entered the fuel bladder and exited in the floor of the rear compartment, passed through the back of the compartment, passed just under the engine, into an exhaust stack, out the engine door, and through the horizontal fin. As the round pierced the fuel cell, burning fuel spilled out, burning away the underside of the aircraft. The pilot continued the dive and the self-sealing tank sealed, and the wind and lack of fuel put out the fire. Pilots in nearby aircraft said it looked like a World War II film of a fighter going down in flames.

When the OH-6A landed at my location, the underside was still smoking, but the fire was out. Because the underside was one large piece of sheet metal with hundreds of rivets, we shipped the aircraft to the depot for repair.

The observer of the covering Loach took this photo of its sister ship after it crashed in jungle in July 1970. Infantry "Blues" were quickly inserted to protect the crew and prepare the aircraft for sling recovery by large helicopter. Evident in this image is a severed tail boom, likely struck by over-flexing main rotor blades on impact. The OH-6A's main rotors are absent, indicating the crew may have removed them in preparation for sling recovery by helicopter. Often, dense jungle such as this was said to "swallow" downed aircraft, ruling out discovery. Various types of helicopter were used to recover downed OH-6As, including, periodically, those of other services. Given the sheer number of Bell Hueys in Vietnam and their cargo hook capacity, often they performed the recovery. (David Dzwigalski)

With a 4,000-pound cargo hook capacity, a Huey could easily recover a downed OH-6A. Usually when helicopters were recovered, it was desirable to have their main rotor blades secured since they could "windmill," which not only hampered the recovery, but was dangerous. With the Loach, main rotor blades were easily removed, being light enough for two to remove. Both Huey and Loach arriving at Đức Phổ in 1970 belonged to 7th Squadron, 1st Cavalry Regiment, 164th Aviation Group of the 1st Aviation Brigade, based at Vĩnh Long. Recoveries of downed aircraft often were dicey affairs with some evolving into major battles. It was not unusual for such operations to encompass days of fighting during which assets from numerous sources came into play to secure hotly contested areas requiring air combat sorties. At times, the operation concluded with the downed aircraft destroyed by Allied aircraft. (Robert Brackenhoff)

It is likely that the armor seat panel of this OH-6A of C Troop/16th Cavalry in 1971 spared the observer serious injury. Personal torso body armor, called "Chicken Plate," along with seat armor panels comprised the bulk of protection from small arms fire. Visible on this Loach's raised collective control levers are the throttles incorporated into the controls. The Loach possessed awesome firepower, but additional armor and protective systems would only compromise the aircraft's performance to the extent that evasive maneuvering would be ruled out. It often depended upon the pilot's skill, and sometimes on pure luck, whether the aircraft and its crew could escape from intense ground fire. (James Sheetz)

BATTERY LOCATED INSIDE

Visible in this view are more than 70 Bell OH-13S Sioux awaiting transportation to a Stateside dock for shipment to Vietnam. In the background are more than 40 Boeing Vertol CH-47A "Chinooks" also bound for Vietnam. (U.S. Army)

Short Flight
by Randy Bresnik

Some of the first Loaches to arrive in Vietnam were shipped by aircraft carriers that docked at the port cities of Qui Nhon and Vung Tau. The first Loach of C Troop, 7th Squadron, 17th Cavalry left the carrier on 8 November 1967. It would log the least flight time for an OH-6A in Vietnam. The overloaded Loach may have succumbed to the high-density altitude that pilots would find vexing in Vietnam's oppressive heat and humidity.

Bresnik picks up the story.

I was on deck with Lt. Col. Johnson and Capt. Bob Young at the time. Col. Johnson really loved the OH-6A. We watched as Capt. Skip Holcomb from C Troop lifted off in number 65-12990 to the south, and started his right 180 turn back toward Qui Nhon.

Even though there was a major storm to the north of us, it was very calm around us that day. What little wind there was came from the south. As he continued his turn, however, he was in a steady, slow descent, and impacted on the absolutely smooth water abeam the carrier's island, about 100 yards west of us. We were shocked by what had happened, because there was never any change in his flight path. Just as we thought we had lost him, he miraculously popped to the surface. The ship's motor launch was already making way and recovered him in short order. We all breathed a sigh of relief. Skip was okay, but I think he broke his arm during the accident.

This artillery base in South Vietnam in 1967 was typical of the remote, crowded sites that Scout helicopters supported. Obvious is the degree of difficulty of landing even a small Scout helicopter, not to mention the closeness of jungle that could hide enemy. (Rodger D. Fetters)

Several Loaches flown by Darkhorse pilot Rod Willis were shot down including three in one day during the same battle. Evident is the OH-6A's design that protected the crew in armor seats, despite extensive damage to the cockpit. (Hugh Mills)

Rough Start
by Tom Pearcy

Just eight days after losing the Loach to the South China Sea, C Troop, 7th Squadron, 17th Cav would record the first OH-6A combat loss. The troop had been flying utility missions, called "ash and trash," and on 16 November began flying combat missions.

Tom Pearcy provides the details, which illustrate that, in the heat of action, not everything goes according to plan.

Fred Nicely, call sign "Blue Ghost One-Seven," was the scout with the first team. When I arrived on station, he briefed me that they had seen nothing while they were screening ahead of the 2nd Squadron, 1st Armored Cav pushing toward a village reported to be an enemy base camp. The terrain was rolling hills covered by thick, tall trees. Periodically there were clearings that held several rice paddies, and a small village with 10 to 12 hootches. There was a reinforced trail or road through the area leading from village to village, and the armored folks followed this road.

I was "Blue Ghost One-Eight," flying scout in an OH-6A for the second team, and Greg Ross and "Wild Bill" Owens were flying a C-model Huey gunship. I made my initial pass over the open terrain toward the village at a fairly high rate of speed because that is what we had been told to do to save our butts. As I neared the village I noticed what I'd never seen before, but had heard about; spider holes. There were four or five of them running along a path leading to the village. I pointed them out to my gunner, Ed Gay, and turned the ship around for a second look. As we came back around, they threw open the covers, came up out of the holes and started shooting at us with AK-47s and bolt-action rifles. Of course,

my voice went up several octaves and I screamed "Receiving fire!" My gunner was so excited that he threw the smoke out without pulling the pin. Greg asked, "Where's the fire coming from?" I said, "Back there! Back there!" not giving him very good directions at all. I made a sort of U turn at the end of the open area and started back toward the village so we could mark it. I did a little zig-zagging this time and we took some hits. Again my voice went up at least six octaves and out went the smoke. But, for some reason, it may have been a dud, or it sank in water before it could completely ignite.

There was just a little wisp of smoke from the grenade.

So I turned around just before the village and started back again. This time the smoke did get out in the correct area. I flew with my head turned, looking left and adjusting Greg's rockets; "A little more to the left." "Add 50 to that pair." And my gunner, Ed, said, "Mister Pearcy . . . uh . . . tree!" I looked up and saw the biggest tree I've ever seen almost dead in my flight path! So I hit all controls left and missed the tree by what seemed like inches, but was most likely a couple of yards. This, however, was part of the VC plan, as they had a claymore mine or something hanging in the tree.

It exploded and sheared off our tail rotor drive shaft. Just as the ship was starting to yaw, the engine made this terrible winding sound and quit. That corrected the yaw and I went straight another 50 or so meters before running out of most controls. The words of my civilian flight instructor at Wolters came to me: "There will always be a place to put the aircraft down in an emergency." I remember thinking, "Yeah, if you're so right you so-and-so, why am I going right into these trees?"

I did a zero-airspeed autorotation and pulled everything I had at treetop level. We fell about 30 or 40 feet through the trees and

Gunship support of Aeroscouts initially took the form of UH-1B and C model Hueys. Armed with 38 rockets, this UH-1C is easily identified by its broad shark-mouth as belonging to the 174th Assault Helicopter Company. (Robert Brackenhoff)

then went inverted, with the rotor blades sort of chopping a hole as we came down. When we came to a stop, I turned off the electrical system and started working with my safety harness. Unfortunately, the seat belt part had been installed in the aircraft backwards and I was hanging upside down in it, worrying that the ship would catch fire and explode. The maintenance people later said that I almost had the webbing in two. My fingers sure were bloody. I remember that. The cyclic had banged up my shin a little; my observer had

Despite the many safety features built into the OH-6A, some suffered post-crash fires, such as this example in March 1969. Crashed Loaches were a common site at bases throughout Vietnam. (Larry Wagoner)

wet his pants, and my gunner had been scratched by the M60 as it banged around, so we really weren't hurt at all.

We took just a few smokes and our weapons. I remembered from the E & E (Escape and Evasion) training at Rucker to move away from the aircraft about 50 yards so if the VC came and shot up the aircraft, we wouldn't be hurt. We let off the smokes and were sad to see they were all green, which didn't do much under the tall trees in the area. Greg did see the smoke. A few shots were fired in our direction and we were definitely scared.

A little later I heard an APC (Armored Personnel Carrier) moving up the trail about 50 to 75 meters away. The foliage was so thick that we couldn't see each other. I waited until it got just about even with us and fired a clip from an M-16 into the air. The APC kept going toward the village, turned around and came back. When they were again close to us, I fired in the air again. They kept going down the trail, turned around and started back. I fired the third time and was surprised to hear their .50 caliber open up all around us. I was just trying to signal them but they were scaring the hell out of us. They later told us they were taking fire. The thought that it was my fire never occurred to me. Greg saw what was happening and screamed at them to cease fire, which they did.

We heard them let the rear ramp down, so we knew we'd be seeing infantry pretty soon.

The thought then occurred to me, "How am I going to make contact with these guys?" If I stood up and yelled, "Hi guy, I'm over here," they'd blow me away. We could see and hear them walking toward us. Finally, when the point man was about 20 yards away, I said, "Psst! We're over here." We made radio contact after a while, were extracted, and the Loach was retrieved.

On rare occasion, OH-6As in Vietnam were used for missions other than scouting. This Loach of D/1/4 "Quarter Cav" at Lai Khê in 1969 mounted loudspeakers for psyops (psychological operations) missions. (Hugh Mills)

Accolades
by Bob Hoffman

Bob Hoffman was an infantry officer when he went to flight school in 1965. His first assignment was to the 118th Assault Helicopter Company at Bien Hoa, Vietnam, where he flew "Slicks" for six months, and then "Guns" for six months. He then went through fixed-wing transition and became a tactics instructor at Fort Rucker. After OH-6A transition and instructor training, he was assigned commander of the U.S. Army Republic of Vietnam (USARV) OH-6A Team, called the "Superbees." Hoffman used the call sign "Superbee 6." In Army aviation, the number "6" denoted the commander's slot. His position provided Hoffman the opportunity to gain a unique, broad perspective of Loach operations in Vietnam. Here, he provides insight to his involvement with the Loach.

The USARV OH-6A Team was the in-country transition unit and it produced instructors.

Our combat role was limited, and the real story of the Loach is the one written in blood by some of the bravest Army aviators ever to buckle on a helmet; the Cav Scouts. As chief standards pilot for the Loach in Vietnam during 1969 and 1970, I was very much acquainted with the technical details of the aircraft, and went throughout the country to re-qualify instructor pilots (IPs) and standardization instructor pilots (SIPs). The team consisted of one major, two warrant officers, a team sergeant/maintenance supervisor, and four crew chiefs. The team had been based at Vung Tau since its inception, and the USARV AH-1G Cobra training team, the "Snakes," was also located there.

What struck me about the units I visited was the consistently high quality of the aviators.

Bear in mind that these guys were combat pilots first and instructors second. The average Loach pilot seldom had an opportunity to do autorotations to the ground, or tail rotor failure training. They were very good at high-gross-weight and high-density altitude work, and I learned a lot from them. These were such good people, from the crew chiefs on the birds to the unit commanders. I've never met better people or better aviators.

A typical day for our instructors began at 07:00 and ended about 17:30. Maintenance was done mostly at night, and we were lucky in that there was a depot level maintenance unit on the airfield at Vung Tau. We did not do any tactical training. That was left up to the units. They were better at it than we would have been anyway. We had done some minigun training, but stopped after we realized that most of the units did not use them.

We concentrated heavily on autorotations and forced landings. All were to the ground. It was not unusual for a student to do 15 to 20 autos a day during the course. I kept track of how many autorotations or forced landings I had either given or done and stopped counting at 12,000. I figured I did about 20,000 before I left. We had one tail rotor strike and that was with a student flying.

We were actually very busy, and although we did not have the threat of combat over us, we were under a lot of stress. I flew about 1,000 hours during this 18-month tour. Couple this with the 1,300 I flew with the first tour and I have about 2,300 hours in country. I consider this opportunity to have been one of the greatest honors I could have been given.

To have served with these men, to have watched them strap that Loach on every day and go forth to war made me very, very proud of the Cav pilots and crews that flew the Loach. We will, hopefully, never see that kind of war again, but we saw the legacy of those men in Desert Storm. They were, quite simply, the best.

Medical evacuation (Medevac), or "Dustoff," was high risk regardless the type of aircraft attempting to rescue wounded in a combat zone. Aeroscouts often were involved in Dustoffs, often rescuing their own, especially in hotly contested areas. Typically, any helicopter could function in the Dustoff role if it was available. Even AH-1G Cobra gunships are known to have rescued trapped and wounded comrades. The Huey, however, proved itself the initial platform for medical evacuation, forming dedicated Dustoff units. This UH-1H hovers over treacherous terrain while soldiers of the 173rd Airborne Brigade "The Herd" load casualties following a battle on Hill 875 in November 1967. Throughout the war, any aircraft that happened to be in the vicinity of ground troops who were requesting Dustoff could respond to assist, and, when possible, pick up wounded. (U.S. Army)

Curt Knapp poses with OH-6A S/N 66-17795 of A/2/17 at 2nd Brigade, 101st Airborne Division at LZ Sally in 1968. Unlike most Loaches in Vietnam, Number 795 had a long life, known to have served with three combat units in Vietnam. After A/2/17, it went to the 11th Armored Cavalry Regiment where it was named *WARGASM,* and then F Troop, 4th Cavalry where it bore the legend *Kill or be killed.* This Loach, not having the minigun system, relied upon a crew chief/gunner and gunner, where each was positioned often was a matter of pilot preference or unit policy. Aircraft flown by the famed 101st Airborne Division proudly displayed their "Screaming Eagle" emblem on the aircraft. It was worn on the OH-6A's tail boom, while other designators, such as geometric symbols, adorned engine panels. (Curt Knapp Collection)

None the worse for wear, pilot Curt Knapp and aircraft were reunited 30 years after having served as a team in Vietnam. In post-war service, Number 795 served the Tennessee Army National Guard, after which it was acquired by the Homestead, Florida, Police Department. The aircraft later went on to join the Army warbird inventory of the Army Aviation Historical Foundation based in Georgia. The OH-6A is seen here painted in the scheme it wore in Vietnam. Only a small number of OH-6As are known to have flown the warbird circuit. More of the aircraft have served out their usefulness in the hands of law enforcement agencies across the country, while a large number ended up with the U.S. Border Patrol. (Curt Knapp Collection)

A Loach comes home the hard way. Downed aircraft recovery was a vital operation during the war. This OH-6A of Headquarters Company of the 101st Airborne Division's 3rd Brigade is sling loaded to Camp Eagle in August 1969. Squatting on the skid of the 5th Transportation Company UH-1H Huey, the crew chief guides the load to a safe landing. (Joe Gwizdak)

Stupid Rules
by Curt Knapp

Regardless the assignment and type of flying done by scout helicopter pilots in Vietnam, it was never lost on the prudent ones that forces existed of which they had to be constantly aware. Smart pilots knew that Pandora's box could be opened at any time, and it didn't have to happen under combat conditions. Often, it was then that foundational rules that went largely unheeded by helicopter drivers came into play. Those rules would have special meaning for scout pilot Curt Knapp. After graduating from his Warrant Officer Class in 1967, Knapp was among the first three pilots assigned to the Headquarters Aviation Section of the 101st Airborne Division's 1st Brigade. The group arrived in Vietnam and set up shop at Phu Bai just in time for Tet, named that year for both the Vietnamese New Year celebration and for the enemy's historic major offensive.

The Aviation Section flew the Hiller OH-23G Raven until July 1968; two months earlier, the unit had received its first OH-6A Loach, serial number 66-17795. Knapp explains how confronting the unknown caused him to develop a special bond with "Ol' 795" and renew his respect for rules.

The Hughes OH-6A was my favorite type of helicopter. I flew only about five different Loaches in Vietnam, but, by far, the one in which I got the most hours and the one closest to my heart was number 66-17795. Anyone associated with the Cayuse can appreciate the difference in the transition from the OH-23 to the OH-6A. It was like going from your father's Chevrolet to a brand new Porsche. I got only about 200 hours in Ol' 795, but that helicopter and I got into and out of a couple of close ones.

My entire tour was with the Aviation Section, 2nd Brigade Headquarters, 101st Airborne Division. Although it wasn't as exciting an assignment as, say, a scout pilot in the Cav, it provided me with a variety of missions and a ring-side seat safely above the battles of 1968, including Tet.

As an observation helicopter pilot for the 2nd Brigade, there were only a few times when I was in any great danger. This was one of them.

Almost every day when the brigade commander wasn't using the helicopter, he would "loan me out" to one of his battalion commanders. I would work all day in the field, performing various missions such as aerial observation, ash and trash, and even flush and shoot sorties.

On 3 June 1968, I'd been out all day with one of our infantry battalions southeast of Hue.

The CO had held me past my release time. It was getting dark and it was starting to rain.

And . . . I broke one of those numerous rules they taught us back in flight school by succumbing to "get-home-itis." Shoot, my base at LZ Sally was just a ten-minute or so trip from Camp Eagle. I'll just go IFR (I Follow Roads) up Highway 1 and maybe be home for dinner.

You see, in my secondary capacity as Aviation Section Maintenance Officer, I had driven the route between Sally and Eagle many times, picking up parts at the 801st Maintenance Battalion. So, with my trusty landing light leading the way, I got suckered into making it from Camp Eagle to Highway 1, over the southern suburbs of Hue, across the Perfume River, and then over the old city itself. The wind, rain, and pucker factor had been increasing proportionally along the way. But when I got hit with a wall of wind and water and lost sight of the ground, I knew I was in deep trouble. I was really scared 'cause the forces at play here were a lot bigger than I was.

I also realized it was about time to start following some of those stupid rules. So of course, the first one I thought of was a funny one; an instructor at Fort Wolters told us, "When your engine quits at night, turn on your landing light and follow it down. If you don't like what you see, turn off the landing light!" Well, I couldn't see jack diddley squat, and I didn't like it. So I turned off my landing light and grabbed some pitch.

Now, the OH-6A has some gyroscopic instruments but it's technically not an IFR approved aircraft. So the second rule I observed probably saved me: when entering inadvertent IFR conditions, perform a 180-degree turn. Of course, with that little Loach getting tossed around like it was, I swung through a 180 a couple of times before I trusted my gauges indicating "wings sorta level." And sure enough, a while later I popped out of the jaws of death into a fairly big hole in the clouds surrounding those three tall radio towers just off Highway 1, across from Camp Eagle. Whew!

I loosened my vise-like grip on the controls, circled the towers, and submitted to my third rule of overconfident aviators: admit you screwed up and call for assistance. Phu Bai GCA was, of course, out of service that night just when I needed it. But after trying several empty FM channels I finally got a hold of some guy on the ground at Eagle who volunteered to go out in the rain and guide me in. Although those towers are lighted and on flat terrain, the 101st Division base camp is blacked out and sits on hilly ground.

Several minutes later, my attention was diverted from my rapidly dwindling fuel supply by a call from my friendly savior informing me that he can't find the keys to unlock the chained steering wheel of the jeep he needs to illuminate my landing spot. Hmmm. What a Catch 22. You chain up the jeep so that it'll be there when you need it. And now that you need it, it's chained up!

Well, he ended up popping a couple of hand flares, and I shot an immediate approach to his immobile headlights, then hovered over to an acceptable landing spot. I spent the night on an empty cot in a tent full of drunken cavalry with guitars. And let me tell ya – I was never so happy to be loudly singing those corny songs like "She'll be Comin' Round the Mountain" as I was that night.

In July of 1998, my buddy, Bill Savedge, was at the 101st reunion at Fort Campbell, Kentucky, when he spied a Loach on display. Well, by golly, after 30 years it was Ol' 795. Sure, it had been through a few changes – haven't we all? But there it was and lookin' great.

Bill Savedge took delivery of this Loach in Vietnam 30 years earlier. As a young WO1 with the 2nd Brigade, he flew serial number 66-17795 during his entire Vietnam tour.

After serving as the brigade's command and control ship, the aircraft was assigned to the division's A Troop, 2nd Squadron, 17th Cavalry. After the war, its assignments included the Army National Guards of Connecticut, Virginia, and Tennessee.

During most of the 1990s it was a crime-fighter with the Homestead, Florida, Police Department, and then went into private ownership before being acquired by the Army Aviation Heritage Foundation. In the course of the AAHF's restoration, 10 patched bullet holes were found at various spots throughout the Loach. Few stories are told of both Aeroscout pilot and aircraft that made it home.

Among the numerous markings on this Loach of C Troop, 16th Cavalry was "Le Disiple Du Paix," which is French for "The Disciple of Peace." Unusual on serial number 68-17238 is the 1st Aviation Brigade's 17th Cavalry emblem, an inverted triangle. (Author's Collection)

Wearing Army nomex flight clothing and "chicken plate" armor, USAF OV-10A Bronco pilot Ray H. Janes of the 19th Tactical Air Support Squadron prepares for a flight in a Loach of A Troop, 1st Squadron, 9th Cavalry in March 1969. As the Forward Air Controller (FAC) assigned to 1/9, Janes' flights with the unit offered a perspective important to his close support role. Troop A's triangle identifier is incorporated into its crossed sabers emblem. (Ray H. Janes Collection)

Up Close with Aeroscouts
by W. M. Sullivan

Sullivan's nickname was "Gaucho" in 1968 and 1969 when he was a scout pilot with Aviation Unit of Headquarters Company, 1st Brigade, 1st Cavalry Division (Airmobile). The unit was best known as "Flying Circus." In a way that could only be described by someone who was there, Gaucho takes us through a day in the life of a scout.

It has been said that Scouts had "brass ones the size of basketballs, and brains the size of peas." Looking back, here's my argument for agreement with the former, and perhaps some disagreement with the latter.

It started with a quiet nudge from the night ops clerk, around an hour before sunrise. "Now? It seems like I just went to sleep." We were supposed to get up and pre-flight the bird with a flashlight, but I usually took the time to stop by the mess hall and round up a cup of coffee and some of the best fresh-baked doughnuts ever made. The night cook worked as a cement mixer before he got drafted. Pre-flights always went better with coffee and a doughnut.

Weather permitting, we were off with what's known as "Morning Nautical Twilight," which means the ground is still dark, but it's light enough to have a reasonable chance of avoiding solid objects. In the I Corps, we'd work the coast first, and let more light reach into the mountain valleys before we headed up that way. Turning the corner over a low finger into the next draw usually meant a surprise for both sides if someone was there.

Better to do that with some daylight in there. At Tay Ninh, west of Saigon, the fog usually precluded an early start. We'd have to wait until a large tinge of blue could be made out above, and at

least two telephone poles an eighth of a mile away could be made out horizontally. We'd make an instrument takeoff through to the fog tops, usually around 1,500 feet above ground level. The fog bank ended just east of Tay Ninh and south of Nui Ba Dinh (Black Virgin Mountain). So we could drop down to our usual tree-top level and scout the northern and eastern portions, catching up on the western end as the fog burned off. These were known as "First Light" missions. The object was to catch Charlie still moving on his trek the night before, spot the smoke from a late cooking fire, or just look around and spot anything different from a previous look. Every once in a great while, Charlie would resolve the detection problem by shooting at us.

With luck, we'd either be back at home plate, or finish up at a battalion firebase in time for breakfast. Landing at a battalion base meant that we usually had a mission coming up with that battalion. It was a good time to get both breakfast and in-brief completed.

Missions could be an insertion, an extraction, close-in reconnaissance, or a snatch (prisoner) mission. As always, a unit in contact with the enemy overrode scheduled missions. Contact could be anything from a single sniper to an entire regiment. The best information the Scouts could get would be over the radio while they were inbound.

Normally, that only described the grunt's eye view, which, of necessity, was limited to a rather hasty look before both sides went to ground. It would be up to the Scouts to sort it all out before the heavier stuff arrived. That was either Cobras, artillery, or Air Force, or all three, so the other requirement was to locate all the grunts and get them reasonably clear before the Scouts marked targets. Easier said than done. Firefights had a way of getting everyone intermingled

The killer element of the popular Hunter-Killer team in Vietnam was Bell's AH-1G Cobra, the first pure helicopter gunship. Heavily armed, Cobras circled protectively over Aeroscouts as they played their deadly low-level game. Mac McMillan, who flew Cobras with 2/20th ARA "Blue Max" in Vietnam says of his photo of *Tango-One* S/N 68-17046: "This is one of our aircraft on a scramble. She is in the normal takeoff attitude. It's probably over max gross weight. It can't hold a three-foot hover, has just bounced off the ramp and is starting to climb. The red circle tells you it is from C Battery. The Cobra is carrying four 19-shot rocket pods, which was our normal configuration. The outboard pod has 10-pound rockets and the inboard has seventeen-pounders. You can tell by the nose of the warheads sticking out the front of the pod. Our A Battery worked Tây Ninh and B battery worked Sông Bé. After the 1st Cav reduced to just 3rd Brigade, C Battery covered the whole area."

Aeroscout crewmen and "Blues" show off spoils of war taken after a fierce battle with the North Vietnamese Army in August 1969. Besides the SKS rifle and sidearm displayed by this ARP, anti-aircraft weapons were also captured. The Aeroscout pilot in the background carries a .45-caliber sub-machine gun. (Hugh Mills)

as both sides attempted to maneuver against each other.

Most of the sweat came from separating the two sides, and then accounting for everyone before we could bring in the heavy stuff. The first hour was invariably the least organized and the most hairy.

The machine guns and grenades of the Scouts could provide support as close as one could see; sometimes, within 10 meters of the friendlies. However, the Scout's payload was too small for long-duration support. Beyond the Scouts, gunships, either the 229th's "Tiger Birds" or the 2/20th's "Blue Max" Aerial Rocket Artillery, were the best choice for early stages of separation and cover fire. The gunships usually needed only one mark. After that, they were in close enough to make their own adjustments.

Once separation was achieved, the Scouts could call in artillery and the Air Force, which meant a slower pace. The Air Force required a run over the target to drop a white phosphorus grenade, which provided a white smoke cloud against a green backdrop for the fast moving jets. Naturally, Charlie didn't take too kindly to being marked. The routine was to drop the WP grenade when the Scouts started taking fire. Either the jets would take their cue from the smoke, or a light, fixed-wing Forward Air Controller (FAC) would launch follow-up smoke rockets to continuously mark the targets. Artillery could be called by an Arty liaison officer (LNO) on the ground or in a Command and Control (C & C) ship, or by the Scouts themselves.

Once the dust settled – literally as well as figuratively – the Scouts would scoot back in ahead of the grunts to determine what was left. At the same time, Scouts could provide better Bomb Damage Assessments (BDAs) than the higher-flying FAC could provide. If the heavy ordnance missed, the Scouts would be the first to know. Time to drop back and do it again.

Scheduled insertions were usually quieter, at least from the Scout's point of view.

Depending on the commander, the Scouts could be called upon to give the LZ a quick look just before the artillery prep went in, or

An OH-13S Scout helicopter of B Troop, 1st Squadron, 9th Cavalry, 1st Cavalry Division in its revetment in Vietnam's Central Highlands. A former member of the unit, Melvin Edwards, said they built sandbag revetments after a mortar attack knocked out two-thirds of their ships. (Melvin Edwards)

they would be held back until the first squads were on the ground. Once grunts were on the ground, the Scout's mission was to cover the gaps in the perimeter being formed as the rest of the company was brought in.

A Huey could only carry from four to six grunts in that heat, and four or fewer in the mountains. A 1st Cavalry lift was from four to six birds, no more. Fewer than four was too slow. More than six was found to be too big a target, both *en route* and in the LZ. Units that flew with massive "daisy chains" of lift birds tended to experience heavy losses.

Once the grunt company was in, the Scouts expanded their search, and started working the intended route of the company in more detail. Simply following the intended route of march would be too obvious.

Extractions were the reverse of insertions. The Scouts provided perimeter security, then cleared the LZ to ensure no one had been left behind.

Finally, there was the "Last-Light" recon of the entire Area of Operations (AO), if no contact was occurring. This was similar to the First-Light recon, only now the object was to catch someone moving, or cooking, too early. Particularly in the hill country, Last-Light tours could also mean dropping in on a company commander and giving him a quick aerial view of his positions. Sometimes, we'd get involved in a late evening extraction of wounded, or a firefight would drag into darkness. There were a few memorable nights of working under artillery-dropped flares, but those nights, thankfully, were few and far between. Murphy's Law of night operations dictates that even flares from three separate batteries will simultaneously go "streamer" at least once. Always.

Then there are the post-flight inspections, the debriefs, the schedule for the morning, a little hot chow, a beer or two, or three, and then maybe some sleep. Next was the quiet voice of the Charge

of Quarters (CQ) in pre-dawn darkness. "Again? Now? I just got to sleep."

What else was required? The ability to read a trail – was that grass always bent that way?

How many people made these footprints? How long ago? Are they deep? Was their maker loaded down? Or was he light, as on patrol? Which way do bicycle tracks point? That trailside bunker – old or new? What makes it so? If it is old, then why is some of the dirt at the entrance a different color? Why would there be a bamboo rack above the waterline in a side stream? It certainly is not a fish trap. The classic: Why are tree branches tied together with red tape? Best guess is that the tier is color blind; there was a supply complex underneath. Tracking footprints in sandy terrain was a one-time shot. Get it right the first time; the helicopter's rotor wash eliminates any second read. Does it sound like a job for country boys? We had a few city-bred souls who did it well, too.

In a firefight, one needed the iron discipline not to shoot until one was sure friendlies were not in the line of fire. If that meant flying over the area and taking fire, then so be it.

Toss in the ability to fly among the treetops without hitting them – too often, the gunner's ability to hit anything, at any angle, with the first three rounds or so, the ability to read a map on the fly, and read it three kilometers ahead of the aircraft, and you have a Scout.

No brains? Some. Common sense? Well, the ability to make sense out of fluid situations with mere bits of information, at least. But, not enough foresight to realize that the risks were cumulative.

As to why we kept doing it, I don't know to this day. The notion of getting into someone's back yard and raising hell was some of the appeal. The constant sense of discovery was some of it. Then there were the grunts. Somebody had to cover them, I guess. First, last, and always, the Scouts were not the reason everyone was out there – the grunts were.

At Vĩnh Long, Apache Aeroscout crew chief Charlie Palek ponders his narrow escape from his crashed Loach, S/N 67-16274, in 1970. (Charlie Palek Collection)

Amazing Men and Machines
by John B. Whitehead III

The highly publicized Loach pilot, Hugh Mills, who spent much of his long Army career with the Loach, called it "A Miracle Machine, which could tolerate a gross bending of the rules when it came to operating limits." Besides its proven ability to withstand punishing enemy fire, the aircraft was also known for its lifting ability. Captain John B. Whitehead III of D Company, 229th Aviation Battalion bent the four-passenger rule during an emergency extraction in the heat of battle. Whitehead wrote the following about the incident in a letter to Hughes, the firm that built the aircraft.

I returned from Vietnam in December 1972 and was actively engaged with the 1st Cav Division in the Easter Offensive for the Battle of An Loc, Loc Ninh, and Quan Loi. Your fine aircraft saved my life. No other aircraft could have accomplished the feat. I was given the mission of extracting three wounded American advisors from a trapped position halfway between An Loc and Loc Ninh. Several attempts had been made to extract these advisors, but to no avail; all were driven off by heavy anti-aircraft fire and small-arms fire. There were a total of 18 people on the ground, of which three were Americans. I led an OH-6A in with a door gunner, while 1Lt. Dave Ripley followed with an empty Loach.

The Americans made it on board my ship, as did six South Vietnamese, for a total of 11 people. The second ship picked up a total of five South Vietnamese. My ship actually lifted off after I bounced it down the road for approximately 100 meters. Two of the South Vietnamese were shot off my ship, so I extracted a total of nine people. The ship was hit several times with .51 cal. fire, including a chord-wise hit in one of the blades and one in the fuel cell. The OH-6A was evacuated to Saigon and required a mandatory engine, transmission, and tail rotor change due to the stress encountered. It flew 20 miles with the extracted soldiers on board. No metal chips were found in any of the components. Since I was the pilot of that ship, I feel that it should be bronzed and placed on a marble base. What an aircraft!

Whitehead's letter did not mention that the mission was made more difficult by gas masks worn by the crew to cope with tear gas dropped by jets covering the evacuation, or that his crew chief was clinging to the skids after having been thrown out by panicking South Vietnamese soldiers who had clambered aboard. As Ripley hovered nearby, his Loach too was swarmed by South Vietnamese soldiers, one of whom jumped up into the front seat and grabbed the cyclic control stick to pull himself aboard. Ripley's resultant left skid toward the enemy stopped when the clinging soldier went stiff, his blood splattering across the cockpit as he toppled backwards off of the aircraft. Whitehead was nominated for the Medal of Honor, and his crew chief received the Distinguished Service Cross.

Welcome Home
by Sandee Swanson

It is said among Vietnam veterans as private acknowledgement of each other's service during a time when America found it difficult to distinguish between the war and the warrior. It was said by Brigid Swanson-Jones at Arlington National Cemetery in May 2002 as she looked at the casket holding the remains of her father, Jon E. Swanson, and Larry G. Harrison; "Welcome home, Larry. Welcome home, Dad." Thirty-one years earlier, they were the crew of an OH-6A that exploded over Cambodia when they took on an NVA stronghold. They died in fierce battle, but not before laying waste to a number of enemy positions, thereby saving countless lives.

When one considers the very nature of an Aeroscout's work, it comes as no surprise that some among their ranks were nominated for the nation's highest award, the Medal of Honor. What is more surprising is that more of them did not have the pale blue ribbon hung about their neck. But Aeroscouts, in the purest sense of heroism, did not find their deeds extraordinary. Rather, they accepted danger and trusted their skills, and each other.

Captain Jon E. Swanson exemplified the spirit of the Aeroscout. He was a soldier's soldier. During 1967 and 1968 Swanson served a combat tour in Vietnam with D Troop, 3rd Squadron, 5th Cavalry. He later volunteered for a second combat tour. Then a captain, he became the scout platoon leader of B Troop, 1st Squadron, 9th Cavalry, call sign "Saber White."

On 26 February 1971, Swanson and his observer, scout platoon sergeant SSgt Larry G. Harrison, were flying in OH-6A serial no. 69-16067 over Cambodia's Kampong Cham Province; they were doing what Aeroscouts did best – flying low and slow, searching for the enemy, in support of ground troops. The First of the Ninth Cav was searching for, and found, part of the buildup of forces for the spring 1972 attack on Saigon. When Swanson and Harrison went down, massive efforts to get them out met with fierce resistance, and they were declared KIA/BNR – Killed in Action/Body Not Recovered.

Nearly three decades would pass before details of the battle surfaced, revealing to Swanson's family that he had been nominated for the Medal of Honor. Sandee Swanson, then Jon's wife, and their two daughters, in true Aeroscout fashion, picked up the trail and doggedly pursued a course of action to complete

Capt. Jon E. Swanson, Scout Platoon Leader of B Troop, 1st Squadron, 9th Cavalry with the troop's *Little Caesar* at FSB Mace in 1971.

a mission. Bolstering the effort was the following letter written on 25 February 2002 by veteran Aeroscout Kent D. Converse to President George W. Bush:

Dear Mr. President,

I am writing this letter in support of Captain Jon E. Swanson, United States Army, to be awarded the Congressional Medal of Honor.

I can attest firsthand of Jon's courage. In May of 1967 we shared the same bullet that wounded both of us as we supported the infantry from the air with an unarmed OH-23G helicopter. I was the pilot and Jon was acting as my observer using an automatic rifle and M-79 grenade launcher to provide suppressing fire until the airborne infantry, gunships, or artillery could arrive.

I was very badly wounded and still had to fly the helicopter. Jon was very helpful to me in this situation as I tried to fly and put a tourniquet on my leg at the same time. When I finally got things under control, I finally had the sense to ask Jon if he was all right. He said, "I got shot in the butt, but don't worry about me."

I do not know the exact circumstance as to how Jon lost his life almost four years later, but I saw his coolness under fire, his dedication to country, and his ability to put his circumstance secondary to help a fellow soldier, all in a few minutes in the Delta of Vietnam that day in May 1967.

Yours,
Kent D. Converse

Testifying to the fact that Swanson's comrades viewed him as a soldier's soldier are the words of former Cobra gunship pilot Tom Genetti:

I was the Gun Platoon Leader when Jon was the Scout Platoon Leader. Jon was "Saber White" and I was "Saber Red." Normally, each day we put up four Pink Teams, one Cobra and one OH-6. Some days Jon and I would fly together and other days I would fly with one of his scouts. Jon was a meticulous leader, who stressed attention to detail and professionalism. He came with all the experience from his first tour and didn't miss a beat when he took charge. The Scout Platoon started showing improvement from the day he took charge. The Scout pilots were always good, but they lacked the discipline that Jon brought with him. The reporting improved, information and details of spot reports greatly improved, and morale rose significantly when that happened."

Here, Sandee Swanson provides insight to the world of anguish and frustration suffered by the loved ones of the lost warriors left behind:

When the Army major came to my door early in the morning of 2 March 1971, my whole world collapsed. I was doubled over in pain, not wanting to hear the words . . . "on February 26, 1971, Jon's helicopter was shot down . . . crashed and burned . . . missing . . ." I didn't know what to do, and I sat there cuddling our two baby daughters, thinking "this can't be happening."

As the days wore on, I became determined that there had been a mistake . . . that Jon had managed to get away. After all, he was an infantry officer, Ranger, and LRRP, as well as an Aeroscout pilot! He knew how to survive in the jungle. He had been wounded during his first tour of duty in Vietnam with D Troop, 3rd Squadron, 5th Cavalry, 9th Infantry Division, and I was confident that he would survive this battle as well.

But there was no information coming from the Army until 28 April 1971 when the Army casualty officer visited me to say that they were changing Jon's status from "missing in action" to "killed in action," but "due to intense enemy fire, all attempts to retrieve him had been unsuccessful."

"NO, NO, NO!" I screamed.

Distraught from not knowing what caused Jon's status to be changed from MIA to KIA, I kept asking the Army casualty officer for more details. He finally told me, "Sandee, I have to work through Army channels, and I haven't been able to get any more information." I then decided to call the General of the Army in Washington, D.C. I tried calling him at the Pentagon, but was unsuccessful. I finally reached him at home, at night, and told him what I knew about Jon, and I also told him that if he did not give me more information, I would fly to Washington, D.C., and if he still wouldn't give me information, I would fly to Vietnam to find my husband! He was very calm, and told me that while he didn't have any information that evening, he would look into Jon's status.

He called me the next day, and said that he had just reviewed the "after-action testimonials" given by the men who had been flying with Jon the day he was shot down, and it was his belief that the decision to change his status to KIA was based on the testimonials

of these eye-witnesses. He asked if I would like to receive copies of the testimonials, and when I said "yes," he said he would send them out immediately.

On 27 May 1971, we held a memorial service for Jon at Ft. Logan National Cemetery in Denver, Colorado, where a memorial marker was placed to signify his death.

During the 1980s, we began attending the Government's annual family briefings in Washington, D.C. At first, Jon's file was very limited, and included heavily redacted descriptions of his battle. As the years progressed, more information became declassified and found its way into the file. It wasn't until 1998 we found out that in 1971 Jon had been nominated for the Medal of Honor for acts of heroism that led to his death. The nomination had been recommended and approved all the way up the chain of command, including Admiral Thomas H. Moorer, Chairman of the Joint Chiefs of Staff, but was then downgraded by Committee.

The Army officer assisting our daughters, Holly and Brigid, at the annual briefing in 1998 said that the Army could do nothing further, but suggested that we take Jon's files to our Congressman. Our youngest daughter, Holly, was working as a legislative aide on Capitol Hill. She took the information to the Chairman of the House Armed Services Committee, Representative Floyd Spence, of South Carolina, who told her that it was rare for files to be reviewed, but he would do what he could. A few months later, Representative Spence's Chief of Staff hand-delivered a letter to Holly stating that the Pentagon was going to "reopen Jon's file." Another three years passed with no communication before we were informed that President George W. Bush had signed a bill waiving the statute of limitations for the Medal of Honor to be awarded Jon. Final approval for the Medal to be awarded was being worked up the chain of command and was still months away.

It was also during the 1990s that there were three separate visits to the crash site in Cambodia by the Joint Task Force-Full Accounting searching for remains. We were told that they were able to recover some commingled remains of both Jon and his crew chief, SSgt Larry Harrison, as well as some badly decomposed personal artifacts. In January 2002, we were visited by an Army casualty officer, who flew out to visit us in Denver from Headquarters in Washington, D.C. He went over in minute detail all the findings of the crash site, the commingled remains and the recovered personal artifacts. He then presented the Army's recommendation for a joint burial for Jon and Larry, with full military honors, at Arlington Cemetery. Wow! I could hardly believe that after all these years Jon would finally be coming home!

After 30 years, we were about to have two major events in honor of Jon – the official burial and the awarding of the Medal of Honor – just months apart and both in Washington, D.C.

Our daughters were instrumental in coordinating the events that unfolded during the spring of 2002. Holly worked with the White House, Congress, and the Pentagon on Medal of Honor details, while Brigid worked with the Army Casualty Office and Arlington for burial and funeral services. On what would have been Jon's 60th birthday, 1 May 2002, Brigid, Holly, and I received the posthumous award on behalf of Jon for the Medal of Honor, presented to us in the Rose Garden at the White House by President George W. Bush. Jon was also inducted into the Pentagon's "Hall of Heroes" the following day. On 3 May 2002, funeral services and a joint burial with full military honors for Jon and SSgt Harrison took place at

On what would have been Jon Swanson's 60th birthday, 1 May 2002, Sandee Swanson and her daughters, Brigid and Holly, receive from President George Bush Jon's posthumous award of the Medal of Honor. (Sandee Swanson Collection)

Arlington Cemetery. These events were an opportunity to bring together many of the men Jon and Larry had served with over 31 years earlier.

Since these events in May of 2002, I have been fortunate to meet many of the men who served with Jon during both tours in Vietnam. I have discovered a profound love for Jon, and have learned that they respected him, learned from him, and have never forgotten him. I truly feel that Jon's spirit lives on in the men with whom he went to war and who have all sacrificed.

The citation for the award reads as follows:

"The President of the United States of America, authorized by Act of Congress, March 3, 1863, has awarded in the name of Congress the Medal of Honor to Captain Jon E. Swanson, United States Army, for conspicuous gallantry and intrepidity at the risk of his life above and beyond the call of duty:

"Captain Jon E. Swanson distinguished himself by acts of bravery on February 26, 1971, while flying an OH-6A aircraft in support of Army Republic of Vietnam (ARVN) Task Force 333 in the Kingdom of Cambodia.

"With two well-equipped enemy regiments known to be in the area, Captain Swanson was tasked with pinpointing the enemy's precise positions. Captain Swanson flew at treetop level at a slow airspeed, making his aircraft a vulnerable target. The advancing ARVN unit came under heavy automatic weapons fire from enemy bunkers 100 meters to their front. Exposing his aircraft to enemy anti-aircraft fire, Captain Swanson immediately engaged the enemy bunkers and evading intense ground-to-air fire, he observed a .51-caliber machine gun position. With all his heavy ordnance expended on the bunkers, he did not have sufficient explosives to destroy the position. Consequently, he marked the position with a smoke grenade and directed a Cobra gunship attack. After completion of the attack, Captain Swanson found the weapon still intact and an enemy soldier crawling over to man it. He immediately engaged the individual and killed him. During this time, his aircraft sustained several hits from another .51-caliber machine gun.

"Captain Swanson engaged the position with his aircraft's weapons, marked the target, and directed a second Cobra gunship attack. He volunteered to continue the mission, despite the fact he was now critically low on ammunition and his aircraft was crippled by enemy fire. As Captain Swanson attempted to fly toward another .51-caliber machine gun position, his aircraft exploded in the air and crashed to the ground, causing his death.

"Captain Swanson's extraordinary heroism and devotion to duty are in keeping with the highest traditions of military service and reflect great credit upon himself, his unit, and the United States Army."

Capt. Rick Waite, Scout pilot of D Troop, 3rd Squadron, 5th Cavalry poses for a portrait.

Rick Waite stands beside the Washington memorial dedicated to the 3/5th Armored Cavalry "Black Knights."

Good Student
by Rick Waite

Prudent Loach pilots who flew with their observer or crew chief in the cockpit wasted little time in teaching them how to fly in the event the pilot was hit. Often the left seat cyclic control stick was removed to increase the gunner's latitude, and was substituted by a two-foot length of pipe kept under his seat. On 28 December 1970, Rick Waite, and Observer Bill Hanegmon, of D Troop, 3rd Squadron, 5th Cavalry, went hunting for the enemy in the Plain of Reeds. Waite explains how the flying lessons he had given Hanegmon would soon pay dividends.

We were nearing the southern edge of the Plain of Reeds, about 10 klicks from the junction of canals we called the "Wagon Wheel," when we began to see lots of fresh activity. There were fresh trails through the reeds in the water, sampans parked under some brush, and bunkers and hootches under the taller shrubs and trees. Hanegmon yelled out, "Break left, break left. I've got a man running!" I immediately broke left as he began to fire his M60 at the target. Suddenly there was a loud explosion in a tree outside my door and everything went black. I could hear Hanegmon yelling, "I've got the aircraft, I've got the aircraft!"

I was temporarily screwed up, and finally realized that my flight helmet was on 90 degrees to the direction it was supposed to be. I had jerked my head away from the explosion so fast that my head had turned inside the helmet. As I straightened the helmet I could hear Hanegmon talking to the C & C ship, telling them that I was hit and that he was flying the aircraft. Blood was flying all over the place in our cockpit. It seemed to be coming from my face or head.

I immediately started putting my finger all over my face, trying to find a hole and having very little luck. In the meantime I could hear the C & C ship vectoring Hanegmon to a compound about three klicks from where we had been shot up. I leaned back in the seat, blood still coming from somewhere on my face. I had given up trying to find the hole, and planned to just wait until we got on the ground.

Bill stayed low-level, and was lining up to set the Loach down on a road between two rice paddies, just to the side of the compound. For some reason he chose to land perpendicular to the road. We were about 30 feet out from the selected touchdown on a short final when I heard the engine suddenly stop. We were too low to do a standard autorotation landing, and too high and too slow to do a low-level autorotation. In reality all this was a moot point, since I had neither explained the dynamics of the aircraft during autorotation to Hanegmon, nor had I ever guided him through such a landing. All things considered, up until the time the engine failed, Hanegmon and I figured we had it made.

He had made many similar landings while I was teaching him to fly. Once the engine quit we were committed. As I put my hands and feet on the controls with Bill, I found that the pedals on my side were completely shot away. Thankfully, Hanegmon managed to keep the tail behind us, which is not an easy task at low speed without power.

We pulled in all the pitch we had, but it was not enough. We did manage to land on the road, but because we could not slow our forward speed without rotor r.p.m. to flare to a hover, the aircraft's skids squatted, and the Loach skidded right off the road into the rice paddy on its nose. The main rotor blades struck the paddy water, and then a blade over-flexed and severed the tail boom. The water in the paddy was four or five feet deep.

Water filled the cockpit as the Loach sank. We got out of our harnesses, helmets, and chicken plates, and swam back to the road. Once there, I tried to stand but then I felt the pain and went right back down again. One of our Slick crew chiefs loaded me on his back and carried me over to his Huey, where they began to check me out. Everyone was looking for a hole in my head because of all the blood on my face and helmet. Then finally I noticed a nice, neat hole through my boot. I had been shot in the foot. That's why it hurt! They took me to a field hospital at Binh Thuy Navy (the Binh Thuy Naval Support Activity Base), where they patched me up. I was flying again in three weeks.

Our Loach had taken 13 hits from small arms fire. A hit in the oil cooler had caused the engine to overheat and quit. The trail aircraft confirmed that there had been an explosion outside my door just before a hail of tracers came up at us. We figured that it must have been one of those home-brewed, bamboo-bladed anti-helicopter claymores that Charlie made and rigged in the tree. My rotor downwash had set it off. Shrapnel from them tended to cone upward, but somehow the frags missed the Loach and my rotor disc. All that blood in the cockpit was caused when I jerked my head around; the edge of the helmet hit my nose, causing a serious nose-bleed. And with the doors off the Loach, the blood was being whipped about the cockpit by the wind.

Our Loach was hurt bad enough that it got to go home, but we didn't. If there was one thing in my life that I could be happy about, it was that I had taken the time to teach Hanegmon how to fly. To make that kind of recovery at low-level when your pilot is incapacitated is unbelievable. Bill clearly saved both our butts that day. I doubt there were many like him. Hanegmon later saved another pilot's life by landing a Loach after he too had been shot. He never received an award for either incident. He seemed to be able to do it all. He had it together then, and he's still got it together as a detective with the St. Louis County Sheriff's Department in Hibbing, Minnesota.

Before they left Vietnam, Waite and Hanegmon each received two Purple Hearts. Their scout helicopter, OH-6A serial no. 66-

Bill Hanegmon of D/3/5, Rick Waite's observer, holds a "chicken plate" armor panel hit by an enemy round.

Bill Hanegmon poses for a portrait in modern times.

The Loach, S/N 66-17792, in which "War Wagons" Rick Waite was wounded and which Bill Hanegmon flew to safety in December 1970 after being sling-loaded back to base. Despite the degree of damage, the Loach was repaired and went on to serve the Army National Guard and the Gainesville, Florida, Police Department. Prior to assignment to D/3/5, the OH-6A served A/3/17 as *The Lucky Lady*. (Bill Hanegmon)

Vietnam veteran OH-6A 792 still fighting bad guys with the Gainesville, Florida, Police Department. Some of the small number of Loaches that survived the war ended up in law enforcement. Most had been repaired after crashes in Vietnam and many were found to have patched bullet holes. (Rick Waite/Curt Knapp)

17792, was repaired, continued to serve the Army, and went on to serve 14 years with the Gainesville, Florida Police Department. Waite describes his January 2000 reunion with 792:

Two of Gainsville PD's finest, Dale Witt and John Rouse, gave me the nickel tour of their office area. I then gave them some War Wagon material. We then went to the hangar, where I laid eyes on her for the first time in 29 years. In the dimly lit hangar, she looked almost like a ghost. As I drew nearer I began to feel a rush of adrenaline. Patches on the engine doors and her belly indicated where we both had suffered wounds 29 years ago. She was beautiful. I touched her and just stared at her, glad to see that she too had survived all these years. She had obviously aged much better than I. I had worn my sow belly Stetson and Cav scarf in hopes that she would recognize me. I think she did.

I showed the two officers photos of her in flight over Southeast Asia, and after our shoot-down. They were listening to every word I said. I then took a few pictures of her.

They opened the hangar doors and rolled her out into the sunlight. This little airplane had taken care of me and Bill Hanegmon, and seemed as though she were really alive.

Then it happened! One of the guys handed me a headset and said, "Are you ready?" I was stunned. I was going to get to go for a ride in her. They said, "We're not taking you for a ride. You're taking us for a ride!" I couldn't believe it. Five miles from the airport and at 500 feet, John said, "Go ahead and take her." For the next two hours, she was mine, and I was that 20-year old scout pilot again.

This day was very spiritual. The last flight I had in 792 in Vietnam ended abruptly, with me being shot. I had a long time to go over what had happened, and I thought a lot about those who never got to come home and enjoy the life I have.

Waite and Hanegmon's unit, like them and their Loach, soldiered on. The 5th U.S. Cavalry had been born in 1855 and its 3rd Squadron was organized as the armored reconnaissance unit of the 9th Infantry Division, just prior to "Old Reliable's" deployment to Vietnam. The 3rd Squadron, 5th Cavalry "Black Knights" would serve in Vietnam from 1966 to 1971, in somewhat vagabond fashion under numerous commands. Later it would add battle streamers to its illustrious and distinguished history during the Persian Gulf War, and in Bosnia and Kosovo.

Wearing body armor, Douglas G. Smith of "Ghost Riders" Aviation Section, 2nd Brigade, 1st Infantry Division prepares for a mission in 1969. Since missions often were flown without a gunner, a fixed M60 fired by the pilot was rigged to the Loach.

Graves Registration
by Doug Smith

Not all missions flown by Aeroscouts guaranteed a ride on an emotional roller coaster.

Some, by their nature, had a more moderate, yet lasting, effect. Douglas G. Smith, "Ghost Rider 6," of Aviation Section, 2nd Brigade, 1st Infantry Division, recounts two memorable missions during which he brushed shoulders with what was the last stop in Vietnam for too many warriors.

The 1st Division was a great division to be with. Often I medevaced soldiers. One time an explosion had gone off almost under my OH-6. A GI had stepped on a 20-pound anti-tank mine. He lost both legs and hands. His lieutenant sat on him as I flew to the MASH at Lai Khe. I called in and they were waiting. I would estimate less than 10 minutes had passed before he had stepped on the mine and was at the hospital. Later that evening I checked with a doc at their club, and the man was still alive. The amount of blood that was on the floor of the Loach was incredible. I have often wondered if he is still alive, or met a fate similar to Lt. Puller of the USMC.

One of the worst things was bringing out America's dead to Graves Registration. Their feet would stick out of the sides of the Loach. I made the decision that we would carry body bags, which was quite unpopular with other pilots. After that we didn't have to carry any more of our dead – fate, I guess.

In 1969, after completing an assignment with the 1st of the 18th Battalion, I was heading back to Di An when I received a call that A Company of 1/18 had spotted VC. As I neared the area I saw two GIs pop their rucksacks and run down a trail. Captain Harvey Kelly, A Company's commander, told me his men were in pursuit of the VC. As I circled over the area I saw their fire and cooking pot. It seemed obvious that the VC were in an adjacent wooded area that was full of booby traps. I radioed Harvey, who seemed disappointed, as we all wanted to get some kills.

I mentioned that I could make gun runs at the wooded area with my M60 machine gun.

Harvey thought that sounded like a fine idea, and it would provide some amusement for the troops. He directed his men to take cover as I prepared to make my gun runs. My Loach had an M60 stationary-mounted to its side. I had no aiming device. The rounds went into the area at which I pointed the aircraft. The accuracy was within 10 to 25 feet initially, and then I walked in rounds to the target.

I was filled with pride, as now Ghost Rider Six was center stage. On my first run, one round went out and the gun jammed. I was disappointed and embarrassed. Not wanting to give up, I told Harvey that he could get in the front seat with hand grenades so we could make bomb runs. Harvey agreed, so I landed, got him strapped in, and his men filled his lap with grenades.

Our first run went fine, as Harvey got off about three, and the second run was just as good. However, on the third run things changed.

Harvey pulled the pin from the grenade, and it fell on the floor and rolled toward the pedals. Harvey could not reach it! Time seemed frozen. I recalled reading about a Loach that had blown out of the air when a white phosphorous grenade went off in the chin bubble. I pulled back on the cyclic and the grenade rolled toward Harvey. He kicked it out with his left foot. I don't know if we got an air burst. We both looked at each other with that "Let's not tell what happened" look.

After a couple more bomb runs we called it good, as he had to get his company in its night defensive position, and I had to check my aircraft for holes, and then head for the bar.

A few weeks later, Harvey was killed in action. One of my Loaches carried his body to Graves Registration.

The engine of this OH-6A receives attention prior to delivering food containers to troops in the field on Thanksgiving Day 1969. The Loach was one of four assigned to the Aviation Section of 2nd Brigade, 1st Infantry Division. (Douglas G. Smith)

Divine Intervention
by Don Langlois

Don Langlois was long on experience, having served two tours as an Aeroscout crew chief.

Some would say he was also long on luck. His first year-long tour in 1968 and 1969 was with D Troop, 3/5th Cav "War Wagons," and his second in 1972 and 1973 with H Troop, 17th Cav "Scalphunters." Here, he describes how events played out that make him believe it may not have been luck at all, but something of a higher order.

When I was with D Troop, the last two months of my tour I was doing the mission scheduling for the crew chiefs. Schedule boards were in two places: in the unit area and in WO Eric Blantin's room. It just so happened that Eric and I had become friends while we were at Dong Tam. Eric wasn't known to use language of an offensive nature.

However, after we got a new troop commander (who was hated by just about everyone except the usual suck-asses) it became his policy that EMs (enlisted men) and noncoms (non-commissioned officers) were to salute officers. The officers, except the suck-asses, did everything they could to bring this policy to an abrupt end. Their main argument was that the saluting policy might endanger the officers, who felt that they might be targeted by any enemy outside the perimeter. This, of course, was strictly bull. The officers didn't want to salute any more than the EM did. Needless to say, the policy lasted for perhaps several days.

One day Eric returned from a mission as I was arriving at the flight line. He walked towards me and I whipped him the best salute that I could muster and said, Good afternoon, Sir," to which he replied, "Kiss my ass." As I said, Eric wasn't known to use that type of language. We had talked about getting together after we were back stateside, on the coast of Connecticut, where he was from. We would sit on the beach and eat lobster. But that wasn't to be.

One day in October I went to Eric's room to post schedules. I had scheduled myself for a mission the next day, flying with WO Conrad Wheeler.

When I arrived back at the unit, a fellow CE (crew chief) named Greeno approached and asked about the scheduling. He asked if I would trade missions with him. Some CEs had certain pilots they preferred to fly with. It didn't matter in this case, although Conrad and me got the crapola shot out of our Loach, but we managed to come out unscathed.

I agreed to let Greeno fly the following morning with Conrad, and I would take his mission the day after. I failed to note the change on either schedule board. The next day I was out and about in the town of Vinh Long when one of my fellow scouts said that "Top" (First Sergeant) was looking for me. Apparently it was assumed that I may have been with Conrad in the U Minh Forest when the Loach exploded during the mission. It was then that I found out that Conrad and Greeno were killed. Conrad was twenty years old.

The following month I scheduled myself to fly with Eric, when Greeno's best friend, Jim Dale, came to Eric's room. Dale asked if

Don Langlois (second from left) and a fellow aviator, pose with the Polish contingent of the four-nation International Commission of Control and Supervision in 1973.

I would let him fly with Eric the following day. I really didn't want to switch, but he finally talked me into it. The following morning, as Eric was getting ready to crank up the Loach, Dale was at the left side of the aircraft, having just returned from the storage container with the explosives we carried. As Eric started the Loach, it blew up in the revetment. I was told later that an electrical problem probably ignited its jet fuel. This happened a few days before Thanksgiving.

Since I was scheduled for DEROS on December 7, I may have flown a couple of more missions, but I don't recall flying after the month of November. I guess it was beginning to sink in that for some reason God kept me from flying both times that another CE ended up dead. Since I really don't believe in luck, I can only think that it was God's intervention.

Out of two tours, I managed to get hit one time. That was when I was with H Troop. We had just returned from a mission and the pilot had gone to operations, while I remained with the aircraft. It wasn't long before I could see the pilot walking back to the aircraft, motioning that we were cranking up. I got in, he got in, cranked up, and before long we were heading over the berm at Pleiku. All of a sudden he asked me where my chicken plate was. I said, "Oops, it's in the back." He asked if I was trying to get him in trouble because I knew I was supposed to be wearing that chicken plate. I came up

with a good reply. I said, "Why don't we turn around and land so that I can get my chicken plate on."

He said that we were just going to check on some people seen in the brush, but that it was considered to be a friendly area.

After we arrived in the area, we descended with left cyclic. As we got down within a couple of hundred feet, we were greeted by friendlies all right; with small arms fire from several different positions. Bullets came from everywhere. But whoever was firing from our front right position was doing an excellent job. He shot out the instrument panel and flying glass hit the pilot. I could feel the breeze the bullets made passing by my legs and hitting the console. One of his bullets grazed my left pinkie that rested atop the M60 holding a smoke grenade.

I just couldn't believe that we didn't have more damage with all the firing that took place.

However, once we landed next to the hangar so that maintenance could look over the aircraft, we discovered that a bullet hit the rotor mast several inches below the rotor hub.

This explained the reason for a vibration, which we had attributed to rotor damage.

It is still a wonderment that certain events changed what could have been. I can only say that I should be dead, several times over.

Thirty years later, Louis Rochat III in formal cavalry dress and wife Ann.

Twenty-one year old Louis Rochat III Scout pilot of Echo Troop, 1/9 in September 1970.

Something About the Cav
by Lou Rochat

Louis J. Rochat III, better known as "Rocket," went to Vietnam as a Cobra gunship pilot out of flight school. Seeking what he considered the best of both worlds in Army aviation, he also qualified in the OH-6A Loach, and flew both Scouts and Guns in Vietnam.

Rochat exemplifies the spirit of the Aeroscout, and here he tells about the Loach and how his involvement with the aircraft changed the course of his life.

The most famous Loach in all of Vietnam hailed from my unit, Apache Troop, 1st Squadron, 9th Cavalry. No one pilot could lay claim to this bird, named *Queer John*. It was one of the first OH-6As to be delivered to Apache Troop. It was an old bird when I flew it in 1970 – old meaning it had more than 300 hours on it and made it to Periodic Inspection. But it always came home and, on several occasions, with wounded crew. This Loach actually had a purple heart awarded to it by the 1st Cavalry Division's headquarters. *Queer John* was written about several times in *Stars and Stripes,* and in the 1st Cav Division's *Saber* newsletter. It was still flying when the 1/9 was stood down. It was reportedly with the Cav when it re-invaded Cambodia, and then went into Laos in late 1971, until stand-down in 1972. It had many patched bullet holes (six were mine) and it lost a dozen rotor blades (two were mine), two tail booms, and lots of plexiglas. This bird and its crews were responsible for many 9th Cav enemy kills, tons of destroyed supplies, and just flat out unbelievable destruction of anything in its path.

My regular Loach was named *The Little Green Killing Machine,* and had a red-and-white bulls-eye painted on the belly. My helmet and chicken plate were also painted to give the enemy something to shoot at – something about being 20 years old and in the 9th Cav.

I wanted to transition into the OH-6A and ended up dividing my flight time between both the Cobra and Loach. I would fly the Loach until I took a mess of hits or got shot down.

Then I would jump back into the Cobra until I got bored, while the Scout had all the fun.

Then I'd jump back into the Loach.

Tuesday, 1 September 1970, Lai Khe, Republic of South Vietnam, III Corps. It was a awe-inspiring day, as the personnel 'selected' to form the new E "El Lobo" Troop, 1st Squadron, 9th Cavalry, arrived and gathered around the now disbanded D Company, 229th AHC company area and their flight line. All of the other units in the squadron had been told to provide some of their pilots, air crew, support personnel, equipment, and aircraft to form this new "Hunter-Killer," Search and Destroy air cavalry troop. I was in Apache Troop of the 1/9, located at the red clay and dirt hill of Song Be on the Cambodian border.

We moved there from Tay Ninh after we went in on the 1 May 1970 Cambodian invasion. I was sort of happy to get out of there because of the conditions we lived in, though I would miss the guys and missions we flew.

Though ordered to transfer their best, you can just imagine what the commanders gave up for equipment and people; their hot-rodders, hell-raisers, oldest aircraft, worn out equipment, etc. And I was part of it. Newly arrived second-tour Major Herbert Chole had a Black Sheep troop on his hands, but he rolled up his sleeves and went to work. By 8 September we were putting up five teams a day, and that had increased to seven by 12 September, after we raided every unit in III Corps for parts, equipment, ammo, and anything that was not tied down, including a jeep. Regardless of the amount of coat-hanger wire and "200 mile-per-hour tape" that was hanging off the aircraft to hold them together, we put teams in the air! Two of the Cobras we got were delivered on flatbed trucks, and they were flying within days.

I was indeed proud to be an original member of this elite, illustrious, rag-tag, no-name, no AO, Red-X aircraft, 70-percent strength, 1st Air "Real" Cav unit of short-lived, great-fame-to-come. My call sign with A Troop was "Apache One-Six," which became "El Lobo One-Six" in E Troop.

Our immediate mission was to support/augment the three other "regular" troops, and they gave us missions that were everything but what we were all about – search and destroy, plus troops in contact – the fun part of the Real Cav. We quickly earned one hell of a reputation and were broken off from supporting the other troops, and given our own area of operations, called "AO Chief," around Phuoc Vinh. Within weeks we had stopped all of the incoming fire on Phuoc Vinh, captured an NVA officer, and found one of the NVA's major headquarters, called MR-7. Then the 1st Infantry stood down, and we got our very own big-time turf – the Iron Triangle!

Echo troop was a mixed breed of personnel, and was making a name for itself due to all the talent it had obtained from these transfers. We were getting people who wanted to be there, and who wanted to get it on with the bad guys.

In the following, which Rochat titles "Don't Get out of the Cobra, Unless…," he reflects on a mission on which he departed in a Cobra, and returned in a Loach. Rocket's narrative is flavored with the colorful vernacular of seasoned combat aviators in Vietnam.

17 October 1970: The Bell AH-1G Huey Cobra and Hughes OH-6A Cayuse Loach Hunter-Killer Team, search and destroy mission, was going like many of the other pre-approved, free-fire missions that the newly formed E Troop, 1st Squadron, 9th Cavalry, 1st Cavalry Division (Airmobile) had been flying for several weeks now in the infamous Iron Triangle. The Big Red One had stood down and gone home to the "Land of the big PX."

Their turf was handed over to the now well known "El Lobo" Black Sheep Troop. Rumor had it that a large NVA unit had been in there for years but Big Red One never could get a full, all out, face-to-face fight with them to see who was the toughest kid in the rice paddy. It was Echo Troop's turn for that privilege now.

The team knew that NVA Regulars were around the location they were going to work, as "Sir Charles" had sent one of their Loach pilot buddies home on a stretcher the evening before. Normally the NVA were reluctant to engage a 9th Cav hunter-killer team. This NVA unit was different, as they had wasted no time in putting down WO1 Ric Amos and his Loach just 18 hours earlier. The team knew that if Sir Charles did engage again, they would have one hell of a fight on their hands. Hot damn, it was going to be a good day!

Aircraft Commander Warrant Officer Danny "Rags" Rager was back seat in the AH-1G Cobra, while I was flying front seat. Rags and I were qualified in both the Loach and Cobra, with me flying Loaches 50 percent of the time. I was taking a break from the intense scout driving and enjoying the air-conditioned Cobra.

Down below, in the best damn helicopter ever made, the Hughes OH-6A Loach, was Warrant Officer Steve Ellis and his crew having all the fun reconning by fire with the M60 machine gun, tossing frags into bunkers, burning hootches with Willy Pete and incendiary grenades, popping M-79 rounds into anything, and skimming the trees with the skids; the life of a Loach driver was awesome! Life in a Loach was basically living on the extreme outer edge of the envelope 99.9 percent of all flight time logged. There was no greater aviation challenge. There were few second chances. There was no greater thrill. And Ellis was good at it! It has never been argued that scout pilots and crews all had steel balls the size of basketballs, but it was questionable whether or not their brains may have been made out of the same material and a lot smaller.

Rags and I knew Ellis was a damn good scout pilot and fighter, but, like most scout drivers, he normally wouldn't tell you he had gooks under fire or had taken fire himself until he had finished them off or got shot to hell himself. You had to watch his gunner's barrel for smoke and fire or the aircraft's tail going vertical when the scout pilot pulled in max power to get away from enemy fire.

Steve was just a normal "Real 9th Cav" scout driver who disliked sharing enemy kills with anyone, even his own Cobra gunship. However, the old pilot proverb was about to come full circle for Steve: "There are bold pilots and there are old pilots, but there are very few bold, old pilots."

Then it happened – fast and without warning, as usual; the Loach tail went vertical for about 50 meters and then Ellis flared out just as I was about to pull the 4,000 round-per-minute minigun triggers on Ellis' six o'clock tail position. I saw the door gunner's M60 smoke and then it quit as Ellis stood the Loach on its tail, did a 180-degree about face and headed right back to where he had just been. I stopped the trigger pull on the minigun just in time. Had I fired, Ellis would have flown into a wall of .30 cal. bullets and tracers.

Rags called Ellis as he was aborting the 90-degree left-hand snap-turn roll-in on-target Cobra attack maneuver and hit the radio transmit, calmly asking Ellis, "What ya got, big guy?" "Stand-by a minute," a scout favorite, was the return transmission. Rags really wanted to pound some sand up Steve's behind because we knew what he was up to. Rags then asked if he had taken any hits. "Naw" was the usual answer.

Hunter-killer Cobra crews were always on edge as their flight time was 90 percent boredom at 1,500 feet altitude in a left-hand orbit over the Loach, listening to Saigon Sue or AFVN on the radio and then 10 percent panic when all hell broke loose with the Loach. The Cobra crew was also fearful for their Loach as their life expectancy in the 9th Cav bordered on four to six months before being wounded in action or KIA.

I told Rags, "He's got gooks and he ain't sharing." We couldn't see into the trees from our altitude but I had five months scout experience – most from the Cambodia campaign – and could feel that Ellis had something good and all hell was getting ready to break loose. Rags, no beginner and a former Loach driver, also felt it.

I had just turned 21 after entering flight school at the age of 19 due to being reclassified from a student to 1A draft eligible because I had just changed schools. Now I was sweating in the air conditioned cockpit of the Cobra as I knew they were definitely going to duke it out with Charlie; here, today, at this place, so far from family, and home, where he should be cruising in his 57 Chevy, hanging out with his local high school pals at the DQ or Sonic back home, hitting on the girls. Reality came back as Rags turned off the Cobra air conditioning for extra power; we'll need it for the gun runs. Nam's cold reality is very sobering.

Ellis called, "I just want to look at a little someth…Shhhhiiiit…Taking Fire! I'm hit! I'm Hit!" His radio went dead silent as our overloaded 12,000-pound Cobra was rolling in.

The Loach spun hard right, flying away just as the Cobra was 45 degrees into its attack turn when I pulled the minigun triggers. About 50 rounds went off and the minigun jammed. I hit the 40mm grenade launcher selector and then the triggers again. Five rounds went out and it quit firing – without proper maintenance, turret failures were commonplace on the Cobra. Rags was just rolling out on target and let loose with the first pair of rockets; they went a little wide. Rags was an expert and with a split-second adjustment, the next pair hit dead center into the target area, followed immediately by a full salvo of the 17-pound high-explosive warheads from the inboard rocket pods. Rags broke off the run and was flying through suspended debris from the rockets when I aimed the turret guns straight down and tried both the "gat gun" and the "thumper." Both failed. Rags broke hard right, the blades almost in the trees, the G forces pressing us against the seat armor plate. The aircraft was shaking hard…difficult to hold my head up…unable to even punch the intercom button…mushroomed a little, and then caught good air and was climbing up in a hard right turn, just as a few tracers flew by the main blades.

Rags rolled in again and fired what was left of the wing stores into the target area. We now flew a snake with no bite. I yelled over the intercom, "Rags, Rags, I don't see him, where'd he go, where's that Loach? I know he's hit, Steve's hit, he broke off, flying hurt!"

Rags replied, "I got him hard right, he's landing, the blades flexed but he didn't cut the tail off." I yelled, "Land this son-of-a-bitch! I see him getting out, he's got a towel wrapped around his arm, it's blood red, he's hit, he's down on his knees. Land this damn thing now! We got to get him out, he's only 100 meters from the gooks, there's no time to wait for our Blues and Buck's lift ships!" The Blue Platoon consisted of our UH-1 Hueys led by Captain Buck "Fly into hell and laugh" Elton, and specially trained, ballsy, kickass ground troops called, "Headhunters," that served as a ready-reaction force for anything we needed them for; mainly our own downed bird insertions.

Being a Loach driver, I knew the gooks would do anything to get a 9th Cav Loach or Cobra crew. Charlie had bounties posted on 9th Cav pilots and crews, especially Loach drivers and gunners. He also knew that aviation personnel were practically helpless on the ground, even though the Loach carried a vast array of weaponry and explosives. They were not ground troops, regardless of how good they were in the air. That Loach crew had to be gotten out now!

Rags replied in a sorta what-the-hell-are-we-doing voice as the Cobra was not designed for medevac or passengers – it was a two-seater aircraft only. "I'm landing. For Christ's sake, I'm landing! Mind if I get out of the fuckin' trees first?" Okay, we're at 100 feet and a hot final; got to slow down. Max weight for a Cobra was 10,000 pounds; most of ours weighed in at 12,000 plus. Rags, like so many of the 9th Cav gunship pilots, could fly a Cobra like Ali boxed – he was a king at it.

I come on the intercom, "Rags, I'm outta here, get ready to medevac him. His Loach is still running. I'll try to get it out but he goes first. See ya at the club." Any reply from Rags was not heard as I unplug my helmet.

The Cobra is at 50 feet, in a hot, nose-high, left pedal sideways flare to bleed off airspeed as I unbuckle my seat belt and shoulder harness. I open the canopy door and lock it open.

I climb out onto the side step, hanging onto the armor seat, and then let go at about ten feet above the ground, front-rolling into the long-abandoned stinking farm field and come up running toward Ellis. I take him from the struggling Loach crew chief and yell at the Torque to get on his M60 and provide cover fire. Ellis yells that his arm hurts bad. He has blood on his face and helmet, blown there when a .30 cal. round went through his arm after going through the bottom of the Loach.

I hear, feel, think Rags is shooting some rockets from a hover into the tree line to keep the gooks busy and to lighten the ship of its heavy ordnance, only to learn 25 years later that it was B-40 rockets being fired at us by the gooks. Rags stays put and holds his ground, pointing the Cobra at the hesitantly charging gooks as if the Cobra was fully armed, when, in fact, it was completely expended, except for the jammed turret guns.

Like most Nam Warrant Officer pilots, Rags is only 20 years old, but he's one of the pros with a chopper, just like all the other 9th Cav pilots that had flown longer than 30 days in country without being zipped into a body bag; the others either didn't make it or were non-hackers that got transferred out quickly and quietly.

I half carry, half drag the barely-walking Ellis towards the Cobra. Ellis is in pain. We reach the Cobra as it settles back to the ground and I help push Ellis up into the front seat.

I grab his left leg under his butt to push and feel something not right. As Ellis rolls over into the front seat, I see a chunk of his leg missing and the tibia bone gleaming white in front of my face. Blood and muscle tissue are everywhere. He's been hit twice!

Rags nods as I shut the canopy door and with a final thumbs up to me, Rags pulls the Cobra's guts out, straight up to 75 feet before nosing over towards 15th Medical at Phuoc Vinh.

I turn towards the shot-down Loach and Ellis' crew; fragments of dirt and weeds hit me all over and I realize we are under attack from the gooks that shot Ellis down. Less than three minutes have elapsed since Ellis called that he'd been hit. It seems like years.

I run towards the Loach, firing one of my .45 automatics at the gooks just as I hear the sweet sound of the crew chief's M60 rocking away at the gooks. The observer joins in with a CAR-15 and the gooks hit for cover. I see several gooks take tracers from the M60 machine gun – one tracer has four hard bullets behind it. Those gooks won't fight again. I also spot a uniformed gook – Sir Charles. I shoot him but I know I missed and I also know these guys won't back down and that it's time for all American personnel to un-ass the area.

I jump into the Loach pilot's seat, sitting in blood and muscle tissue from Ellis. I wrap up the turbine throttle from flight idle, check gauges – some are gone from bullet hits and there are bullets hitting everywhere. I smell fuel from somewhere, the engine oil temp is up. I yell for everyone to get on and start pulling in the collective. I can hear and feel metal grinding. The thin main rotor blades are hit and shaking the aircraft; can't read the gauges. Another bullet hole appears in the chin bubble. Dirt and rocks are flying everywhere from enemy fire. The gunner is putting out all the M60 fire he can; the erratic M60 tracers indicate the barrel is overheating and the gun will lock up soon. I already have power pulled in to the top of the yellow caution area of the torque gauge. The blades are coned upward; trying to lift off. Loach transmissions like to blow after that limit has been reached. To hell with it! I pull max red-line power out of the little Loach turbine and it shudders into vertical flight over the 50-foot high tree line and the still-firing, can't-hit-shit gooks.

The gooks charge out of the tree line, firing everything they've got at the crippled Loach.

Only a few rounds hit insignificant areas of the Loach. The gunner is standing on the skid with his almost totally melted down M60 and gives the gooks the infamous American military wave goodbye – gloved middle finger extended proudly!

At red-line power, 40 knots airspeed and 30 feet altitude, the beat-up, shot-up, bloody loach makes its way back home to Lai Khe.

I try all the radios but none work. The Loach shakes so bad that the gauges and instruments are unreadable. I then see the caution panel warning light; the transmission chip detector has activated from all the metal flying around in the transmission oil.

The gunner is pulling pins and tossing out all the ordnance to lose as much weight as possible. Several homemade C-4 Superbombs also go. There is smoke coming from the engine compartment and the aircraft shakes and shudders all the way in for a running landing at Lai Khe. The little bird held together long enough to bring us home.

I never got to let the aircraft stabilize for the required two-minute flight idle cool-down period. Just as I got the collective full down, the engine lost fire. With the blades still turning down to their inevitable full stop, I head for Flight Ops to check on Ellis. Rags had radioed back from Phuoc Vinh that Ellis is going to be okay but he will be going back home minus a few pounds of his ass.

In 1980, while Rochat was completing his third overseas tour, then in Germany with an AH-1S Cobra unit, the nomination for the Sliver Star for this action was found in his records. Rocket was given a full-honors battalion parade in Hanau and Air Cavalry pioneer Brigadier General Charles E. Canedy presented him with a Silver Star. It would be his second Silver Star for combat involving a Loach.

Ellis was nominated for the Distinguished Flying Cross and his crew chief and gunner for their action and bravery under fire. He also received what was called the "VC/NVA Marksmanship badge," the Purple Heart. He was medically retired and flew for a major airline.

Rags retired after putting in 20 plus years, including a second tour to Vietnam as a Huey TOW missile tank-killer, and went on to fly for a major airline. Rocket stayed in the fight and, here, he relates how three months later, his turn "in the grinder" came.

Unfortunately, El Lobo Troop's legend was cut short after only six months of action when everyone merged into a single unit for the massive operation, Lam Son 719. My activity with the unit ended prior to that, in the Iron Triangle, on 18 January 1971. Having less than 99 days left in country made me a "two-digit midget," but I was getting ready to extend my tour when I got back into the Loach for what would be my last time.

It was the first mission of the day, and all of our teams were trying to stir up Charlie. I found a sampan docking point and, after destroying two sampans, flew low-level cover for a Korean team we put in to check out a nearby bunker complex. I will never forget those guys. After insertion they grouped and waited for me to drop a smoke on the target about 400 meters away. I then moved 200 meters away to lessen aircraft noise, yet still be nearby to provide them with fire support. Once they saw the smoke, they fixed bayonets and charged it from the LZ. Those ROKs were awesome!

I was down to about 30 minutes fuel when the "Down Bird" call went out. We were the closest team, as most of the others had broken to refuel and rearm. Captain Paul "Red" Dagnon was my high bird, with the executive officer, Captain Reterrer, in his front seat.

We arrived on station and found that the low bird had been hit, but flew out of the area several klicks before having to set down. His high bird Cobra had to leave, due to low fuel and no munitions. He had shot up everything when his Loach had taken fire. The Loach pilot was brand new; hadn't been in the unit more than a week or two, and was still peeing stateside water. This was the first time he had taken fire and got hit. I spotted him outside the aircraft and

counting bullet holes. He gave me a sign count of over 10 hits in the engine doors. I knew right off we were not dealing with VC, but NVA, and they wanted him down, otherwise they would have put all those rounds in the cockpit. He would not get on the radio to tell us what he saw, and where it was, but through hand signals between him and my torque, he pointed in the direction from which he flew. We headed out after I checked around him for one klick to make sure no bad guys were after him.

Red said everyone was in refuel and rearm, but that Captain Larry Brown, my scout platoon leader, had his Cobra almost refueled and rearmed. It would be only a few minutes before they took off. Both of our 20-minute warning lights were already on. I told him we needed to check the area to find out what the hell was in there so we would know what it would take to end the bad-guy situation, and that I would do it at 60 knots; I normally did a lot of hovering in Loaches to make Charlie take a shot.

Red was still apprehensive, but I wanted to get in there to find out what was there and, possibly, to rack up some kills. Red could see where the other team had been firing, and guided me in there while I was low level. I went in at 60 knots, but was up to 90 knots within seconds. All I could tell Red was that it was like being in Cambodia again. I had bunker openings, uniforms hanging out to dry, campfires with food cooking, stacked AKs, heavy-use trails, and NVA equipment and gear everywhere. I had my torque start "recon by fire" with his M60 just to keep the bad guys' heads down, as I had not seen any yet, but the hair on the back of my neck was standing up. I could feel and smell the little commies everywhere.

Red wanted to put down some of his flechettes, but I had him hold off, as I was about to get the hell out of there and live to make an R & R in Bangkok, when it all went good and bad at the same time. I had flown the entire Cambodian campaign, and had learned a lot of the unwritten tactics you use to survive as a Loach pilot, but still get body counts. We had been out of Cambodia for a while and my edge wasn't as keen as it had been then. I made an error that would cost me dearly.

I was on fumes and getting ready to split when a group of five to seven NVA packing full gear and AKs, came out of nowhere and appeared to be running away from us. I fell for it and stood that Loach on its tail, slowed, and started hovering sideways as the torque started putting them down. Just as the last gook went down I either heard or felt the rocket coming. I went nose over and pulled 102 pounds of torque to get out when the rocket hit the tail. I learned later from Red that all he remembers seeing was a gray-black cloud, and my tail boom section flipping through the air.

Everything went into slow motion. The aircraft was nose-over with a ton of torque to the blades, and the rocket blast flipped the Loach into a forward flip. During the time it was upside down I took one .30 cal. round through my right hand, and it came through what would have been the top of the aircraft. My thumb and little finger were the only thing letting me hang onto the cyclic. I remember the aircraft finishing the flip and heading down as parts of the dash, instruments, and radios started flying everywhere from rounds coming through my side of the cockpit. I felt several tugs at my left leg, and then a whack in the chest and head. Just before impact I pulled in the collective and rolled the nose forward and to the right to impact on my side, nose down, to help keep my crew alive.

Just as I was getting a good look at the ground, my left leg fell over, and the cyclic came out of the floor and a lot of stuff hit my face. I recall the aircraft hitting, bouncing, and rolling several times before it came to rest on its left side. During this part of the "controlled crash" I remember getting a good rap on the head. After stopping, I saw that it was one of the rotor blades that came into the cockpit. Everything was still slow motion; the dust and debris was settling into the cockpit, as all the plexiglas was gone, but then everything returned to normal speed.

I was hurt bad and I knew it. I braced and had my observer reach up to unlatch my seatbelt as I started to crawl through my "greenhouse" roof window. A bucket of blood landed on my observer as I moved my left leg up. That's when I saw it and knew that it was blown in half, and that I was bleeding to death. I stuck my head through the window and saw the damn rotor head still turning and clanking and grinding. No tail boom, no skids, no rotor blades, and a smashed bird, and the engine was still running at flight idle. I had to turn back around and shut the engine off before I could get out. I could hear my torque shooting the M-79 grenade launcher and wondered why I wasn't hearing the M60, when I saw it pinned under the wreckage. I rolled out of the aircraft, and my observer was right behind me. I could smell burning grass and hear AK rounds hitting the top of the aircraft. Red was really working out with the Cobra, but I could also hear return fire after he broke his run. They were shooting both .30 cal. and .50 cal. at him.

My left foot was turning the wrong way, and I flopped it over the right way, knowing that only my flight suit and blousing rubbers were holding it on. I used the observer's boot lace to tie my leg above the knee, and locked it down with my bayonet after I stuck it into my flight suit to free my good hand. I saw a bomb crater, and told the observer to get any guns he could find and head for the crater. I dragged myself into the crater, and then realized that dirt and bamboo were falling on us from Red's covering fire. Damn, he could shoot! Or, as he says, "How'd ya like that dazzling display of aerial rocket artillery?" At that moment I couldn't get enough of it. It must have been their third gun run while I was laying in the crater with my observer and torque, as I remember how awesome it sounded hearing the rockets fire, break the sound barrier, and then impact.

You would hear a split second of the thunder the Cobra made in a dive, and then the minigun and "chunker" would go off as they broke off the run. As the sound of the Cobra left us, the enemy guns opened up, and then the debris from the gunship would float down on us. We even heard shrapnel flying through the air. It was fantastic!

Then I got scared for the first time. I couldn't hear Red. My torque was shooting his M-79, and I had been shooting left handed with my handgun, as I lost my Thompson in the crash. The observer had lost his rifle in the crash, and I gave him my empty handgun to reload when I heard the sweetest sound there was in the world; the high-pitched whine of another Loach. The pilot made one pass over us and went on his tail in a right-hand circle, coming down on top of us. He half-landed half-hovered over that bomb crater while my torque and observer picked me up and literally threw me into the back of that Loach.

My butt landed in the grenade box, and my legs were pointing out the gunner's door. I looked around and saw a full load of ammo, weapons, and fuel. I had maxed a Loach before, and knew this would be too much. I was still cringing when I felt the wind blowing after all the shuddering and vibrating that Hughes OH-6A went through to get us airborne. I do not honestly believe that takeoff could be repeated, given the circumstances. Being scared can get all kinds of things done! Something was wrong with the aircraft, as it would not maintain trim, and the wind coming through the gunner's doorway was blowing blood all over my face and helmet. We tried to get my visor down, but it was history, as two .30 cal. rounds had gone through my helmet from front to rear, and there was a crack on the right side from the rotor blade hit.

We landed at 15th Med, Phuoc Vinh, where I was carried into the only building I never really wanted to see, but had been in many times with our wounded and KIA. The smell inside was one you would never forget. They removed my chest plate, and I saw the damage to it. They hesitated to remove my helmet due to its extensive damage, and being covered with gore, they must have thought that part of my head was gone.

Suddenly I heard, "Hey, Rocket! How's it going?!" There stood Red holding his shoulder and chicken plate, both covered in blood. He had taken a round through the shoulder, and his face had been sprayed with plexiglas fragments. He and his gunner had taken over 20 hits in the cockpit area, and they lost the main hydraulic system on their last gun run.

They were setting the Cobra down several kliks away when the second hydraulic system's warning light came on and the controls froze. He rolled off the throttle to get it on the ground. That made three birds and eight people down within a 10-minute period.

I saw Captain Reterrer, and he had a look on his face that told everything about the worst nightmare any commander could have. He had just lost some of his best pilots and aircraft in the blink of an eye, and he almost bought it at the same time. He was like most 1/9 commanders and flew with us, not above us.

I had been hit seven times and was still kicking! Bullets hit my heel, left thigh, right hand, chest armor (which broke ribs), helmet, and the biggie, a .51 cal. that blew my left leg in half. One artery still connected pumped blood to the foot, so they left the leg on to see if it could be saved.

I would not have survived if it had not been for Larry Brown's compliance with a division rule that we wear gloves, roll sleeves down, not wear jungle boots (their nylon melts in a fire), and wear chicken plates. Brown caught me walking out to the flight line and asked where my plate was. He was new to the unit, but we had hit it off, so I admitted not having it with me, instead of lying that it was in the aircraft. Instead of ordering me to go back to get it, he handed me his. Less than two hours later it had several hits dead center!

I didn't see Brown again until years later at a Vietnam Helicopter Pilots Association reunion. He was, and still is, a commander, leader, friend, and brother. I found the Loach pilot who came in and got me and my crew out on one load on that OH-6A. The Army said it would try to save my leg, and they did, after two years in a hospital. It healed crooked and short, but it healed, and I eventually got back into aviation and flew Cobras.

I was a maintenance tech, but at least I was where I belonged. The Army gave me 17 years of use with that mess of a leg, and I lost it in 1987 while I was a police officer.

I would not trade one moment of my life for any other. It seems that there is no way for me to get close enough to someone to be a total friend unless they have been there. We trusted each other with our lives – how many people around you right now can you trust that much?

Cool Hand Chole, Buck Elton, Rags Rager, Iceman McNeal, Fanny Farmer, Super-X

Linder, Rasberry Jones, Weird Oz Osborn, Sugarbear Shugart, Mad Dog Brown, Harv Hopkins, and all the others – we spent a short moment in time together, and we had a unity that can never be duplicated, but is the envy of many to this very day.

The *Montana Mercenary, Vagabond Virgin, 442 Doctor Death, Peacemaker, Little Green Killing Machine, Queer John, Triple Nickel, Timujin Ship, As Ye Reap, Family Car,* and all the other birds, are gone but not forgotten.

Through the Vietnam Helicopter Pilot's Association, I found that I could again associate with the type of people that I could respect and care for because they had earned their place and survived "The

Nam" just as I had, without the "There-I-was war story BS," which doesn't mean anything.

There were many different and unique parts of our unit. Yes, I was hanging it out all the time as a Loach pilot, but I'd spend 10 hours of Loach time in the Dog's Head before I would want to spend 30 seconds of hover time in an LZ that our Blue Lift pilots did daily. I'd spend 20 hours of Loach time in the Fish Hook before I'd hump the jungle where our Blues Headhunters were inserted. And, I'd spend my entire tour in Laos before I'd spend one day as a nurse in a Nam medical facility.

Health problems did to Rocket in May 2010 what hordes of the enemy could not. Before checking out, Rocket wrote his own obituary in which he stated that his life "…has been some party." Something about having been in the Cav.

A 1st Cavalry Aerorifle platoon, "ARP" or "Blues," prepares a downed OH-6A for sling-load recovery. A yellow triangle on the Loach's "doghouse" identifies S/N 66-7837 as belonging to the division's A Troop, 1st Squadron, 9th Cavalry. (U.S. Army)

This OH-6A, S/N 68-17234, of B Company, 123rd Aviation Battalion wears the unit "Warlords" emblem on its nose. Skid gear was painted yellow and black and all glass framing was painted a light color, possibly off-white. Loaches replaced B Company's OH-23G scout helicopters, which also flew under the call sign "Skeeter." The unit's parent command was the 23rd Infantry Division, better known as "American." All infantry divisions in Vietnam had included on their organizational charts an Aeroscout unit as a component of an aviation battalion. Scores of other units of all sizes and purposes in country also had loaches on their inventories. Their missions often veered from the scout role and included everything from unit hack to psychological warfare (psywar). (Author's Collection)

A "Warlords" Loach is secured against typhoon winds with sandbags in its revetment at Chu Lai on the Vietnamese coast in 1970. The Scout element of the 123rd Aviation Battalion under American wore the Warlord unit insignia, which was a skull-like, helmeted knight superimposed on white wings. By 1970, Chu Lai's flight line had seen improvements, with Pierced-Steel-Planking, or PSP, replaced by broader plank panels. Revetments, which remained necessarily low for main rotor clearance, were made up of sand- or concrete-filled 55-gallon drums on pallets. At most bases, aircraft parked on flight lines, as well as buildings in company areas, presented tempting targets for enemy gunners and sapper squads. At many bases, a heavily armed Huey helicopter lightship would fly perimeter security, or pilots and aircraft would be designated for alert duty. (Michael Stanley – "Warlord 3-0")

A Loach of Apache Troop, 7th Squadron, 1st Cavalry Division flies near the Vietnam-Cambodian border during the Cambodian Incursion in late 1970. Pilots often preferred that their observer/gunner be positioned at the same side of the aircraft. The pilot could then point out targets to his "Oscar" and direct his fire. The observer shows the photographer a 40mm round for his M-79 grenade launcher. Firing the weapon from the Loach required a great deal of skill. The M-79 was one of a number of weapons used by heavily armed Scout crews. Number 66-17793 wore its A/7/1 Apache unit emblem on engine compartment covers, which were painted black. "WO1 WILLIS" is painted on the rotor pylon, known as the "doghouse." (Bill Staffa)

Last Laugh
by Ed Sweeney

Combat affects people in different ways, despite their beliefs, and often alters the perspective of others. Ed Sweeney remembers this about a Scout pilot who was a Mormon.

Christmas 1969. A cease-fire was declared in Vietnam from 6 PM Christmas Eve to 6 PM Christmas Day. We still flew on Christmas Day, just to ensure the peace was kept. I was the Scout Platoon Leader of C Troop, 3rd Squadron. 17th Cavalry. We flew Hunter-Killer teams. Just before the cease-fire ended on Christmas Day, I received a radio call from one of my Scout pilots. He reported that he found a Vietcong lying in an open bunker with an AK-47 in his arms. He was calling to get permission to continue low-level circling of the enemy soldier until the cease-fire ended, some five minutes away. I granted the request and five minutes later he called me back. He reported one dead gook.

Sweeney describes two other incidents that likely were not mentioned in official mission reports.

While breaking in new Scout pilots, we always had a full-fledged Scout pilot fill the role of observer, flying left seat. I was riding left seat one day and just as soon as we got low level, I saw a huge herd of deer to my left. My platoon felt that if we killed edible wildlife, we were taking food from the mouths of our enemies. Without thinking about the new guy next to me, I immediately said, "Break left, break left!" Well, the pilot did just as I asked, and I opened up with my Car-15 on full auto and started spraying the deer.

Meanwhile, the newbie has no clue what is going on so he continues increasing bank.

Before I know it, the helicopter's rotor blades are now between me and the deer. I'm still firing, meaning that I am now making numerous large holes in our rotor blades.

As we level off, the helicopter starts vibrating violently and we are forced to land in an enemy infested area. We only briefly stay on the ground before we decide we would rather take a chance trying to limp back to base rather than chance the gooks. Off we go again – boom, boom, bang banging it back home.

In the meantime, our gunship is covering from 1,500 feet and screaming, "What the hell is going on down there?" I think fast and say we are taking fire. Cobra rolls in and dumps half his load of 40mm, minigun, and rockets on the area. The gunship reports back to base that I had received fire. The command group then decides to insert the infantry. I said, "Oh shit!" What am I going to do now?

I decided to just wait and see what happens. We flew back to the refuel/rearm point and shut the Loach down for inspection. We found numerous holes in the blades and had to have the aircraft sling-loaded back to base camp for rotor replacement.

The infantry was inserted but thank God the platoon leader was a friend of mine. When they got back to base he came over to the Scout area and invited us all to a venison dinner. It was full of holes, but quite tasty.

The CO (commanding officer) never said a word to me. He was a good guy, and because I was the laughing stock of the unit that day, I'm sure he knew about it. I may be the only Loach jock who has the dubious distinction of shooting himself down.

Another time, Thanksgiving Day 1969, we were assigned a mission, which will forever live in my mind. We usually flew all over 90 percent of III Corps. For some strange reason, this particular day

An OH-6A, S/N 67-16161 of C Troop, 2nd Squadron, 17th Cavalry "Condors" of the 101st Airborne Division at Camp Eagle's Scabbard Pad in 1971. Aircraft of 2/17 were identified by colored bands on tail booms, with light blue indicating C Troop. (Doug Kibbey)

we were told to fly the other 10 percent. This was the only day in my entire year there that we flew this AO.

It was a free-fire zone, which was exciting, but also scary. Exciting because most of our flying was under that foolish "Don't fire unless fired upon" rule. We knew that if anything moved we could shoot and ask questions later. Scary because being a free-fire zone, it was probably overrun with gooks.

We arrived in the AO, as usual, around dawn. As soon as we got low level, it was apparent there was plenty of fresh activity. We kept our airspeed up initially because we were sure the gooks were there. It didn't take long to figure out the gooks had taken off quickly. They must have heard us coming and jumped into the many spider holes in the area. They left behind beaucoup logging trucks and associated equipment, as well as a lot of personal belongings. There was even a very unusual gasoline-driven car and a motorcycle. Being a free-fire zone, we proceeded to have a ball. We and the Cobra took turns dumping ordnance into the area. There were so many targets that we must have refueled and rearmed four or five times that day. We ended up logging 10 hours of flight time, the most I had flown in one day during my entire year.

On our last visit to the area, our gunship pilot had a bright idea, he wanted us to swap places with him. We would play the role of gun and he would go low level and become the scout. We should have known! Bright idea, all right. But we did it. We went to 1,500 feet and he went low level. He wanted his front seat copilot/gunner to have fun with his minigun and grenade launcher. Was it ever fun. It looked like a reverse fireworks display.

We were all hooting and howling for about 15 minutes as they shot up all their ordnance.

We then returned to base camp for a great finish of a great day – Thanksgiving dinner.

After post-flighting, we heard moaning and groaning from the gun crew. We went over to investigate. We stopped counting at 199 shrapnel holes on the Cobra. Who would have figured that their grenades would go off in the tree tops and pepper the helicopter with shrapnel. Of course, the Scout crews laughed all the way to the mess hall, leaving the Cobra jocks saying, "What the hell are we going to do now?"

We got to the chow hall and sure enough, ol' Cookie and company had saved the special dinner for us, with apologies for all the boiled shrimp that had been eaten before we got there. The last laugh was on them. The next day, the Scout and Cobra crews were the only ones not suffering from shrimp food poisoning.

Joe Crockett of D Troop, 1st Squadron, 4th Cavalry of the 1st Infantry Division "Quarter Cav" poses with the Vietnam Cross of Gallantry he had just been awarded. Crockett wears jungle fatigues designed specifically for troops in Vietnam. Standard fatigues worn by first arriving troops in the combat zone quickly proved unsuitable, prompting the development of clothing that was mildew resistant and dried quickly. On his fatigue blouse, Crockett wears black metal rank insignia on the collars, the 1st Infantry Division patch on his left shoulder, and locally-made, unofficial unit patches on breast pockets. Boonie hats or OD baseball caps usually topped off the tropical uniform. Jungle boots were part of this uniform, but leather boots were worn while flying. (Joe Crockett Collection)

They're Good but We're Better
by Joseph Crockett

Crockett was a Loach crew chief/door gunner of a Hunter-Killer team of D Troop, 1st Squadron, 4th Cavalry of the 1st Infantry Division, simplified in military jargon as D-One-Four. Stationed at Phu Loi, the unit was nicknamed "Outcasts." Crockett offers an example of a skilled Scout's ability to read sign and sense something out of place.

We flew with two crewmembers in a Loach; the pilot in the right front seat and the crew chief/gunner directly behind him in the rear. On the opposite side was mounted a minigun. We were on station about 90 miles north of our base, flying outside of a town called Quan Loi, which had been overrun by the Viet Cong the week before. It was known that there was heavy enemy activity in the area. We were cruising down on the deck at a speed of about 40 knots. Usually I had to adjust my eyesight to see down through the triple canopy of trees and jungle. Suddenly we came across a clearing and something caught my eye. I couldn't place it, it happened so quick. I hit my mike button, telling the pilot to bring the bird around again. I grabbed a red smoke grenade and had it at the ready. The

pilot came back around in a clockwise rotation, circling on the tops of trees, right on the outside of the clearing. As I scanned I noticed a small row of bushes in the midst of the clearing.

I stared hard, knowing I had seen something of merit. I was just about ready to give the pilot a clear signal when I saw one of the bushes move ever so slightly. Turning my attention to it, my hunch played right. There was a squad of Viet Cong crouched down camouflaged with bushes strapped to their backs. I grabbed the red smoke, flipped the pin out and rolled it out the door. I swung my M60 around and squeezed off my first rounds. That was all it took. The enemy leaped to their feet and started running for the tree-line. I was in perfect position, my pilot pushing in the tail rotor and staying in a hover, and I brought the entire squad down, either wounded or killed.

I heard the pilot come up on the mike, saying that the Cobra gunships were inbound, and I could feel the Loach pull in power as we headed out of the kill zone and up to altitude.

As was our practice whenever we had confirmed kills, we would trail red smoke as we made our approach back to our home base. Today was a good day – let's see what tomorrow brings.

Wearing jungle fatigues adorned with D/1/4 "Outcast" patches, veteran Aeroscout crewmen Joe Crockett and Jimmy Parker pose at the Vietnam Veteran's Memorial in Washington, D.C. in 2005. Vietnam vets attending special events at "The Wall" often were reunited, affirming the brotherhood to which only Vietnam combat veterans could relate. Behind the pair stands the famous statue at The Wall that represents those who served in America's protracted war. Over time, helicopter crewmen of the Vietnam War found a renewed sense of brotherhood and a collective voice in various organizations such as the Vietnam Helicopter Pilot's Association (VHPA) and Vietnam Helicopter Crew Members Association (VHCMA), of which the author was one of the original members. (Joe Crockett Collection)

Serial number 67-16254 minus its main rotor blades after being sling-loaded to Camp Eagle in 1969. Assigned to Headquarters Company of the 101st Airborne Division's 3rd Brigade, this Loach was later pressed into service with the division's 326th Medical Battalion. Since Hueys attempting medical evacuations with rescue hoists suffered high losses, it was hoped that a smaller, faster Loach had a better chance of getting wounded out. After only 20 missions, however, the dedicated Dustoff Loach was shot down. (Joe Gwizdak)

Hard Lessons
by Danny L. Aiken

Aeroscouts knew that until they gained combat experience, they were a liability to their fellow Scouts. And they knew that one mistake made by an experienced Scout could prove fatal. Danny Aiken was a crew chief in a small Scout unit, called "Primo Aviation Ltd," which was attached directly to the commander of the 11th Light Infantry Brigade. Aiken was seriously burned on a mission that went bad as a result of his new commander's inexperience. The commander was killed. Aiken says, "I only knew him on the way to where he got killed – 30 minutes. A lot of things happened that you will never find in any military records, and you will never find the people involved. That is why I have had no luck all these years finding the men I flew with." After a 33-year Army career, Aiken talks about the death of Primo Aviation Commander Captain John L. Wadsworth.

On 8 July 1970 at LZ Bronco, Duc Pho, Vietnam it was a real hot day as usual for that time of year; hot and muggy. Getting into the Loach with the blades turning overhead was a little cooler. The mission for the day, I was told, was a search for a six- to eight-man patrol that got washed away in a flash flood, and drowned. They had been missing for about three days. I was not told until later, after I got out of the hospital, that it wasn't a patrol, but a Long Range Reconnaissance Patrol (LRRP) team that was massacred, chopped up, and thrown into a mass grave. They were good men. I knew some of them; even ate and drank with them. The mission covered hundreds of miles of rice paddies, at high speed, low level flight. It got so that all we could see was green, and we couldn't tell one paddy from the next, until we came into a free-fire zone.

Nobody was supposed to be in that area, except farmers, during the daytime.

On this mission we had two ships, a white team, both Loaches, one with a minigun, and the gunner, Frank, and pilot, Warrant Officer (WO) Glenn, on the right side. My aircraft had me as gunner and Mister Gregg as the WO. A third person, Mister Mike, was observing in the left rear seat. The mission, as usual, was for the low ship to go down and look around, searching for any clues. If we found anything, we got TOC (Tactical Operations Center) on the line for further instructions.

We had been flying since early morning and had not had breakfast yet. We were getting tired, and it was getting hard to think, getting a little punchy. We needed to get something to eat and go back out a little later. The pilot said, "Let's go in and get something to eat."

We headed back to LZ Bronco. We did a 90-degree left bank and as we did, we spotted a VC flag under a tree line as we passed over a French villa compound. The tree line led right to this villa, which had a well near its front. Well, before going back to the LZ, we had to knock down that flag.

Mister Gregg informed TOC of what was going on, and we were told to go down and look around. As we approached the villa, a girl was lying near the well like she was trying not to be noticed. It didn't work. We hovered over her and I motioned for her to go out to the nearby field so the high ship could pick her up and take her back to MACV (Military Assistance Command, Vietnam) for questioning. I pointed my M60 at her and having to fire at her to get her to go out to the field didn't help, but unless in full contact, we were not allowed to land or expose the aircraft. The high ship came down and picked her up as a prisoner, and headed for the

MACV compound.

We were ordered to work the area to see what happened. People were in the villa trying to find a way out while facing my M60. They would not come out and we were down to half fuel. The villa structures were made of brick and mortar with hard clay tile roofs that the M60 rounds bounced off of. My pilot said that if he could knock some tiles loose, I could stand on the skid and drop a grenade into the hole. Two VC ran out the back door and tried to escape down an escape hole. The people refused to surrender and continued to try to escape. This was the hardest time of my life; the 10-minute warning fuel light was on, the high ship was not back on station yet, and the VC were trying to hide something. When they tried to run for a heavy covered tree line, I shot at and hit them, killing them both. Then we landed and Mister Mike ran over to the dead, while I covered him with my M60. He grabbed the bag the dead guys were hanging onto so tightly. We lifted off and headed at very high speed for LZ Bronco. We were just about out of fuel; in fact, as we landed at Primo Aviation, the aircraft quit, with not even fumes left.

You would think that was enough for one mission. The report came in from TOC that the bag we had captured from the VC had a list of 118 VC operatives in the area, a VC flag, 1,000 piaster, and a grenade ready to be pulled. I wish someone with a real pair of balls would have stepped in and said "end of mission," but no luck. The new CO, Captain John Wadsworth, with no air combat experience, decided he had to better what was done. As our aircraft was refueled and rearmed, I had a Coke and we were back in the air, going back to the same hot spot we were so lucky to have gotten away from without taking hits.

The SOP (Standard Operating Procedures) of recon dictated that if something was not attached to someone's arm, you do not touch it without EOD (Explosive Ordnance Disposal), or a grappling hook. Also, once you hit an area, you do not go right back to that area because you are going to be set up. And if you break all the rules, you let the crew chief try to protect the aircraft the best he can by always facing him into the fire; he has all the firepower. All of these rules were broken that day. We were on a hot mike so TOC knew what was happening, so all the blame does not go to Captain Wadsworth; there was plenty to spread around, to include

The shadow of an OH-6A's tail points to the bodies of four Việt Cộng soldiers attacked on a trail in 1969. The Loach belonged to the Aviation Section of the 2nd Brigade, 1st Infantry Division. (Douglas G. Smith)

myself.

We did once around the villa, when Wadsworth spotted a bag on the ground close to where the two dead VC were laying. But before I could get the grappling hook out and thrown, the aircraft landed with me facing a field, not the action. The new Captain Wadsworth got out and ran over to the bag. He brought it back to the aircraft and as he set it down in the aircraft, it exploded, killing him and blowing the fuel cell. Fuel blew over me and set me on fire; the whole aircraft was now on fire. Armor plating between me and WO Gregg protected him from the direct blast and flame. I got out onto the ground, rolled around, and put out the fire. Gregg pulled the straps loose from his seat and got out. As he and I were on the ground, not far from the burning aircraft, VC and NVA troops fired at us. The high ship put down suppressive fire, which was very good, because we had only one .45 cal. pistol between us. All the other weapons were inside the aircraft, burning and exploding.

The high ship landed close by in the field and gunner Frank, like John Wayne, came running over to us, firing all the way. Frank stopped to see if the CO was still alive; no such luck. As a result of this mission, Captain Wadsworth, the son-in-law of a congressman, died at 28 years old. WO Gregg received a minor burn on his nose, but he shook from combat trauma the rest of the time we flew together. I spent two months in the hospital recovering from wounds, and went back into combat shortly thereafter. Mister Glenn and gunner Frank never received awards for their heroic action that day, but I thanked them.

Ed Gallagher poses for a portrait in his Air Force dress blues with the decorations from his service and accomplishments in both military grades. (Ed Gallagher Collection)

Ed Gallagher's broad military career comprised two stints in the Air Force and one as an Army Slick and Loach pilot in Vietnam.

Combat Track Meet
by Ed Gallagher

After serving in Vietnam as an Air Force advisor, Ed Gallagher did what he calls an "encore" tour as an Army pilot in 1970 and 1971. He "drove" slicks during the first half of his tour with the 175th Assault Helicopter Company (AHC) "Outlaws" and then flew Loaches with D Troop, 3rd Squadron, 5th Cavalry at Vinh Long using the call sign "War Wagon One-Three." Gallagher's career was cut short as a result of the Army's 1971 Reduction in Force. Bent on a military career, he returned to the Air Force where he started out near the bottom again, and retired 30 years later as a Chief Master Sergeant.

The Hueys had just completed the troop insertion and were leaving the LZ to refuel and rearm. With no landing to cover, we decided to form a "Pink Team" and look for targets of opportunity. We were a flight of two OH-6A Loaches and two AH-1G Cobra gunships.

Since I was flying trail, the last ship in a right echelon formation, my job was to watch the other aircraft and monitor communications. So I tuned in Radio Saigon and was busy listening to some rock and roll when Cobra Lead dove hard and started yelling about some guy running around down below. As I pulled out of the dive and let my stomach return to its normal place, I noticed this one lone individual running a zigzag pattern across an open field, and he was really moving.

Now a Cobra is an awe inspiring sight with guns, cannon and rockets bristling from everywhere. So to be an all-alone enemy troop in the middle of an open field with not one, but two of these man-eaters closing in on you at 200 m.p.h. must be highly motivating.

The first Cobra opened up with his miniguns, which sprays bullets at 4,000 rounds per minute. A cloud of dust kicked up all around the guy but not a single shot touches him and he's still running. The second ship lets go a volley of rockets and flame, dirt and smoke envelope the speeding figure. "He's had it now," I say to myself, and then sit slack-jawed and incredulous as I watch him pop out of the smoke, running faster than before. The lead Loach dives in dropping hand grenades like a mini-bomber yet the lone speedster goes on unscathed. It's my turn now and I've got him all lined up. I slowly squeeze the trigger for my minigun just as he steps into my sights and the damn gun jams. We are all wild with frustration as he ducks into a small thatch hut on the edge of the field.

The Cobras line up and dive in to blow the hootch to hell when out pops the moving marvel who is now wearing a white shirt. Now this sophisticated disguise may have fooled many others, but not us. I mean, let's face it. We're all high school graduates. The Cobras blow up the hootch and he's off and running.

This Loach of D Troop, 3rd Squadron, 5th Cavalry crashed on Easter Sunday 1969 after its engine was hit by an RPG round. Fortunately, the round did not detonate and the crew lived to tell about the experience. The engine panel the round went through leans against the aircraft. The emblem of the 9th Infantry Division, to which D/3/5 was assigned, was worn on the rotor pylon. (Michael Galvin)

He's now heading back down the field he had just run up. Again the gunships attack and the field literally explodes in a fury of munitions and again, miraculously, this Viet Cong voodoo goes untouched. He leaps over a row of hedge and dives into a small, deep stream covered with vegetation. Now the Cobras must climb back up into their element and let us Loaches do what we do best.

We slowly scout every inch of the stream bank for our hidden prey. I'm reflecting on his impossible escape from our firepower and am amazed at his skill, speed, and good fortune. As I follow the lead Loach, I begin to sense the feeling of being watched. I stop dead and snap right just in time to see the top of his head disappear under the water. I say nothing to the others and hold my position. My heartbeats tick off the seconds. He raises his head, gasping for air and his eyes suddenly go wide with terror. I'm not 10 feet away.

He has no place to run and certain death is staring him in the face.

His eyes mirror the disbelief and confusion he feels as I turn my aircraft left, away from him. As I turn my head to face him, I touch my right hand to my helmet visor in brief salute, smile, and fly on. Tomorrow we may meet again and death may not be cheated, but for today he has earned the comfort of another sunset. As for me; it will remain my secret as later, when we gather to tell of our daily exploits, I'll listen to the other pilots tell the story of "the one that got away."

In contrast, Gallagher relates this story, which he calls "Lifetime."

October 1970 in South Vietnam's U Minh Forest. It looked like a Kansas wheat field just before harvest. An endless sea of tall yellow growth slowly swaying on a warm midmorning breeze; an undulating mass to mesmerize and soothe the watcher. But this isn't Kansas, it's the Mekong Delta. It isn't a field of golden wheat but a fetid morass of coarse swamp grass. In this place there are men waiting and wanting to kill me.

We've left the safety of altitude and are diving towards the decaying moor, jinking and twisting to throw off the enemy's aim. We scouts are part of a hunter-killer team made up of two Cobra helicopter gunships and two light observation helicopters. The gunships stay high, a constant threat to the bad guys. We go low and ferret out enemy activity and supplies. In short, we're bait! The enemy, the Viet Cong, actually has a special medal for those who shoot down helicopters. Because of the gunships, the award is usually posthumous.

Today, because the area is so large, we've abandoned our normal routine of slow movement and hovering at ground level. Later, troops can be inserted to do the close up work if we find anything now. Lead scout is flying a fast crisscross pattern and I am close up behind him, a little off to his right in the five o'clock position. The downward wash from his rotor blades cleaves the tall grass like a giant, invisible scythe. Even at our higher speed, I'm getting a good view of what's in the swamp. Lead pops up over a small mound as I pass on the side. Suddenly I see a little guy with a big gun and it's

An Aeroscout crew of D/3/5 *Charliehorse* poses with OH-6A S/N 69-15993 at Camp Evans in 1971. After the 1st Cavalry Division relinquished control of the unit in 1966, it fell under various parent commands, earning it the title "Bastard Cav." The large red and white triangle represents the 17th Cavalry, a designation taken on by D/3/5 in late 1971. (Hugh Mills)

pointed right up Lead's tail pipe.

"Break, Break, Break!" I shout into my helmet mike. This designated command alerts the whole team of danger and allows me to take over as Lead. I stab the stick hard left and the sky and earth change position violently. My gunner, who sits next to me, grabs hold of his seat as I roll the ship over 100…110…120 degrees of bank. The bad guy is now shifting his weapon towards me. I bottom the pitch and kick it out of trim to slow us down. I'm trying to draw a bead on this guy with my minigun. At 4,000 bullets a minute, I can vaporize him. His gun steadily moves towards me. I'm almost in position. I pull the trigger anyway. He's getting too close. I feel pressure on my finger. The trigger moves.

The silence is deafening. A circuit breaker pops. The damn gun is jammed. I kick the pedal hard right to let my gunner get this guy. His gun is up and ready. If we fly much closer, he won't have to shoot him with the gun; he'll be able to beat him with it. Flame erupts from the barrel of the M60 machine gun and I watch a tracer dance at the bad guy's feet. But, just as quickly as it started, the firing stops. The usual five or six-second burst has only lasted two. The M60 has jammed. The bad guy's weapon is aimed directly at me and I'm staring down a black, endless opening, waiting for the flash that will end my life.

Time has stopped. My hands and feet move as in slow motion. The rotor blades pass haltingly overhead. The air turns into syrup. Heartbeats pound in my ears, one slow beat at a time. In my mind, I see the windshield shatter, my head snaps back, my body slumps forward and the ship slides into the mound and explodes. This time it's over.

But then, heartbeat by heartbeat, I notice the muzzle easing away from me! The enemy's feet leave the ground. His gun drifts from his hand as his twisting body topples from the mound and slides into the swamp. Yes, it's over, but for him.

Eleven empty cartridges are found in the ship. Eleven rounds fired before the gun jammed. Eleven rounds that made me the victor, not victim.

The pounding in my ears fades away and the rotor blades resume their furious pace. The battle lasted but a minute. A deadly minute that cost a life, but, for me, will be lived for a lifetime.

Ed Gallagher also penned this reflection of the cost of war. He calls it "A Day in the Forest."

The folks in New York City were almost friendly to each other as they enjoyed the cool respite of the fall weather after a hot and arduous summer. They even failed to complain about the lateness of their particular mode of transportation, which was reacting with predictable mechanical reluctance to the first chilled whispers of a coming winter.

At the same time, those of us half a world away suffered no transportation delays although we readily wished we could. Our mission for the day, which had looked to be boring, tedious and extremely safe, was canceled in exchange for an immediate divert to the southernmost part of the country, the U Minh Forest. Flying around that area in daylight was almost as much fun as jogging in Central Park at night. We followed the compass south but it was done with no joy.

We landed at Ca Mau, refueled, rearmed and in general, tried to act cool. The boss called all the pilots together and tried to explain

The "Seawolves," HA(L)-3, was the Navy's only attack helicopter squadron of the Vietnam war, having been commissioned and decommissioned within South Vietnam's Mekong Delta region. The Seawolves flew all three Huey model heavily armed gunships, often from the tight quarters of ships. Initially developed for maritime duty as part of the "Brown Water Navy" controlling Vietnam's waterways, Seawolf detachments increased in number, allowing widespread coverage of the country's IV Corp Tactical Zone. The author, while assigned to the 240th AHC at Camp Bearcat, recalls often working in concert with Seawolf units throughout the Mekong Delta region. He found especially interesting the wide variety of weaponry that formed the Navy Huey's muscle. And staging from a naval base guaranteed better food, along with ammunition for exotic weapons not normally found at Army installations. (U.S. Navy)

what was happening. The Navy had sent in some Huey gunships to find the bad guys in an area we called "VC Lake." They did their job well and found a whole bunch of them, which resulted in the shoot-down of a gunship and crew, now missing. The downed crew had to be located before we could let loose with all our firepower into the area. All eyes turned towards the Scouts. As one of the senior Scout pilots, I knew this one was ours. I pulled out my revolver, spun the cylinder and in my best John Wayne voice said, "Let's mount up." The Cav was on its way! As I headed toward my aircraft, I wanted to light a cigarette but my hands were shaking too much.

We got to our aircraft and had a meeting of the Scout crews to discuss options and strategies. Just about midpoint in our conversation, a lone Navy gunship approached our gathering. At first I was annoyed by his noisy interruption, but as I looked up I realized his problem. Hung over the right skid, secured by a strap held by the gunner, was one of the missing crewmembers. He was young, he was American, and he was dead.

As the ship hovered a few feet above us, I could see the anguish in the gunner's eyes. This had been his buddy. The ship couldn't land due to the position of the body, yet no one moved to receive its ravaged cargo. The gunner's eyes were too plaintive to ignore, so I stepped into position, opened my arms and accepted his sorrowful burden.

As he released the strap, I realized for the first time what "dead weight" really meant.

Despite his youth and slight frame, his body filled my arms and bowed my legs.

I cradled his head and looked at his face, a face that would never grow older. It was slightly whiskered and his pale blue eyes were opened and fixed in an eternal stare. His lips were poised with final words the world would never hear. The others came up to take him from me. They had spread a poncho on the ground to receive him. Even as I staggered under his weight, I was reluctant to let him go. I knew that after I released him, the warrior boy would cease to exist. He would be bundled and bagged and become just another dead statistic; never to be held in anyone's arms again.

The flight back to base that night was unusually quiet. A large pumpkin-colored moon rose as we watched the night claim the land below us. On the other side of this world the sun was just rising, bringing a new day. And to the young sailor's home; visitors. A Navy chaplain, a personnel officer and a telegram that reads in part, "We regret to inform you…"

That night we spent drinking but didn't party. We talked but in muted tones, and the conversations were of home and loved ones, not of daily heroics. Tomorrow we would do the hardest of tasks after being closely touched by death; we would continue living.

Two Battles
by John Lindgren and Henry Leigh Ballance

The struggle to continue living challenged not only a Loach crew called "Phoenix Four," it set in motion a major rescue operation comprising elements of both the U.S. Army and Air Force. Since chopper pilots who shared Vietnam's unfriendly skies are of like ilk, regardless of service, this Loach story is told by U.S. Air Force helicopter pilot John Lindgren and U.S. Army helicopter pilot Henry Leigh Ballance. Lindgren rescued Ballance. Given that time, for them, is a great illusion that can be folded to make 40 years look like last week, they create an interesting dual perspective of the event.

The OH-6A belonged to the Aviation Section of Headquarters & Headquarters Battalion, Division Artillery of the 23rd Infantry Division, popularly called "Americal," based at Chu Lai. Under the call sign "Phoenix Four," its crew comprised pilot 1Lt. Ballance, forward artillery observer 1Lt. Peter R. Perez, and gunner/observer PFC Buster Leroy Scott.

Ballance begins by saying that on 3 June 1970, the trio was sinking sampans in the Song Thu Bon River at the bottom of a steep valley. The aircraft took hits in the tail rotor section and it went into a spin. Ballance continues: "I held the power in and we bounced off the mountainside at least twice. It was during these violent maneuvers that our gunner was thrown out of the aircraft from where he sat in the doorway. When we crashed, everything came off the aircraft, but we landed upright. We looked for the door gunner and heard the enemy shouting. We spotted a bomb crater when we went down. We were climbing up the mountain when we came across the large bomb crater and we decided that would be a good place to be picked up by helicopter. We climbed about 50 yards above the crater and that's where we spent the night."

Perez, who had ground experience as a forward observer, had offered that their chance of survival was better if they spent the night on the mountainside. Throughout the night, the pair hung onto a sapling; from their precarious perch, they could hear activity in a village below. More unnerving was the continuous bird calls the searching enemy used to signal one another in their closing circle. Ballance estimated that the enemy closed to within 15 meters of their position.

Although their headquarters had not been aware of their last position, Ballance and Perez hoped that rescue forces would be searching for them come daylight.

When daylight broke, the pair heard a Loach hunting in the area and made their way down to the crater. They spotted the enemy below and lobbed two white phosphorous grenades, hoping to start a brush fire that would keep the enemy at bay. Ballance says:

"The Loach crew first thought it was an artillery shoot and started to leave the area, but the pilot decided to make one more pass, and that's when we were sliding down the mountain to the bomb crater. We had just arrived at the crater when the Loach flew by and saw us." *In later conversation with the Loach pilot, Ballance discovered how close they had come to being shot by the Loach crew; since details of their downing were sketchy, the Loach wasn't searching for the pair, which had camouflaged their faces.*

Unable to land, the Loach crew threw down a radio, an M-79 grenade launcher, and smoke grenades.

U.S. Air Force Air Rescue was alerted, and the Rescue Coordination Center (called "Queen") on Monkey Mountain near Da Nang scrambled the Alpha Force. The message read, "Phoenix 4 with 3 SOB (souls on

Capt. John Lindgren poses with a Sikorsky HH-53C Super Jolly Green Giant during his time as a pilot with the 37th Aerospace Rescue and Recovery Squadron (ARRS) in Vietnam. Only 44 HH-53Cs were built to serve as the long-range SAR version of Sikorsky's Model S-65. Often called "BUFF," the HH-53C supplemented the famed HH-3E Jolly Green Giant rescue helicopter of the ARRS. As a major element in SAR operations, the HH-53C with a crew of five was all-weather, air-refuelable, and well-armored. The BUFF arrived in Southeast Asia in early 1968. (John Lindgren Collection)

BUFF pilot John Lindgren, after C-141 and UH-1 and H-3 experience, went to Eglin AFB, Florida for combat crew training in the HH-53. Early in 1970 he deployed to Udorn RTAFB and was wounded on a rescue mission in March. After ferrying new HH-53s from Thailand to Đà Nẵng AB, Lindgren was assigned to the 37th ARRS there. Later, he put in a tour with the 40th ARRS at Nakhon Phanom RTAFB. (John Lindgren Collection)

A USAF Sikorsky HH-53C from the family of Air Rescue Jolly Greens that in 1970 rescued two OH-6A "Phoenix Four" crewmen of the 23rd Infantry Division's artillery section. Rescue came in all forms in Vietnam, with the HH-53 considered the king of rescue aircraft. (Stephen Miller)

board) down 20 west of 74 – hostile area." Seven minutes later, "Jolly Green Six-Five" and "Six-Six," huge Sikorsky HH-53Cs of the 37th Aerospace Rescue and Recovery Squadron, were airborne from Da Nang Air Base. John Lindgren was the copilot among the crew of five aboard JG 66 and he picks up the story:

"Ninety-nine percent of the time the Army took care of their own guys that got shot down. The only times that they called on us were situations that were too hot for them and they needed the industrial grade close air support. In addition, not very many Army choppers had the heavy duty, long-cable rescue hoist, and there were situations when they just could not reach the survivors. We knew that if the Army called, it was not going to be an easy mission."

Air Rescue mission number 1-3-046, the rescue of Phoenix Zero-Four, 27 miles southwest of Da Nang, quickly took shape with "King Three-Three," an HC-130P Hercules airborne command post, heading to the area to assume command of the search and rescue effort. King advised the Jollies to establish a "feet wet" (over-water) orbit 20 nautical miles north of "Channel 74," which was the code-name for Chu Lai's TACAN station. A pair of A-1 Skyraiders, "Spads 11" and "12," had been scrambled and were inbound. Meanwhile, "Blue Ghost Two-Six," an AH-1G Cobra gunship of F Troop, 8th Cavalry at Chu Lai, had located the survivors and maintained radio contact with them.

Cobra Lead advised that he was putting in ordnance. The survivors reported the same, and that they had spotted movement on the mountainside above them. The enemy was tightening its circle, bent on either capturing the Loach crew or using them as bait to attack the rescue forces they knew would come.

When Spads 11 and 12 arrived, Cobra Lead briefed them on the survivor's location, ground fire, and enemy troop movement. The Cobras, low on fuel, expended their remaining ordnance before leaving to refuel. Another Blue Ghost Cobra Lead reported inbound with four Cobras and a Huey gunship. Meanwhile, the pair of Skyraiders rolled in, attacking with cluster bomb CBU-25, miniguns, rockets, and 20mm cannons. When the Cobras arrived, they were briefed by Spad

11 and then put in an air strike, saving most of their ordnance for the Jolly Greens' run-in.

Jolly Green 66 and 65 had taken up a closer orbit. There was no time to waste; a Cobra pilot reported spotting 40 to 50 enemy troops moving toward Ballance and Perez from about 300 yards away. The pair clung to a tree halfway up the steep slope and the enemy fired from the opposite slope, above their position. This put the rescue chopper in a most dangerous position since the enemy would shoot down at the hovering chopper.

Regardless, the pickup attempt had to start immediately since the enemy was closing in.

Jolly Green 65 (the high bird) remained in orbit, while Spads 11 and 12 laid a smoke screen on the enemy's slope, and then joined with Jolly 66 to begin the run-in. Jolly Green 66 jettisoned its auxiliary fuel tanks, dropped down to treetop level and slowed for the approach, while the Skyraiders flew a protective daisy chain, blasting the enemy with CBU-25 and cannon fire.

Due to the terrain, the crew of Jolly Green 66 was unable to spot the survivors during the run-in. The battle raged around Ballance and Perez, but what they didn't realize was that another battle was taking place in the Jolly Green passing overhead. On approach, JG 66's pilot slipped into a mode that was all too familiar to those around him; a dangerous mode marked by erratic behavior and thought to be the combined result of fear and a flawed system that didn't always identify and address unstable, and subsequently dangerous, characteristics. Aircrew avoided flying with the pilot, whose flying skills were known to be lacking. His knowledge of procedures and aircraft systems, and his control of the aircraft, left much to be desired.

Lindgren picks up the story: "Prior to our run-in, everything had gone right by the book, and all normal procedures were followed. As we approached the survivors, we started seeing enemy tracers as we took ground fire, but still no hits. The pilot started jerking the aircraft around to the extent that he knocked the flight mechanic halfway out the doorway; if he had not worn a gunner's belt, he would have left the aircraft. The mechanic was on hot mike and yelled for help, the pilot screaming at him to shut up. At that point we overflew the survivors and neither the PJs (pararescue specialists) nor I could get the pilot's attention over the yelling on the hot mike. One of the two PJs finally helped the flight mechanic back into the doorway and shut off the hot mike. The Spads had been calling on the radio to tell us that we were flying over the survivors so the pilot finally got us slowed down. The ground fire continued all over the place, but still no hits.

"We hovered back and the flight mechanic spotted the survivors, went back on hot mike and started giving directions to position us over them.

"The pilot was now in a very agitated state and his control was getting worse. The aircraft was jumping up and down due to excessive, rapid collective movements and he was having difficulty maintaining a lateral position over the survivors. These two guys were on a steep slope, hanging onto a tree and they could not move to grab the hoist cable – it had to be dropped right on them. The flight mechanic kept saying 'left 20 feet' and then 'right 20' and 'forward 20' as the aircraft jumped around. The pilot then started swearing at him on hot mike, saying 'make up your mind' and calling him a 'dumb bastard.' At that point, I grabbed the cyclic and tried to dampen out his inputs and settle things down and then he yelled at me, saying things like 'get your hands off the controls or I'll court martial you!'

"I responded by saying he needed to flex his fingers and relax a bit and take a break, take a deep breath. Finally, a crewman came to our rescue and said on the interphone, 'Sir, if you don't stop flinging us all around back here, we will never get out of this place.' The pilot

relaxed on the controls and I managed to settle things down so that we got the penetrator down to the survivors. As they were coming up the hoist, the pilot took the controls back. The stream of ground fire and tracers coming through the smoke screen never stopped."

The Cobras provided covering fire while the HH-53 was in a hover, which was made difficult by the updrafts and the steep slope. On one side the treetops brushed the aircraft, while on the other side, the treetops were a hundred feet below. Lindgren noted, "Our main rotor was very close to the side of the valley and the trees. The HH-53 had a 72-foot rotor diameter and it was very difficult to judge exactly where the tip path was at the sides of the aircraft."

The penetrator was dropped into the survivors' hands on the first precise hover attempt. Lindgren added, "This saga wasn't over. As the flight mechanic and a PJ were pulling the two survivors through the aircraft's doorway, we heard on the interphone 'ohhh shit.' The pilot asked, 'What's going on?' and the reply was 'standby, standby, standby, okay, let's go.'

It turned out that one of the survivors came up the hoist with a grenade in his hand with the pin pulled! The lead PJ grabbed the grenade and slowly got the guy to release it. He then walked to the rear of the aircraft and tossed it out the ramp as we pulled out. The survivor said the enemy was so close that he was ready to toss the grenade down the hill when the rescue chopper showed up."

Ballance went on to fly more Loach missions, Lindgren went on flying rescue in the Jolly Greens, being credited with five combat saves, earning two Distinguished Flying Crosses.

Scout Observer PFC Buster Leroy Scott was never again seen alive; his body eventually was recovered. The fate of Perez and the erratic pilot is uncertain.

Friend to both grunt and downed airmen was the Douglas A-1 "Skyraider." Able to carry its own weight in ordnance and endure tremendous punishment, the Skyraider, or "Spad," as a key element of the rescue force, was known for providing superior close support. (Tom Hansen)

Henry H. "Rick" Roll is captured in a photograph taken while he was assigned as a pilot to D Troop, 3rd Squadron, 5th Cavalry of the 9th Infantry Division's 9th Aviation Battalion. When flying OH-23G "Ravens," the troop's call sign was "Spook." Besides his varied and interesting flying assignments, Roll joined the fraternity of flyers who had the good fortune of experiencing the fact that one good turn serves another. Roll began his combat experience early enough in the long war to fly the vintage reciprocating engine-powered Hiller OH-23 Raven. Having first flown Huey gunships provided perspective and an understanding of other elements of helicopter operations. Undoubtedly, amassing such experience benefited his fast track in Army aviation. (Rick Roll Collection)

Fast Track
by Rick Roll

In every walk of life there seem to be certain individuals who rise above the rest, exuding a rare balance of intellect, tactful responsiveness, cool headedness, and intuitiveness; in short, they have it all together. In Army aviation, such an individual was Henry H. "Rick" Roll. Roll graduated at the top of his flight school officer's class of 71 students, and left the Army in 1968 with the rank of Captain after serving only three years of active duty. And Roll was exceptional in that he was awarded two Distinguished Flying Crosses in less than two weeks while flying as an Aeroscout. Roll finds his second DFC incident more remarkable. On 27 May 1967 he was flying in support of an armored column that came under siege. Continually exposed to the firefight, he flew with the squadron commander on board who controlled the operation, and he marked targets for gunships and adjusted artillery. During the battle, when ground troops called for a medevac for a seriously wounded officer,

Roll heeded the call, descending almost vertically into a small clearing. Roll tells it best.

I was a helo pilot as a 1Lt. with D Troop, 3/5th Cav in 1967. For the first four months of my tour, I was an AC (Aircraft Commander) and Fire Team Leader, flying UH-1C gunships. I switched to Scouts for a change of scenery and action. I flew our Hiller OH-23Gs in combat for two months.

On this mission, near Ap Binh Son, despite all the hostile fire, I got out of the hot LZ in the pouring rain with four passengers on board: our squadron commander in the left seat, me in the middle, the medic in the right seat, and the wounded 1Lt. on a litter strapped to the right skids with our web belts. We had no specialized medevac equipment on board.

The medic initially did not want to board the aircraft but I told him to climb in so he could keep the lieutenant from falling off of the litter; his leg was dangling by a few sinews under the makeshift tourniquet.

Like many combat aviators, Rick Roll pursued his passion for flying after leaving military service. Here, nearly three decades after the Vietnam war, he is seen with a Bell 206B-3, a sleek civilian derivative of the OH-58A Kiowa family, familiar to many Army rotary-wing aviators. Obvious on this Bell Jet Ranger III is the wire strike protection kit, which was initially developed for the Kiowa and other Army helicopters. The Kiowa's introduction to the Army, while not as controversial as that of the OH-6A, had its own complexities. First developed as the OH-4A as a competitor against Hughes' OH-6A, the type was the first to fly in the LOH competition, making its maiden flight on 8 December 1962. Undeterred by its entry being passed over, Bell Helicopter began work on the civilian version it labeled the Model 206A. During 1970, Bell's 206A would get its reprieve and began augmenting and eventually replacing the OH-6A. (Rick Roll Collection)

The Hiller is a three-man lifter, max, including the pilot, on a cool, dry day, but it is only a two-man bird in Vietnam's hot and humid conditions. I had to climb over 100 feet vertically in a 100-foot wide hole in the jungle, which had been flattened by several M-48 tanks. Before I could clear the treetops, my rotor RPM headed for the basement. My flight school training stepped in and I kicked my right pedal, thus reducing the load on the tail rotor, which gave me just enough extra power to make it out, although we were spinning to the right about two to three rpm. The lieutenant lost his leg but survived the war.

Later in his Vietnam tour, Roll himself would have to be rescued. If dedicated air rescue forces were unavailable, any available aircraft within reasonable flying distance responded to the universally recognized "May Day" distress call. Flying without a crew in an unarmed OH-23G, Roll one day had to send out that call. The result was that Navy rescued Army, and rescuer and survivor would be reunited decades later. The mission was at the behest of John Paul Vann, for whom Roll flew an OH-23G the last four months of his 1967 tour. Vann, the protagonist of Neil Sheehan's Pulitzer Prize winning A Bright Shining Lie, was the Deputy of the Civil Operations and Rural Development Support (CORDS) in Vietnam's III Corps Tactical Zone. The unique civil-military operation was USAID's largest endeavor of the war. Immensely controversial, Vann was seen as the David who stood up to the Goliath of the shameful politics of the war. Vann's war, and that of his Scout pilot, ended on a rainy night in June 1972 when their low-leveling OH-58A Kiowa crashed into a stand of trees guarding a Vietnamese cemetery. Rick Roll tells the story.

In early July, after John Paul Vann interviewed and flew with several OH-23G combat-seasoned pilots, I was recruited by him to be his personal pilot and aide, flying Hillers that were provided to me by my old troop. John refused to upgrade us to a UH-1 because he felt the Hueys did not fit the pacification efforts he was spearheading as CORDS Deputy. Flying Vann, on multiple levels, was more dangerous than flying the guns and scouts I had flown previously. He, in my honest opinion, had a subconscious death wish.

In October of 1967 Vann sent me on a highly classified mission to Can Tho, deep in the Mekong River delta, to pick up a South Vietnamese Army colonel and fly him to Saigon.

En route to Saigon, right after crossing the Song Be River, and less than a minute after I tuned to the Dong Tam firebase frequency, the engine of my Raven failed catastrophically. I made a successful zero ground speed autorotation to the center of a rice paddy that was submerged under a foot of water. I ended up, sitting dry as a bone, in the middle of the paddy. All I had for personal protection were a half dozen HE grenades and a 9mm Swedish K submachine gun. During the very rapid autorotative descent, I recall making a 180-degree turn and checking my airspeed for 60 mph, but I remember nothing about the flare and pitch pull, a credit to my flight school training.

I had broadcast multiple "Maydays" on the way down and in less than 10 minutes, a solo U.S. Navy "Sea Wolf" UH-1B gunship shot an approach to our right-hand side to pick us up. After I pulled my radios, I don't think my boots got wet as I raced across the rice stalks. The Sea Wolf flew us back to Dong Tam, a U.S. Army colonel grabbed my ARVN colonel, and I hitched a ride on an Army Caribou back to my base at Bear Cat.

Ever since that day I have had a deep need to find and thank that anonymous pilot and his crew. In 1999, better late than never, I posted a message on the Sea Wolf Association's website in an attempt to locate my savior.

Much to my great surprise and pleasure, on 20 April 2007, I received a letter from Mike Stock, "Sea Wolf Six-Two," informing me that he was the pilot who picked me up on 17 October 1967. I called him immediately and talked to his wife, Barbara, and learned that he was on a corporate flying trip and would return in two days. I then asked her what was Mike's favorite adult beverage and she told me he enjoyed Chardonnay wine. After hanging up with Barbara, I arranged to have a case of Kendall Jackson's finest Vintage Reserve Chardonnay FedExed to the Stock residence in Michigan.

I called Mike on the 22nd and, as you might imagine, we had a great conversation. He's now retired from the Navy and, after flying multiple aircraft, helos and fixed-wing, literally all over the world, has settled in Michigan. He flies de Havilland Beavers on floats in Alaska during the summers; a real pilot's pilot, to be sure!

During this first conversation, I learned, for the very first time the details of Mike's side of this event. He was alone in his Navy UH-1B at Dong Tam, approximately 10 miles from my location, hovering a short distance to refuel, when he heard my radio transmission. Knowing that I was going down in very nasty Viet Cong territory, he pulled pitch and went searching for me; just himself and his crew chief. His miniguns were still wrapped in their protective canvas coverings.

He worried *en route* that the covers might fly off and hit his main rotor or tail rotor but he knew he had to get to me and my passenger very quickly. He saw my flare – I had forgotten I had even fired one – and made the pickup. On his way in, he told me he saw multiple armed VC moving towards my location along the paddy dikes, some within 100 meters of my position. After dropping us off at Dong Tam, he manned his helo with the rest of his crew, teamed up with two Army gunships, and headed back to the paddy to fend off the VC until an extraction team was dropped in to secure the area and pick up my chopper. While the extraction crew was doing its work, it was mortared by the VC but neither the extraction team nor the Army platoon securing the area were hit.

Hearing this narrative for the first time, 40 years later, made my skin crawl. No other aircraft had responded to my Mayday so if Mike had not been on frequency at that time, I probably would not be alive to tell this story today. I owe him my life. Fittingly, Mike's wife, Barbara, had told me that he had been awarded the Silver Star for his actions in rescuing me. I wish I had pinned it on his chest!

To bring this story full circle, Mike and Barbara visited us in Wyoming, Delaware, in April of 2008. Shaking his hand for the second time – the first was through his cockpit window in 1967 – was a very special moment for me and my family.

Before the Stocks arrived, my eldest son, Adam, asked me, "What do you say to a person who, were it not for his heroism, you would not even exist?"

My wife, Pat, and I threw a big reunion barbeque for the Stocks, and after the tables were cleared, Mike presented me with his framed Seawolf Drinking Flag that he has signed, "We share a bond that few will ever know." Mike had carried this flag with him everywhere since he left Vietnam in 1968.

Mike and I correspond regularly. As a side note, the Stocks' youngest child, Julie, is a U.S. Army Captain and just got back from her second tour in Iraq.

Walker Jones, a warrant officer Loach pilot with C/1/9, poses with fellow Aeroscouts and one of their OH-6As in 1970. The "First of the Ninth" was a much heralded Scout unit, not only having pioneered many Scout tactics, but having seen much combat. The veterans of 1/9 continue to lay claim to the unofficial boast of the 1st Cavalry Division: "If you ain't Cav, you ain't shit!" When the division deployed to Vietnam, its 1st Squadron, 9th Cavalry was authorized 30 OH-6As, believed to be the largest number of Cayuses assigned to a unit in the combat zone. The division's maintenance battalions were assigned eight, and division aviation battalions were authorized three OH-6As. (Walker Jones Collection)

Navy Rescues Army
by Walker A. Jones, Ph. D. and Robert Clark, CDR, USN (Ret.)

In another case of Navy rescues Army, we're reminded of the commonality in the character of combat helicopter pilots. Their professionalism and sense of comradeship shines through, despite the bureaucracy responsible for their sometime awkward alliance. Here, we're treated to a dual perspective of an ad hoc, yet effective, partnership that not only accomplished the mission, but reinforced the bond between airmen when it mattered most.

Jones was a young warrant officer who in 1970 and 1971 piloted an OH-6A for C Troop, 1st Squadron, 9th Cavalry Regiment, 1st Cavalry Division, called in Army parlance "Charlie Troop, First of the Ninth." Jones explains:

"This unit developed the Scout tactics for the Vietnam war, beginning with the old OH-13 in 1965, and there exists a world of stories, tragedies and heart among those crews that did most of the subsequent scouting with OH-6As. We all love that old Loach – it saved our lives too many times. I'd like to comment on the OH-6A, as the crash I relate describes much about why this helicopter sometimes kept us pilots and crews alive – design characteristics that would have left us dead without them. Helicopters that had

to go down in trees frequently caused fatalities because the rotor blades would strike something hard, and the torque action would cause the aircraft to flip over. Also the tail boom would often hit something more substantial than itself, and pitch the aircraft's nose down, causing it to crash through trees 'pilot-first.' And, being of magnesium alloy: burn city!

The LOH was designed to be very crashable – when crashing into trees – to allow its tail boom to break off, its rotor blades to fold up, and the skids and seats to collapse in sequence, just short of a human's body to collapse. They also designed the 'over-running clutch,' a breakaway device placed between the transmission and rotor system. If the transmission seized, the torque due to the sudden stoppage in motion would break the rotor system away from the transmission, allowing the blades to freely 'pinwheel,' and with precise and proper piloting, could uniquely allow the ship to be put down with no power. Of course, if no open level ground was underneath, one had to place it above trees or water, and then hope for the best."

Bob Clark flew Navy helicopters, specifically, in this case, the Kaman H-2 series "Seasprite," a medium-size helicopter used successfully by the Navy for utility, search and rescue, gun spotting, and carrier plane-guard duty. Clark begins his narrative by providing insight into the background of this unique Army-Navy arrangement, followed by his

Walker Jones and Bob Clark reunite in San Diego in July 2010 aboard USS *Midway* Museum, where they they pose with a displayed Kaman UH-2 "Seasprite" similar to the one Clark flew during his Navy service. Periodically, inter-service units and their equipment joined forces to conduct a mission. In this case, the Seasprite's submarine detection system was used to locate enemy installation in dense jungle. The multi-mission UH-2 served in Vietnam as a plane guard and flying highly risky rescue missions in North Vietnam. Since the services like to "play with each other's toys," the Navy eventually acquired OH-6As for its helicopter pilot training. Conversely, during the early 1960s the Army acquired a few UH-2 Seasprites for evaluation as gunships. (Walker Jones Collection)

aerial perspective of the event.

In late April of 1970 President Nixon authorized the U.S. military to launch a campaign to locate and destroy North Vietnamese Army sanctuary sites in Cambodia. On 1 May 1970 the campaign was launched into Cambodia to seek out, engage, and destroy NVA military targets, with the stipulation that all U.S. forces must be out of Cambodia by 30 June 1970. Because of the narrow window for the campaign, a call went out to all services by the Commander U.S. Forces Vietnam for any technology that could help locate enemy weapons cache sites.

In the spring of 1970, CNO (Chief of Naval Operations) Development Project (D/V 98) was initiated to validate the Light Airborne Multi-Purpose System (LAMPS) Mark I concept. The D/V 98 project was to be carried out in three phases, using modified HH-2D Seasprite helicopters. Each phase would separately evaluate the three technologies that made up the LAMPS mission suite: the ASQ 81 Magnetic Anomaly Detection (MAD) unit, typically used to hunt submarines; Antisubmarine Warfare (ASW); and the Electronic Support Measures (ESM) and radar. Additionally, the ability to operate helicopters independently for an extended period of time off of low freeboard ships would be evaluated.

In May 1970 the fliers from HC-5 who had been selected to be the D/V 98 Phase A project pilots were at Naval Air Development Center, Pennsylvania, undergoing familiarization on the ASQ-81 MAD. Late in the afternoon on Friday, 22 May, the project pilots were notified immediately to fly the ASQ 81-equipped HH-2Ds to the Kaman Aerospace facility in Bloomfield, Connecticut, to be modified to operate with the Army in South Vietnam; this was the first we had heard of this. At noon the next day, the pilots received a call from a former HC-5 commanding officer, who worked for the CNO, directing them to return to San Diego. He said, 'We need pilots to fly the birds and can't think of a better group than the pilots already familiar with the equipment.' When you get a call from the CNO's office volunteering you for a mission, how do you say 'no'? The HH-2Ds were flown by C-5A cargo aircraft to NAS North Island to pick up the maintenance crew and support package and continue on to Vietnam. On 26 May the pilots departed San Diego International for Saigon. After the HH-2Ds were modified by Kaman, they were flown to NAS North Island in a C-5A to pick up the maintenance crew and support equipment. They were given radios with which to communicate with the Army, and a piece of armored hard face to provide a modicum of protection from small arms fire to the MAD operator in the cabin.

The detachment was hosted by the 1st Air Cavalry Division at Phuoc Vinh, located in III Corps. The Army named the operation 'Iron Barnacle.' During June we flew our missions in Cambodia, always under the watchful eyes of an experienced Army Hunter-Killer team consisting of an AH-1G Cobra and OH-6A LOH. Our mission profile was to fly at 300 to 400 feet above the triple canopy (measured on our radar altimeter) with the ASQ 81 deployed in order to have the maximum possible sweep width of the MAD.

Because of the density altitude, blade stall was always on our mind, so we flew at maximum possible speed. The Army deemed our operations in Cambodia a success and on 1 July we were notified that our deployment was being extended to support operations in South Vietnam. For many reasons, this was not a crowd pleaser with the detachment, but as military professionals do, we saluted and carried on.

An Iron Barnacle crew – consisting of LCDR Phil Olson, LT Bob Clark, LTJG Leroy Anderson, AT1 Arnie Hardin, and me – was assigned to a search-and-locate mission in III Corps, northeast of Phuoc Vinh. The search area was in the general vicinity of the southern extremity of a spur off the Ho Chi Minh Trail where NVA activity was suspected. Late in the afternoon and approaching "Bingo" fuel state, Arnie Hardin got a MAD contact. He threw out a smoke to mark the location and we climbed to altitude so the LOH could descend and conduct an expanding circle search around the smoke. After a few minutes the pilot of the LOH reported strong signs of enemy activity. As it was late in the day and all three helicopters were at bingo fuel, we broke off the search and returned to base. Evidently the report the LOH pilot made to his operations upon returning to base was impressive enough that a troop insertion mission was planned for the next day. Since the location of the site was deep in the jungle, with no landing sites for the UH-1 Slicks, the Air Force was tasked with creating an instant landing zone using a 10,000-pound bomb dropped by parachute from a C-130.

The following morning the Iron Barnacle HH-2D crew joined up with a Hunter-Killer team from Song Be to relocate the site of the previous day's contact. Once in the general area of the previous day's contact, the HH-2D started its MAD search. It wasn't long before Arnie Hardin reported a MAD contact and threw a smoke. We climbed to 2,500 feet and the LOH descended to start a search. Shortly after starting the search, the LOH pilot reported smoke in the cockpit and requested a vector to the nearest clearing in the jungle. The closest clearing was approximately five miles away and a heading to that site was relayed by the Cobra pilot.

The LOH started a turn toward the heading, still at a very low altitude and just over the top of the jungle canopy. The LOH passed behind a tree in a 90-degree bank and didn't reappear on the other side. The Cobra pilot immediately got out a "Mayday" on "Guard" and we started a search for indications of survivors. At that moment I didn't have much confidence that the crash through a 250 to 300-foot jungle canopy was survivable. To everyone's surprise, within three or four minutes we started hearing static on Guard as the LOH crew tried to make contact and then we started seeing pencil flares. The LOH had come to rest on its skids in a small stream.

Since we were in a suspected area of NVA activity, immediate rescue of the LOH crew became an overriding consideration. The delay while the Army got a helicopter with a rescue hoist to the scene was unacceptable. Phil immediately informed the Cobra pilot, the on-scene commander, that we were equipped with a rescue hoist and carried trained rescue aircrewmen, so we would give it a go. Because the rescue hoist cable on the HH-2D can only be extended 90 feet, it was necessary to execute a hover-down through the jungle canopy. This was going to be exciting enough, but the prospect of enemy reaction really raised the level of adrenalin flow. Phil executed a flawless hover-down maneuver with Arnie calling clearance on the left side. I was monitoring engine performance, communicating and looking out for any sign of enemy activity. On the first attempt, Phil stabilized the hover with tree limbs extending just below the rotor system and the tail rotor almost touching the trees. We only had a horse collar on board so Arnie rigged for rescue and lowered the cable to the maximum. Three problems became apparent: the hoist cable wasn't long enough to reach the ground, the LOH crew couldn't move the few feet required to get to where the horse collar was because of very thick undergrowth, and we couldn't slide the helicopter to get over them because of the trees. We broke hover and prepared for another attempt. As Phil, Leroy, and I worked to get a better fix on the location of the downed LOH crew, Arnie busied himself demonstrating the out-of-the-box thinking that makes the U.S. service member special. He decided to extend the reach of the rescue hoist cable by attaching a gunner's belt to it.

After getting some direction from the LOH crew, we had a good fix on their location.

Phil started his second approach and hover-down maneuver. This time we were able to hover-down deeper into the trees. Phil stabilized the hover with tree limbs so close that I could reach out and touch the one on the left. Leroy had provided direction so the tail of the helicopter was in the "V" between two limbs of a tree behind us. Arnie's quick thinking to extend the length of the rescue cable allowed it to reach the ground, allowing the LOH crew to be extracted from the jungle. After winching the three crewmembers aboard, Phil did a vertical climb to clear the trees and we returned the downed crew safely to Phuoc Vinh for medical evaluation.

Here, then, is Jones's perspective of the experience, which shows dramatically the difference of a few hundred feet:

During 1970, the Army jumped in bed with the Navy and spawned a joint operation that placed a Navy submarine-detector helicopter with an Army Hunter-Killer team to try and locate Charlie's arms caches. The romance didn't work out too well for my crew and me.

A dark, shiny-blue Navy Seasprite with MAD gear worked with Hunter-Killer (Pink) teams of troops of 1/9. We Scouts in Charlie Troop considered it an out-and-out "Romeo Foxtrot" (Rat-Fuck). I was the last unit Loach pilot to have to accompany them. My turn finally came. We pulled pitch at first light: an OH-6A LOH, an AH-1G HueyCobra, and a Navy Seasprite (a "Blink Team?"). My roommate, Mel Wyatt, was the front seat, high bird. After getting to the assigned AO, we cut doughnuts while the Seasprite winched down that torpedo-like thingy. We smoked cigarettes, listed to the ADF, and cussed our bad luck. No KBAs today.

In no time, they had a reading. So I spiraled down to the treetops, raced over without expectation toward the smoke, and had just started pulling back on the stick, slowing at the mark, when there was a "pop-pop." I don't think that I'd even stuck my head out to look down yet. It was a little unusual to hear discreet pops, and not the more familiar clackity-clack of the AK. I don't remember even calling "taking fire." I asked my gunner, Wilkes, if heard fire, but he wasn't sure. Neither of us had felt a hit. We probably didn't even throw a smoke to mark the spot as we usually did.

I don't remember exactly why I decided to lift tail and di-di away, but I did. Maybe it was a Scout's sense. Yet soon I began to feel an unusual vibration, so I started to get some altitude, and asked Mel for a vector to the nearest firebase, Garry Owen, I think.

During my ascent, the vibration got quickly worse. The grinding sound in my ear soon transferred to my butt, then to my hands and feet. Then there was the acrid white smoke that put the cockpit in IFR. The idiot lights on the dash began blinking and whining. Scout pilots didn't normally read their instruments, so that part wasn't so exasperating. It was the violent vibrations that were getting me a little tense. I hollered up to Mel – he's from Kentucky, and I'm from Mississippi, so we "holler" – if he could see any smoke.

That was the last communication between us, as I toggled the battery off, wishfully thinking it a possible source of the white,

stinging smoke. I kicked in pedal to clear it, but the vibrations were by then a scream.

The grinding-thrashing-smoking reached a violent crescendo that suddenly, and dramatically, ended with a sudden "Snap!" leaving total quiet; a smooth tranquility.

Stunned at yet another dramatic change in my situation, I noticed that my needles had split and one was doing a fast, as the British say, anti-clockwise motion. I so vividly remember turning my head and stared at my left hand, still holding up the collective, and through some force of will, told that hand to push that damned lever down. Pucker time.

Training took over the rest of the way. The farm was bought, and I had seconds to decide which of the million trees below looked softest. This would be my first crash experience.

I've never remembered flaring and pulling pitch – thank you flight school, and Cecil Smith. But I vividly remember the seemingly endless fall through the center of the earth.

I'd tensed up for the impact after falling through the trees, but it didn't come; just greenery flapping up through the blasted-out Plexiglas, endlessly, endlessly, falling and falling. I finally woke up with JP-4 dripping over my face, and the sound of smoke grenades spewing from right behind me. I yelled, "Get the fuck out!" and dived out the open door, only to be rudely reminded that I was still buckled in. I popped loose, thinking I'd burn to death, and fell face first into clear water, maybe a foot deep.

We had flipped and flopped through all the trees and somehow crashed upright in the bed of a creek that was coursing tunnel-like under the jungle, unseen from above. Later I'd realize I'd subconsciously headed toward a lighter green area which was evidently bamboo along that hidden creekshore. The JP-4 jet fuel all over us was water. We had fallen through 150 feet of greenery, and somehow splatted upright in the middle of that under-jungle creek. We were in the center of a tunnel formed by the creek that wound through a ravine forged underneath the thick trees higher up, and bamboo alongside. Big treetops lapped way overhead. Mel later said that the jungle "just swallered ya'll up."

The creek curved out of sight about 50 meters in each direction so I sent my gunner and observer to position themselves at the bends in each direction to watch for Ho's guys making their way to us. But I soon realized it was danged unlikely the dark creek-tunnel was an NVA transportation route, and absolutely no one could penetrate up or down the steep, thick sides. I relaxed. I shot some pen flares that never penetrated the trees. I yapped into my survival radio on Guard, "Don't drop no danged bombs on us!" The noise way overhead from what sounded like every helicopter in Vietnam was so GREAT. That sweet, most comforting sound. THAT was part of what we now define as the Brotherhood.

I stood off to the edge and snapped a picture with the Spotmatic. In the foreground was Richard D. Wilkes, his back to me, standing in the dim light and shallow water, looking at the broke-dick, tail boom-less, skid-splatted, rotor blade-less, leaf-filled Loach, one hand on his sidearm, the other on his cocked head, like "Jeez, how did I survive that?!"

The poor Loach was bottom-flattened to my seat. Tree limbs and leaves filled the cockpit.

And really neat rays of parallel light beams were angling in from above. The color smoke marking grenades Wilkes had hung on the wire behind my seat had jerked loose upon impact and expended themselves. Each of those jungle-penetrating light rays became multi-colored laser beams – colorful spotlights on the tragic-comedy of this now calm war moment. We're alive because he had the sense to not hang WPs, frags, superbombs, etc., up there, too. The cacophony of every helicopter in III Corps hovering way overhead made transmission on my survival radio impossible.

It was clear that our rescuing Blues could not rappel this deep, and we could not see much sky. So I decided that we had to somehow climb through the thick bamboo and trees and make it to higher ground. Upon moving out, I was stunned by a loud voice saying, "DO NOT MOVE AWAY. STAY WHERE YOU ARE!" I thought at first I was hallucinating, and God was speaking to me. But it was that damned Navy Seasprite with a freaking loudspeaker. Scared the spit out of me.

The Seasprite pilot had managed to open enough foliage to see down some, and soon started deploying their rescue hoist. Subsequently, we each went up in turn, me last, taking pictures all the way. Our other guys flying overhead later told me that the Navy pilots were yelling incredulously that some damn fool down there was taking pictures, while they had sucked their seats up to their goozlepipes, no doubt.

The next day, curly-mustachioed CW-3 Dave Lawley came over while I was laid out in my hootch, and brought me the twisted overrunning clutch that had saved our lives – thank you Mr. Hughes. Seems that all the fast-spinning metal thingies in the transmission had rioted over the abrupt exit of their lubricating fluids, causing a transmission meltdown, and the subsequent violent vibration and smoke. I later quit smoking cigarettes because of that day. After transitioning to Cobras, I found that when the front seater would light up, I would break out in a cold sweat. I knew it was because

the smoke told me that I would burn up before I could get back to earth.

I no longer have the photos I took in that jungle creek that day, but I do have a photo of that spit-shined Navy Seasprite on a pad at Song Be, and of old number 290, finally slung back, sitting on the tarmac in front of the maintenance hangar at Phuoc Vinh.

One bullet hit was no big thing. But sometimes it was. As I slowed over the smoke, one bullet found my transmission and as I gained altitude, the transmission seized after the fluid drained out. I had not radioed that I had taken a hit, so the Navy guys didn't realize I'd been shot down. And, thank goodness, as their assholes were puckered up enough as they hovered over us for so long. Now, a belated thank you, Navy. I sort of regret that I didn't write you up for some medal, as I now realize that you were probably more tense than I had been. But the job we 1/9 Scouts – and others like us – did each day made that little incident just a good club story. I had insisted that it should be classified as a "ditch" because I landed in water and had to be rescued by the Navy. But the incident review board in the O Club was never able to come to a consensus. Hey, we're Cav!

Bob Clark, on the Navy side, later added, "Because the LOH crew operated out of Song Be, it was disappointing to the Iron Barnacle detachment that we were never able to meet them over beers to exchange war stories. To us 'Squids,' the Iron Barnacle experience left a lasting impression and deep respect for the professionalism and tenacity of the Army aviators whom we worked with during our short period of joint operations."

Clark, who was one of the Seasprite pilots that day, and Jones finally did meet, aboard USS Midway *during a Vietnam Helicopter Pilots Association reunion in San Diego in July 2010.*

The Loach in which Walker Jones and crewmen Wilkes and Mitchell were flying while working with a Navy Seasprite helicopter was sling-loaded to Phước Vĩnh after it crashed in July 1970. Later the Loach was transferred to 1/9's B Troop and was shot down and destroyed in 1971. (Walker Jones)

Don Callison flies an EC-145 for Orlando's Florida Hospital, years after Vietnam. (Don Callison Collection)

Don Callison and *Pig Pen* S/N 67-16398 of D/3/5 in August 1970. (Don Callison Collection)

History Lesson
by Don Callison

Often, a traumatic event stamps a single, indelible impression on someone's mind. Such an impression was made upon Loach pilot Don Callison, call sign War Wagon One-Four, after he went toe-to-toe with the enemy. From May 1970 to May 1971, Callison flew the OH-6A with D Troop, 3rd Squadron, 5th Cavalry, or D/3/5, which served the armored cavalry element of the 9th Infantry Division. The troop was coined "Light Horse" and the Aeroscouts "War Wagon." Operating in the southern IV Corps region of South Vietnam, the War Wagons lived up to their name.

It looked like it was going to be a typical day in the Delta of the Mekong River for our air cavalry troop. We were based at the Army airfield near the small town of Vinh Long. Out of bed at 04:30, perform the three S's, grab a rusty can of Coke, and head for the flightline. I made a quick swing by the mess hall. Yuck! One sniff was enough. No breakfast today. My alcohol-soaked stomach just couldn't handle it. I'd sneak a box of C rations from some unsuspecting Slick crew later, at the staging area. I hopped in the back of the scout platoon's old three-quarter-ton Dodge truck, affectionately called the "Loach Coach," and said my "Good mornings" to grumpy fellow War Wagons as we headed for the Cav pad in the dark.

I was happy because today I would be flying *Pig Pen,* my favorite Loach. Painted flat black with tail number three-nine-eight, it had been affectionately named after the *Peanuts* cartoon character. Pig Pen had the reputation not only as the scout platoon's dirtiest, beat

up, and nastiest looking helicopter but it was also the most powerful. I had inherited *Pig Pen* from Smitty when he DEROSed (Date of Estimated Return from Overseas).

We needed plenty of power because of the load of combat equipment that we carried on each flight. Our unit was unique in that we did things a little differently than other Scout units. Not better, just different. Most Scout units operated with a gunner/observer seated in the left rear door with an M60 machine gun and an assortment of air deliverable weapons. Some units also carried an additional gunner/observer in the left front seat. The pilots flew from the right front seat. Nearly all of the other units made right-hand turns while they were low level and scouting. In D/3/5, the War Wagon Scouts carried their gunner/observers in only the left front seat with the pilot in the right. With the rear of the ship nearly empty, there was always room for picking up a crew that had been shot down.

Each aircraft had a 7.62mm minigun mounted on the left side. The gunner had an M60 machine gun and we only made left-hand turns. Left-hand turns required a little more power but the possibility of encountering a "Hughes tailspin" was minimized. The tailspin occurred during slow right turns at high power settings, finally resulting in loss of tail rotor effectiveness and the helicopter spinning out of control. Not a good condition when flying very close to the ground.

In addition to the heavy guns, the War Wagons carried an infantryman's field pack filled with hand grenades. Called the "frag bag," it rested on an armor "chicken plate" which lay on the floor between the gunner's feet. The frag bag usually contained 20 to

This Loach, S/N 67-16398 nicknamed *Pig Pen,* wears the white and red stripe designator for D Troop, 3rd Squadron, 5th Cavalry "War Wagons." Despite its unflattering name, the OH-6A was a favorite among War Wagon pilots due to its exceptional handling characteristics. Scout helicopters normally were flown without doors allowing not only ventilation, but rapid egress in the event of a crash. (Don Callison)

25 fragmentation and concussion grenades. Strands of wire were stretched across open spaces in the cockpit. Hooked on the wires was an assortment of non-explosive type grenades: 20 or more trip flares, incendiary, smoke, tear gas and thermate canisters hung ready to be dropped on targets. Five white phosphorous grenades were crammed under the pilot's armored seat, while the compact area between the seats may have contained an M-79 grenade launcher, plus 10 rounds of High-Explosive ammo, or perhaps a couple of homemade bombs.

The crews also carried personal weapons. The gunners carried .38- or .45-caliber pistols.

The pilots usually brought along cut down and modified AK-47 assault rifles in addition to their pistols. Scout pilots were issued CAR-15s, which were short-barreled versions of the M-16 with a telescoping, collapsible stock. Most crews found the CAR-15 to be useless for our mission since its main purpose was to be a backup weapon for a malfunctioning M60. The 5.56mm CAR-15 couldn't bust bunkers or stir up debris while reconning by fire as well as the 7.62mm AK. Our customized AKs had shortened barrels and no butt stocks. Those loaded guns were secured on top of the helicopter's instrument panel.

With our basic load of ordnance, plus 2,000 rounds of 7.62 for the minigun and 1,500 rounds of ammo for the M60 machine gun, we were heavy. But after we added our sidearms, chicken plates, canteens, cameras, knives, C rations, and other personal gear, our average takeoff weight was approximately 300 pounds over the maximum weight allowed for the OH-6A. We carried no survival gear of the official type; no vests, survival radios, flares, etc.

I went into our large metal storage container box and got my helmet out of its locker. I'd gotten soaked in the rain the day before and there was a fresh growth of hairy, greenish gray mold growing inside the headphones. As I used an old oily, dirty rag to wipe out the headsets, I hoped there wasn't anything incurable growing in them. I slung my flak vest, with its extra large chicken plate in the front section, over my shoulder and headed for *Pig Pen.* Sp4 Rene Garneau was scheduled to fly with me and he was already at the ship doing his pre-flight inspection and getting the aircraft loaded.

We had landed in the middle of a thunderstorm the previous night and Rene, who, like the other gunners, was also a crew chief and had probably worked on the bird until late last night while we pilots were living it up and getting drunk at the officer's club. Never has enough been said about the tremendous job our enlisted crewmembers did, and their dedication for getting enough helicopters flyable for each day's mission.

I just said "Howdy" and started my own pre-flight inspection.

The flightline was alive with activity. The roar of rotors, the whine of turbine engines and the smell of jet fuel filled the humid pre-dawn air. Lots of helicopters were running, some hovering out of the protection of their revetments and lining up behind others preparing for takeoff. I could see activity in the area of the 7th of the 1st Air Cavalry, home of the Apaches, Comanches, and Dutchmasters. Some Hueys from the 114th Assault Helicopter Company were just lifting off from the main airstrip. On a recent morning just like this one, a War Wagon Loach exploded during pre-flight, killing the gunner and pilot who were standing nearby. Pre-flight checks were now done very carefully. Because of the poor condition of our Loaches, we rarely flew at night. The windshields were scratched nearly opaque from low-level grit and grime, and

Despite the appearance of the AH-1G Cobra for gunship support, Huey gunships were a mainstay in Vietnam and often an element of Scout missions. Adorned with striking markings, this UH-1C, S/N 65-9507, of the 174th AHC prepares to depart Đức Phổ in 1970. (Robert Brackenhoff)

few, if any, exterior or interior lights worked. We were scheduled to take off at the very first glow of dawn's light.

Our unit "hired out" to Army of the Republic of Vietnam ground units located throughout the Mekong River's delta region of the IV Corps region. The "package" we provided consisted of a Command and Control (C&C) UH-1H Huey flown by the Air Mission Commander (AMC), four AH-1G Cobra attack helicopters (call sign "Crusader"), four UH-1H troop-carrying Slicks (call sign "Long Knives"), and four War Wagon scout ships. The maintenance platoon (call sign "Scavenger"), was responsible for the excellent aircraft availability the unit enjoyed.

Today our mission was in support of an ARVN unit in the notoriously nasty, Viet Cong-infested U Minh Forest near the southern tip of Vietnam, some 70 miles south of our home base.

The C&C and the Crusaders had departed earlier. The Long Knives and we would be leaving soon, although we rarely flew as a group.

Garneau and I strapped in and fired up ol' *Pig Pen,* hovered out of the revetment and set the ship down and waited for the rest of the flight. The four Loaches consisted of two teams. Each team had a Lead ship and his wingman was referred to as Tail. I was senior Lead today and after we were assembled, I made the radio call: "Vinh Long tower, War Wagon One-Four with a flight of four sperms at the Cav pad for west departure and left turnout." The tower cleared us and we lifted off, turned south at the airfield boundary and climbed to 1,500 feet. We flew in a diamond formation. I was at the head of the formation; my wingman was tucked in tight at my four o-clock position. Second Lead was tucked in tight at seven o'clock and the newest Trail was doing his best to squeeze into the slot at

my six. Ed Gallagher, my trail, radioed that we had a complete flight and I nosed *Pig Pen* over to 100 knots for the 45-minute flight to the AO.

We taught all of our gunners to fly. They used foot-long pieces of sawed-off mop handles stuck into the copilot's cyclic stick receptacles and handled the ships really well. On this morning I was pretty well hung over as usual and gave the controls to Garneau, while I leaned back, smoked a cigarette and contemplated a nap, knowing the other gunners were probably flying too while the pilots were taking pictures, reading pocket novels or eating breakfast. All except the new Trail pilot. He was probably working his ass off trying to stay in formation and re-learning how to fly.

As we approached the airstrip at Ca Mau, I maneuvered the flight to the POL refueling point where each Loach took on a full load of JP-4 jet fuel. The fuel gauges on OH-6As were notoriously inaccurate so we never stayed airborne for more than two hours. A scout mission, or Visual Reconnaissance (VR), was normally planned for an hour and thirty minutes, with the second team relieving the first on station to continue the mission.

After refueling, we repositioned to a clear area, shut down and wandered over to where the guns and slicks were parked, and tried to bum some food and maybe get a clue as to what we were doing today. The C&C had flown off to meet with the Ground Mission Commander.

My roommate, Russ Allison, was the Long Knife flight leader. I visited him at his aircraft and tried begging some grub but he told me to wait until I was really hungry. He had a feeling that because of the AO we were in, I'd be getting really hungry later. I had recently confided in him that lately when we got a kill, I would

Wearing the triangular unit designator for 3rd Squadron, 17th Cavalry, 1st Aviation Brigade, OH-6A S/N 66-7782 sits in its revetment made of wooden rocket cases at Lai Khê in 1968. The Loach was lost on 11 August 1971. (Norm Stewart/Bill Tuttle)

get really hungry. It seemed that the nastier or smellier the kill was, the hungrier I got. I was afraid to tell anyone else, fearing they would think I had some kind of cannibalistic tendencies.

I noticed very little activity around the Crusaders; some guys were sacked out on open ammo bay doors, while others were writing letters or reading books. Some new guys were checking over the rocket pods and just poking around the ships. The familiar thumping sound alerted us that the C&C Huey was coming back from the briefing. The pilot landed at POL and stuck his arm out of the Huey's window, and made the familiar twirling motion with his index finger, indicating to crank 'em up.

While C&C was refueling, my trail and I started our helicopters. The Crusaders got their Cobras running and we all took off together. I lined up our two Scouts behind C&C in a loose trail formation as we headed for the AO. The two Cobras were effortlessly cruising at our altitude about a half mile off to our right.

We received our mission briefing over the UHF radio; C&C described the area we were to recon and he explained that we were looking for remnants of an enemy unit. Their activity had been reported in the area the previous night. We were told that the "Rules of engagement" were "Specified Strike, which was a more stringent rule than "Free Fire."

Under the rules of Specified Strike, we could not shoot just anybody we found but had to get permission to fire on personnel based on the descriptions we gave to the Ground Mission Commander who was riding in a rear seat of the C&C Huey. Of course, we were allowed to return fire when we were fired upon. Specified Strike rules were designed to prevent killing innocent civilians who may be living in the area.

The area we were going to work in was a cleared, partially cultivated rectangle surrounded by dense double and triple canopy jungle. The clearing was approximately 100 yards wide and 300 yards long. The long side lay along a 50-yard wide river. The eastern edge of the clearing was bordered by a narrow canal that intersected the larger river. Finally, the southern portion of the area was divided by yet another smaller canal emptying into the north/south canal. Next to the small canal was a small shack, or "hootch," constructed of thin sticks for walls and a nipa palm thatch roof. From altitude I could see a small sampan that had been turned on its side and leaned against one wall of the hootch.

I was cleared to go low level, and knowing that my wingman Ed would have a hell of a time keeping up with me, I grinned to myself as I rolled back *Pig Pen's* throttle and entered autorotation. At 100 knots and loaded the way we were, our rate of descent was more than 2,000 feet per minute. With a power recovery just prior to ground contact, we were in the area in less than a minute. We could come out of the sky like simonized manhole covers.

I headed for the hootch and saw that the bottom of the sampan was still wet. I was about to report it when C&C radioed for us to come back up to his altitude. Nuts! We hadn't even gotten started. As we climbed, I asked what was going on and C&C said that an ARVN unit at a firebase 20 kilometers (klicks) away was in a firefight and they needed our Cobras for close air support. We did not work low level without our gunship cover so we headed in the direction of the quickly disappearing Crusaders. The C&C radioed to scramble the second team of Cobras and they arrived near the clearing about 20 minutes after we had left it. We orbited four or five klicks north of the area, waiting for C&C to get back on station.

Perched on a makeshift pad of PSP and sandbags in 1967, this OH-6A is assigned to C Troop, 1st Squadron, 9th Cavalry. Besides its serial number, 65-12936, blade cuffs and pilot door window strengthening ribs identify this Loach as part of the initial production batch. (U.S. Army)

We were finally cleared to go back into the clearing and had received clearance to do "Reconnaissance by fire," meaning we could shoot the place up to uncover clues of enemy activity and maybe draw some fire. This time I took the team low level about a mile from the clearing and popped in from the north. I had great respect for the enemy and a smart scout tried not to use the same ingress and egress routes more than once.

As soon as we were low level I immediately saw that the sampan had been moved a few feet and was now lying upside down, flat on the ground. I looked all around the clearing; no bunkers and no other apparent activity. I cautiously meandered over to the sampan and saw in the mud next to the boat fresh footprints that had not been there before. I had caught bad guys hiding under boats in the past so I had Garneau fire up the sampan with his M60. The skiff flipped over and sure enough a dead enemy soldier was under it.

There was something very different about this soldier. He was wearing an NVA uniform.

The majority of the enemy we encountered during late 1970 were Viet Cong. It was indeed a rare occasion to find a uniformed NVA soldier. I felt the illegally long hairs on the back of my neck stand up because I also knew that NVA soldiers rarely traveled alone. I wondered where his buddies were. I reported the KBA (kill by air) to C&C and worked my way along the smallest canal, turned left and headed along the mid-sized one.

I glanced over my right shoulder at the forested bank on the opposite side. For an instant I locked eyes with a uniformed soldier who was standing about 50 feet from me in waist-high brush. As we looked at each other I caught a glimpse of the black automatic pistol in his hand as he used it to make a chopping motion. A guy lying on the ground in the bushes opened up on us with a .30 caliber, bipod-mounted weapon. His buddies joined right in with an assortment of SKS and AK rifles and RPG (Rocket Propelled Grenade) fire. I vividly remember the muzzle flashes, hearing rounds go by, the WHOOSH of the RPG, and feeling bullets hit the aircraft. On the radio I yelled, "TAKING FIRE! TAKING FIRE!" I snapped a quick left pedal turn, shoved the stick forward, and hiked in full collective pitch while squeezing the trigger on the minigun. I heard and felt the RPG explode harmlessly off to my right side. I wondered how Ed and his gunner were doing while I was wildly zigzagging to escape. We were starting to haul ass but things seemed to move in slow motion. Just like in the movies I could see the enemy's bullets hitting the ground beside me as the gunner tried to get his range on my helicopter. Garneau was hanging out of his door, firing long bursts from his M60 to the rear. The minigun was great to have because it was so loud that it drowned out the sound of the enemy's guns. I had that trigger pulled all the way back, which made the gun fire 4,000 shots per minute.

After three seconds it automatically stopped. I could still hear the NVA firing so I strangled the trigger again. Between squeezes I could hear Ed's guns going and he was yelling enemy positions to the inbound Cobras. After what seemed like an eternity, I heard the comforting sounds of the Crusader's rockets impacting the area behind me.

After we had escaped from the area, the Air Mission Commander directed us to go to altitude and to return to the staging area. The Cobras were needed to cover the Long Knives who were going to insert ARVNs near the firebase of the earlier firefight. We never returned to the canal area. I figured those NVA troops just went on their merry way.

Back at the staging area, Ed, the gunners, and I excitedly talked about what had just happened and counted the many bullet holes in our aircraft. I told Ed that I'd had the strangest thought while we were bugging out of that clearing. I felt that the NVA leader may have taken a page from American history and had instructed his troops, "Don't shoot till you see the whites of their eyes."

They did exactly as they had been told.

Steve Nagle poses with the Bell OH-58A Kiowa, S/N 68-16910, of which he was crew chief while serving with the 12th Aviation Group based at Long Binh North "Plantation" in 1971. The Kiowa's arrival late in the war only added to the reluctance of Aeroscout crewmen to accept it as the OH-6A's replacement. Eventually, the OH-58A, like the OH-6A in the hands of skilled aircrew, would be heavily armed and fly the low-level Scout mission. Like the OH-6A, Kiowas flew the Scout mission without doors, with only protection for the pilot derived from seat armor panels. To its credit, the OH-58 not only went on to serve as the Army's primary helicopter trainer, its vastly improved models distinguished themselves in conflicts in South America, Europe, and the Middle East. (Steve Nagle Collection)

Kiowa Tales
Steve Nagle

Some things never change. Throughout history, military units have struggled to keep equipment operating, including aircraft flying. Sometimes the only way to do that has involved side-stepping official logistics channels, relying instead on a supply system mentioned only in guarded conversation. Steve Nagle, who served as a crew chief with the 12th Combat Aviation Group "Blackjack" at Long Binh's "Plantation" heliport during 1971 and 1972, explains how it was no different in Vietnam.

My days as a crew chief on the OH-58A, serial number 68-16910, were always interesting. Each morning, after breakfast in the chow hall, we met at the Blackjack flight line. Reporting to the Flight Sergeant, we would get missions for the day. As a headquarters group, the missions were never the same. Many times flights transferred documents to the "Hotel" heliport in Saigon. Several times a week we flew to Phu Loi or Tay Ninh. As a crew chief, my responsibilities included the mission readiness, topping off fuel, and dealing with any red X notations in my log book. Usually I flew right seat with the pilot. I was ground security when we landed and would wait around the ship until we flew our next leg of the day.

In a war zone, supplies that were critical never seemed to get to those in need. Stories of wool blankets being shipped to the tropics were all too common.

As an OH-58A crew chief, my performance was based on something called "Flyability."

If your ship was unable to fly, the readiness of the unit was at stake.

Especially during the monsoon season we were challenged to keep tail rotor bearings from keeping the ship "Red X'd." The exposed bearings supporting the tail rotor shaft were poorly designed and failed more often than we could keep them in stock. Many of our aircraft sat waiting parts. Supply said they were being shipped to units more in need.

Bob Brown was our flight line tech sergeant. He was in the middle of his second or third tour in country. I think he had received a "Dear John" letter somewhere along the line and decided to stay. He had a girlfriend off base. He always seemed to have connections. A four-ton air conditioner appeared in his hootch one day. His room was kept around 55 degrees! But that's another story.

One afternoon Bob asked if I wanted to go on a little trip. He stopped at the flight line and I helped load 10 cases of Budweiser beer in the back of our flight line jeep. We waved at the MPs at

Steve Nagle in modern times, poses with an updated version of the Kiowa he crewed during the Vietnam war. Over time, the Bell OH-58 underwent vast improvements through successive models, serving in our Middle Eastern conflicts in the Aeroscout role and as heavily armed gun support platforms. Outfitted with advanced systems, modern Kiowa Warriors bear little resemblance to their clean-lined ancestor of the Vietnam era. Nagle, like many Vietnam war veterans, learned from the lessons of war and easily connected with their past, proud in the recollection of their accomplishments. He, along with fellow Army aviators presented here, is typical of the productive, successful Vietnam veteran. (Steve Nagle Collection)

Bell OH-58A Kiowas arrived late in the war to assume Scout duty. Although unable to match the OH-6A's nimble performance, the Kiowa, in the hands of skilled crews, performed the scout mission nonetheless. Crewmen of the 12th Combat Aviation Group at Long Binh gave this Kiowa an edge for night security missions by rigging a spotlight cluster to the aircraft. (Steve Nagle)

the gate as we rolled out on Highway 1 going southeast towards Saigon. It was about a 35-minute drive. I was driving and remember slowing down to make a left turn. I stuck my left arm out as we had no signals and we were in heavy traffic. I felt a tug on my arm to see a young teenaged boy we called "Cowboys" running around the corner with my Seiko watch!

Bob directed me down some back alley and told me to stop. I was to wait in the jeep. He disappeared into the back of a noisy bar. A couple guys came running out to help unload the beer. It was getting towards dusk and I was sure uncomfortable thinking we'd be out in this neighborhood at night. Bob came out with a box, which he threw in the back seat.

As I let out the clutch to engage the gears, I heard a noise under the jeep. The jeep did not move. We crawled under the jeep to check things out. The universal joint had broken and the driveshaft was lying on the ground. Bob got real excited. We really did not want to be stuck there, especially with nightfall closing in. I reminded him that this was a 4 x 4 vehicle and we should be able to drive home as long as we put the jeep into four-wheel drive. I shifted the transfer case, let out the clutch and we started moving. We threw the old drive-train in the back seat and headed home.

As we started home I asked Bob what that was all about; the beer and the box trade. He reached into the box and pulled out 15 tail rotor bearings. They were still in their sealed military packages!

Within two days we were 100-percent flyable. Nobody asked questions. Our sister units could not understand how we were able to requisition and receive parts so quickly. Welcome to the Black Market!

We did what was necessary to accomplish each mission. We served with pride and smile today about some of the methods that were employed to keep mission ready. One of those methods, although unconventional, proved the versatility of the Kiowa and the resourcefulness of its crews.

Tet 1972 rolled around and we at the 12th CAG were concerned as rumors of a VC push circulated. Our perimeter ran along Highway 1 with open fields on two sides.

Down at the flight line we got the idea to build a light ship. We started with an OH-58A that was not used on a regular basis. Landing lights from a Huey were fasted to a tail rotor drive shaft. The vertical post was fastened to the Kiowa on the left hand side. The power was pulled from the main buss behind the rear seat. The operator sat on the floor since the rear seat and door were removed. By straddling the vertical post, the light could easily be maneuvered into position. The gunner held an M60 across his lap with several hundred rounds draped over his shoulder.

It was quite a feat hanging onto the free 60 while switching the light on and off. We rigged a seat belt fastened to the floor, but when the pilot swung around, it would be easy to slide out the door.

We flew it twice a night for several nights. We flew our missions at random times to avoid setting a pattern.

After three or four nights, it was my turn to fly as gunner. We found a pilot who would fly our perimeter for 30 minutes or so. It was about 1:30 AM when we took off for our security perimeter run. Normally we had a gunship circling above in case we got into any trouble.

We had flown for about 10 minutes at about 200 to 300 feet off the ground. We could not get coverage from the gunship for some reason so we felt very much alone. We kept all lights off as we flew out over the open fields around our base. Every so often I would turn on the lights for a brief moment to keep us from being

Like their predecessor, OH-58As in Vietnam often mounted the M27 minigun system. The forward skids of this Kiowa, S/N 69-16114, at An Khê in 1970 were painted red. (Michael Belis)

an obvious target. As the pilot banked and turned I had all I could do to keep from sliding out the door. The M60 was getting hard to hang on to and the belts of ammo slapped in the wind. When I turned on the lights, it really lit the place up. As we circled around in the dark, the tension seemed to rise.

We were running parallel to Highway 1 a couple of klicks to the north when I turned on the lights. There in the grass was a squad of men. I pulled back the slide sending a round into the chamber. My pulse quickened as I started to squeeze the trigger. The soldiers started to jump up and down and wave wildly. I eased the pressure on the trigger as I saw they were a squad of ARVNs on night patrol. We had no idea they were out there. I quickly switched off the lights, plunging the sky back into darkness. I remembered stories of ARVNs shooting at us and I didn't want to be a target. We made our way back to the flight line and packed our gear for the night. It was only then I got the shakes realizing that I could have wiped out a group of friendlies that night.

Our perimeter patrols soon faded as the Chinese New Year came and went without major incident. Little did we know that in less than three months the Easter Offensive of 1972 would see Soviet tanks crossings the borders along An Loc, but that's another story.

This remembrance by Nagle reminds us of the covert nature of the war and how blurred were the identities of authority.

On a day in February 1972 I was met at the flight line by a pilot who was taking 910 for the day. I had never seen this man before. I wondered who authorized this flight, as I knew all the pilots in our unit very well. Something strange bothered me as the tall dark middle-easterner wore no name or rank. His flight suit was a dark

blue one-piece style I was not familiar with. Strapped to his side was a non-service issue revolver.

The stranger was a man of few words. As I untied the blades and helped with the preflight I asked if I was needed for the flight. He looked over the flight log and shook his head in a negative manner. I was not needed. He mumbled "Clear" and began to crank the engine. The throttle was rolled to flight idle. He pulled pitch and slid out of the revetment. After a momentary hover, the nose dipped and the blades beat a steady rhythm as he flew across the flight line and rolled to the right, clearing the compound as he headed northeast.

The day on the flight line for me was uneventful. I pulled inspection covers on a Huey for a major inspection. After lunch I helped another crew do some service on the flight line jeep.

It was close to dusk when I heard the familiar buzz of the OH-58's blades. Looking up I saw 910 crossing the flight line and hovered to the revetment. I walked over as the mystery pilot was walking away, leaving the blades slowly turning. After tying the blades, I looked at the log book to note any entry of the day. No time was logged, no comments written. It was as if the day never existed.

What alarmed me the most were a half dozen spent brass shells in the chin bubble. I picked up several and they didn't look like any rounds I had ever seen. My mind raced trying to figure out the what, where, and when of the day. The post flight revealed no battle damage. Any inquiries about the flight were ignored. The flight time on the clock said 4.8 hours. I never did learn what happened during that flight. There were many things I never understood about the Army; yet another mystery in my Vietnam tour.

Peter Bales poses in the Loach he pilots with 3rd Squadron, 11th Armored Cavalry Regiment in Vietnam in 1970. (Peter Bales Collection)

New Guy
by Peter Q. Bales

As an Army helicopter pilot in Vietnam, Peter Bales' flying duties were divided between the cockpits of a UH-1 Huey and an OH-6A Loach, thanks to the unique operating procedure of the combat cavalry unit to which he was assigned. Many years later, Bales took a step back in time when he acquired one of the few OH-6As flown by his unit in Vietnam.

Despite having been extensively damaged by a booby trap, the aircraft, serial no. 67-16026, survived the war and began new careers in the Army National Guard and law enforcement. Bales painted his Loach in its original warpaint. In his narrative, it becomes obvious how he quickly made the transition from new guy in Vietnam to seasoned combat aviator, developing a sense for doing what was necessary. That sense, and his ability to learn quickly how to think on his feet, earned him the Distinguished Flying Cross.

I graduated from the U.S. Army helicopter flight training course at Fort Rucker with WOC (Warrant Officer Candidate) Class 69-29 on 23 September 1969. Almost my entire class was assigned to stateside duty instead of going directly to Vietnam. I was assigned to D Troop, 2nd Squadron, 9th Cav at Fort Riley, Kansas. This was an armored cav unit with an aviation section. We had about 50 young aviators and three operational OH-13s and a couple of H-34s. Needless to say, getting any flight time was a real chore. It did not take long for most of us to figure out ways to get reassigned to Vietnam where the real flying was going on. I made a call to the Warrant Officer Branch to see what could be done. There was an opening for the OH-6 IP (Instructor Pilot) course, and I jumped at the chance to get out of Kansas. I was to report to Fort Rucker on 23 March 1970 for the seven-week course, and to be on my way to Vietnam on 15 June.

Peter Bales connected with his past as a combat Loach pilot years later when he acquired one of his unit's OH-6As, S/N 67-16026, which he painted in original unit markings. (Peter Bales Collection)

These two Loaches serve with Headquarters Company, 3rd Brigade of the 101st Airborne Division at Camp Evans in 1970. The OH-6A in the foreground, S/N 66-17781, survived the war, while the other, S/N 67-16068, crashed and burned when it encountered a booby trap. (Joe Gwizdak)

My first impression of the OH-6 was that it was very quick to respond and a treat to fly. It had lots of power compared to the piston-powered TH-55 and OH-13s I had flown. I was impressed with the skill of the instructors and their genuine concern that we learn not only to fly and instruct others to fly, but how to stay alive in Vietnam. After successfully completing the course, I had orders to report to the U.S. Army, Republic of Vietnam.

At the replacement center in Vietnam, I found that I had been assigned to the 3/11 ACR (3rd Squadron, 11th Armored Cavalry Regiment). In fact, I had been assigned for some time and they were waiting for me, literally. The driver was already there to pick me up.

To my surprise, the driver was a former classmate in the 10th WOC "White Hats" at Fort Wolters, Texas. He was booted out of flight school and had put most of his year in Vietnam as a tank driver and was finishing up his tour as the squadron commander's driver. It was good to see a familiar face in this very foreign place. As we made our way to a place called Di An (pronounced Zee-On), he filled me in on the 11th ACR.

The 11th ACR was made up of 1st, 2nd, and 3rd Squadrons, Air Cav Troop and Regimental Headquarters, along with several support units that were attached to the 11th ACR. Each squadron was made up of three APC (Armored Personnel Carrier) troops, a tank company, a Howitzer battery, and Headquarters and Headquarters Troop (HHT). Each of these units was company-sized. The Aviation Section was part of HHT. The aviation section of each squadron had two UH-1D/Hs and two OH-6As and a total of six pilots. We had a captain as a section leader, a couple of lieutenants, and the rest were warrant officers. The squadrons were

independent of each other and we very seldom ever worked together or even saw the other units, as they all had their own AO.

The 3/11th had lost one of its two Loaches to enemy fire. The aircraft had disappeared on the evening run from Fire Support Base Susan in Cambodia to Quan Loi, the rear headquarters where the aircraft were based. They found the aircraft the next morning with the pilot still in his seat; they found the gunner about 300 feet away. The pilot probably had been shot while in the air and had made what appeared to be a controlled crash. I was told that the gunner survived the crash and was heading for cover with his M60 and some ammo when he was shot in the back. Both the pilot and the gunner were stripped of all personal items and the weapons. This loss during such a busy time in Cambodia put the 3/11th in a bind for pilots. Not all the pilots in the aviation section were Loach qualified, and they were short a Loach pilot.

The Aviation Section was housed in what was left of a French plantation house. I was to take the bunk of the guy I replaced. I was directed to Headquarters for in-processing and was issued my flight helmet, hard hat, .38 pistol, a chicken plate, survival gear and emergency radio. I met the flight crews as they returned and they were happy to see me there to help with the flying load. They were a tired bunch having flown in excess of 10 hours a day. This was my first night where there was a war going on. The section leader, Captain La Chance, told me I would fly with him in the Huey in the morning for my orientation flight, and would fly the OH-6A in the afternoon on my own. There was not a lot of conversation with the guys because by the time they got back, fueled the aircraft, and got some chow, it was bedtime because we had to be off at first light around 04:30.

During 1969 and 1970, Apache Troop of 7th Squadron, 1st Cavalry flew minigun-armed OH-6As, with a gunner occupying the left pilot seat. The gunner's cut-down infantry style M60A machine gun hangs from a strap in the doorway, while a variety of grenades are strung between the armored seats. Belted M60 ammunition lying on the deck was draped across the gunner's lap. (Charlie Palek)

We went to bed to the sound of constant machine gun fire, M60s and .50 caliber machine guns going off all around the perimeter of the compound. This started at dusk and would continue until dawn. Whoever was assigned to perimeter guard would sporadically fire into the dark. This, along with illumination flares, would discourage the VC from a ground attack.

Somewhere around 12:30 I was wide awake lying in bed. It was hot. I was in a cot with mosquito netting tucked in around me, the ever present smell of 55-gallon drums of burning shit drifting through the broken windows, the constant firing and flares on the perimeter, coupled with a body clock that says it's the middle of the day, added up to no sleep. I heard for the first time a sound that I would hear many times over the next year; a far off thump, thump, thump, and then small explosions but much closer, and then a bed-shaking explosion. I was up and partly dressed when I heard a wavering siren. Everyone was up now grabbing their weapons. Someone shoved an M-16 and a clip at me and told me to get my hard hat and get in the bunker.

Outside on my way to the bunker I saw massive flames shooting up near the flight line.

The perimeter was lit up by what seemed to be hundreds of flares and a constant ring of tracers going out 360 degrees from the compound. I took all this in during my dash to the bunker, a six-foot circle of sandbags four feet high. To my surprise, there was only one enlisted guy in the bunker; the rest of the pilots and crews headed for the flight line. The guy in the bunker told me the wavering siren meant ground attack, a steady siren meant rocket or mortar attack. I could hear helicopters cranking. I peered over the sandbags and in the glow of the fire I could see Cobras lifting off.

The tracers around the flight line had stopped.

A million things run through your head at a time like this: had the VC overrun that section of the perimeter? Which way will they come from? Do I remember how to take the safety off? How long can I make one clip last? The Cobras were firing rockets as they took off. It had been only three minutes since this all started. It was then that I realized that all the war stories I had heard in basic training, flight school, and on the plane coming here were not stories; they were true. Here I was my first night in the field and the flight line is burning, the siren is wailing, the whole perimeter is lit up with everything we have. The Cobras are now in a daisy chain blowing up the countryside with HE rockets. No one I had met that day was anywhere in sight and I'm in a small bunker with one clip of rounds, with a Spec 4 with Coke-bottle glasses looking to me for some leadership.

The siren stopped, the Cobras landed and our guys returned from the flight line. There was no ground attack but mortars had found their target, hitting five Hueys, none of ours, and the fuel dump. The perimeter went back to its normal sporadic fire. Everyone went back to bed. I was wide awake thinking what have I gotten myself into.

I had some breakfast with the guys, got acquainted with the four-holer and found the source of that ever present smell. On the flight line the crew chief had the aircraft ready to go, and after a short preflight we were seated and strapped in the Huey. I was ready to read off the checklist when Captain La Chance yelled "Clear" and hit the starter before he got any response from the crew. I didn't know you could start an aircraft without a checklist. This wasn't flight school any more. We hit our altitude of 2,500 feet before even reaching the perimeter. Captain La Chance was a short-timer and he was going to have as much going for him as he could. This wasn't much of an orientation. He flew it just like the mission it was, with a few pointers here and there.

The squadron commander, a lieutenant colonel, used the Hueys for overall squadron command and control. The Loaches were assigned to the squadron executive officer (XO), a major, for his use in C & C and artillery spotting. Both of the aircraft types provided a variety of services when not in use by the CO or XO. Generally, we flew one of each every day. If we were in contact with the enemy, all of us flew every day. It was June of 1970 and all of the 11th ACR was working in Cambodia. President Nixon had made a speech announcing to the world that the Americans would be out of Cambodia by the end of June. This announcement with a definite date was the death sentence for a lot of our troopers. The enemy was lying in wait along the departure route. All the flight crews were flying almost every day because one or more of our squadrons were engaged in battle daily.

Loaches flew with one pilot and one crew chief/gunner with an M60 machine gun hung from a bungee cord out of the left rear doorway. The gunner was on the opposite side of the pilot because, in theory, and sometimes in fact, he would be shooting at the direction of the squadron XO, who sat next to the pilot. The pilots were issued snub-nose 38s. All the pilots also had some sort of automatic rifle that was not issued but handed down from other pilots as they left country. Over the course of the year I was there, I had a .45 caliber grease gun; you could actually see the bullets as they were fired. I also had a carbine with a small clip, and, finally, the tanker's version of the M-16, the CAR-15, which had a short barrel. I used this because it was reliable and it fit well with the strap over the side of the armored seat of the Loach, within easy reach if we went down.

I was anxious and apprehensive about my first flight in the Loach and my first solo to the AO. The crew chief met me at the aircraft and told me it was ready to go. We had plenty of time before I was to depart and I did a flight school preflight. The crew chief watched patiently but I wondered what he was thinking. He was really the guy that had to introduce me to this helicopter setup. He had his M60 hooked to the bungee and there were several strands of safety wire twisted together and strung across the back of the front seat bulkhead that had about 10 smoke grenades and four white phosphorus grenades hooked over the wire by their handles. These were used for marking areas to guide Cobra strikes or air strikes, or to mark the wind for landing aircraft. We did not carry regular hand grenades due to previous bad experiences. Some of the crew chiefs and gunners used to place a grenade in a glass jar with the pin pulled. They would be able to drop them from a greater height and when the jar hit and broke, the spoon flew and armed the fuse. This gave the crew more time to get away from the blast. Apparently, some jars broke in the aircraft with bad results and we were banned from playing with real grenades. We carried several metal canisters of ammo for the M60.

The crew chief always flew in the back manning the gun no matter what our mission was.

I liked this guy. In fact, all our crew chiefs and gunners were hard working and always gave the proper respect, never questioned an order, and were good guys. In the Loach there was just the two of us most of the time and we were a team. I was counting on him for a safe aircraft and firepower, and he was counting on me not to fly stupid.

We got strapped in and, like the Huey, I found the armor seat a bit restrictive at first. I went through the prestart checklist and the run-up checklist until I had no more checklists to stall. I had to make that call for takeoff. Over the intercom I called "Coming up," and the crew chief responded, "Clear Sir." I remember how heavy the aircraft seemed with just the two of us; the TOT (Turbine Outlet Temperature) was much higher than I remember back at Ft. Rucker and I was a bit concerned with the gauges at first. The aircraft was much heavier; we had armor seats, some armor in the engine compartment, and a bunch of bullets and grenades in the back, and it was really hot. We had none of that with training aircraft. I would get used to being near redline TOT and well into the yellow on torque much of the time when hovering.

I got off my radio calls and was cleared for takeoff. I climbed out somewhat like we had this morning, but I noticed that most of the aircraft ahead of me were not making as steep a climb-out. Being a short-timer does that to you.

The trip up to Cambodia was easy; just follow the road but when the road ended, the anxiety level went up. I searched for landmarks and after identifying them I called FSB Susan on the FM to let them know I was five minutes out. They told me to keep it running and that the XO would meet me at the aircraft. My approach and landing were normal and I didn't do anything yet to let everyone know I was the new guy. The XO was there with his helmet and grasping his map. He always had that map in his hand; it had all our unit's locations, their routes of travel and the locations of known enemy and friendlies, along with their radio frequencies marked in different colored grease pencil. He climbed in and said, "Oh, you're the new guy." No introduction, just "Let's go." So we went.

He directed me to where the tanks were making their way down the road. It was slow going because guys with metal detectors were sweeping the road for mines. He spoke with the tank commander on FM, decided they were okay, and we went on to check on the rest of the APC companies. Things were going well with all the units making their way back to FSB Susan to make that damn deadline the President set. There had not been any enemy contact that day.

We were on our way to the last troop in the field. The major was tuning the FM radio to make contact with them when his map went out the door. My first thought was that that had happened to me a couple of times in flight school. No big deal, he can get another one. But he about crapped! He was yelling, "Go back! Go back!" I made a hard left turn so he could keep his eye on it as it fluttered to the ground. And the crew chief had it in sight as we made the turn. We were in the middle of nowhere. He had not made a call to tell everyone he lost his map, so we were on our own. This was not jungle, but scrub brush and the map made it to the ground where we could see it.

I circled and found the only place to set down, about 50 yards away. The crew chief cleared me into the confined space. Hey, this was just like primary training at Ft. Wolters.

As we touched down, the crew chief said, "I'll get it." Then it struck me. I'm sitting in a noisy helicopter knowing that there are bad guys all around. I can't see 30 feet in any direction and the guy with the gun is going for a walk. The XO did get his pistol out and kept looking back in the direction that the crew chief went. There was no talking between us. By his reaction to the map flying out I knew it was a big deal to get it back. If the map were found by Charlie, it would have a lot of information that would be used against us. I felt stupid to relate that map to the Dallas sectional chart that flew out of our TH-55 on a cross-country over Possum Kingdom Lake. I was getting the feel for how serious these guys were. Like the CO, this guy knew his stuff and was responsible for all the movement on the ground. He told them where to go and how to get there and he took the job very seriously. Lives depended on his decisions. The XO said, "Here he comes," and we were both relieved. I remember yanking the collective. It was not a pretty takeoff but we wanted out of there.

We shut down at FSB Susan and I got a chance to meet the CO, CSM (Command Sergeant Major), Foxy the CO's dog and some of the other guys, but not the XO. I don't think we ever really were introduced; we just got used to each other. He was all business, all the time. I respected him too. The Huey came in and shut down. This was really the first time I got to talk to the guys. They were quick to tell the story of the guy I replaced, telling me where he got shot down, and how they found him and the gunner. This was a good bunch of guys and I felt proud to be part of the unit.

I was hoping to follow the Huey back but they had sacks of mail for me to deliver to the various track units, and I was to pick up a guy who was going home. We made the rounds in about 15 minutes, and picked up the guy on the dusty road. All he had with him was his stuff wrapped in a shirt and a big grin. These guys traveled light.

The next day I was assigned to fly the Huey with CWO2 Harrison, who was finishing up his second tour in Vietnam. We met the crew at the flight line, and as was almost always the case, the aircraft was ready to go. Most of the preflight was completed by the crew chief; we checked the rotor head, tail rotor and fluid levels. The crew chief and door gunner would endure more on this flight than you could ever ask of anyone. I remember the professionalism of the crew chief and gunner. They always knew when to announce that we were clear on takeoff and landing, always using the proper terminology and military respect.

We made our call to FSB Susan and were advised that "Bandit Six" would be waiting for us and not to shut down. Upon landing, Bandit the mascot dog ran out and jumped on the Huey. The dog would jump on the aircraft every time we landed. The CO, the CSM and the CO's aide, a captain, were right behind Bandit. Once aboard, the CO directed us to make the rounds as all the units were moving and working their way to FSB Susan to convoy back into Vietnam, and he wanted to see their progress. Susan was being dismantled. I could see activity, with tents being taken down and a lot of cleanup being done.

The CO had to be back at FSB Susan in an hour for a meeting with the regimental commander, all three squadron commanders, and a general. The meeting was about the withdrawal from Cambodia. Each of these commanders had their own Huey, and with WO1 Owens bringing a ship for us to swap, we had six Hueys in the open around the pad, all running. All the commanders and their staff had gone into the compound to meet in the TOC (Tactical Operations Center).

We had switched Hueys, with me in the right seat to take the controls. Harrison had taken the left seat. The crew chief and gunner were in their positions. For some reason Harrison's helmet needed adjusting and he was making the adjustments when I heard something unusual. I looked up to see dirt flying on the far side of Susan. I watched, not yet comprehending what was going on. I could see more puffs of dirt flying and now noticed people running. I still didn't get it, but then saw the lids on the tracks slamming shut, and I got it that we were being mortared. Even at this early stage of being in Vietnam, I reacted by rapidly rolling the throttle from the flight idle position. Harrison, engrossed in fixing his helmet, heard and felt the engine rapidly advance and gave me a "what the hell are you doing?" look. I nodded toward the activity and he caught on real quick. By the time he had his helmet on, I was pulling pitch at exactly the same time the rest of the Hueys were pulling pitch. All six aircraft lifted at the same time and headed in different directions. Harrison grabbed the controls and continued in the direction we were headed. We were making circles around Susan looking for any sign of where the mortars were coming from.

In the meantime, requests for immediate Dustoffs came in. There were multiple casualties and injuries and the first concern was to get the wounded out of there. Owens volunteered to pick up the wounded and other Hueys were picking up their officers. We had no success in finding the mortar team, and were requested to return to Susan to take the KIAs. I would learn that the first priority after an attack like this was to remove the bodies as soon as the injured were taken care of.

We were met at the pad by soldiers carrying stretchers with very badly mangled bodies.

Each stretcher was filled with blood of the soldier that had just been torn apart by shrapnel from the mortars. One by one they loaded while we sat there at full rpm. The crew chief and gunner helped place the stretchers until they had to pile them one on top of another. I remember four stretchers on the first layer, with three on top of them. The last thing I watched was a leg from the knee down, still in the boot and with the pant leg up to the knee being tossed on top of the pile. I never looked after that.

We were loaded and, except for a "Clear right" and "Clear left" from the crew in back, there were no words spoken among the crew for the entire flight. We were instructed to go to something new to me, called "Graves Registration." I had never heard that term but I figured it out real quick. Harrison flew and I just sat there thinking about what had just happened.

I would learn later that the poor souls we were now transporting had been on police detail, cleaning up the area outside the berm. Someone higher up the ladder had decided we were to leave Cambodia cleaner than we found it. The mortars started falling on the opposite side of Susan from the helipad and then walked across the base making their way toward the helicopters, but we all got off before they made it that far. We figured that Charlie had been watching us all along and could not pass up the opportunity to use their mortars when they observed all the Hueys landing with big Brass on board.

We landed at Graves Registration at Long Binh and Harrison rolled the throttle to flight idle and we just sat there with no one saying a word. I was wondering if we would have to go find someone to take our cargo when three guys slowly rolled gurneys out the door toward our aircraft. They were not in any hurry, certainly not in the same hurry we were to be unloaded. It took them a while to get us unloaded but I never looked back to see the progress. They finished and the crew chief came on the intercom and said we were ready to go. We headed for our rear area at Quan Loi where we went directly to our revetment.

Harrison made the call and we landed, completed the two-minute cool down and shut down. Once the battery was turned off, we departed the aircraft. Only then did I realize what the crew chief and gunner went through.

Both of them were completely soaked in blood. The only part of their bodies not coated was where the helmet was and where they had lowered their visors. When we took off, the cabin doors were open as usual. The airflow past the doors sucked the pooling blood out the doors, past the two, soaking them in the process. They could have gotten up and shut the doors but that request never came. It was a solemn moment and they just dealt with it. The entire tail boom was red with blood. The tail rotor blades were red and drips came off the tail stinger. Inside the aircraft were deep red globs of coagulated blood where the stretchers overflowed. These are the kinds of sights and memories that you never forget.

Word of the mortar attack had reached our rear area and most of the flight crew met us when we came in. There was not much talk. The crew chief and gunner went right to work cleaning the aircraft and others pitched in. They ended up getting the truck that delivered water to the showers and mess tents around the base to come to the aircraft to provide water for cleaning. This was my second day of flying in Vietnam. We were back in the air in two hours. We still had to get the 3/11th home from Cambodia.

I did a lot of flying the rest of the week, mostly Command and Control as the tracks and tanks made their way out of Cambodia and headed for our new home at Di An. There would be a 21-day maintenance stand-down. I was taking a liking to flying the OH-6. I had to think about why and then realized it was the mission and the fact that it was just me and the crew chief most of the time. I liked flying a single-pilot ship. I was in control and could do things my way, something that has stuck with me all my life.

During the stand-down we did little flying the first week. We spent our time moving into the new quarters. The base did not present a really secure situation, but we never had a ground attack and we were mortared twice in six months. The biggest threat here was from other U.S. soldiers on the base. During the stand-down, the officers club was fragged by a doped up soldier. We also got gassed with CS a couple of times by drunk pranksters. One of our pilots, a first lieutenant nicknamed "Deputy Dog," got drunk one night and went to the enlisted hootch and lined all the guys up with a pistol. They were a pretty scared bunch. One of the senior CWO2s went in to check on something and took the .45 away from the guy. The Old Man took his pistol away and forbid him to drink the rest of his tour. He left the unit shortly thereafter and no one asked why.

Our flying missions varied; we were there to support the ground troops in many ways.

The routine for the OH-6 was to fly out in the morning to pick up the XO, who would direct the ground units as to what route to take, and when in contact, he would direct air strikes and artillery. We would be the courier from the FSB to the ground units, delivering and picking up documents and mail. And on occasions where the Huey was too large to get in to make a dustoff, we would hover in and pick up the injured. Every day we found an excuse to shoot the '60 out the back. Sometimes it was for practice but mostly it was to keep Charlie's head down while the tracks were in a vulnerable area. The small groups of VC we were up against did not like to give their position away because they were no match for us or the tracks.

By the end of September I was one of the old experienced guys. I had been flying the Loach from day one and had some pretty good opportunities to take charge of some of the air operations. After a while, you don't ask, you just do, and unless you screwed up real bad they would let you run with an operation.

By Christmas we had a new CO who had a heck of a time with the radios. He could never tell who was talking to whom. He would answer someone that was talking to us on UHF but he was on FM and in on the wrong conversation, or just kept saying "Who was that" and we would have to sort things out for him. It helped a lot when we suggested he turn off his UHF switch so he was only listening to one radio, but if he needed to talk to an Air Force FAC or Cobras, he had to use UHF and the confusion would start all over again. I took over the calls to the Cobras and the Air Force. I would ask him on the intercom what he wanted them to do and then make the calls. Eventually I got a feel for what the CO wanted and took care of it. When I was flying the Loach I put in a lot of artillery and air strikes working with both the Cobras and the Air Force, sometimes speaking with the FACs or directly with the fighters. The CO never did get used to the radios.

My flight time in Vietnam was about half Huey and half Loach. I enjoyed the Loach missions more as we got closer to the fighting. We did a fair amount of scout type flying for our own units but without the benefit of a Cobra overhead. Since this scouting was in support of our tracked units, we had to rely on them if we took fire or found a bunker complex. We often would scout ahead of the tracks, looking for RPG teams that may be lying in wait for the column of tracks to go by. When the tracks were in jungle, the going was slow as they had to "bust jungle" by knocking down trees as they went. There were two occasions in one week when I had to make dustoffs with the Loach.

The jungle area that one of the troops was working had been defoliated and the tall trees were dead. As the tracks hit the trees, they would break into pieces and fall straight down, instead of going over like a live tree. A large section of a tree that was hit fell onto the track and hit one of the guys riding on the outside, breaking his neck. This was an urgent dustoff situation and the request was made for our Huey.

It was clear to the Huey crew that that they could not get in there to pick up the guy because the space was too small for the Huey to even hover down. There were two options: wait for a hoist-equipped dustoff bird or try getting a Loach in there. I was shut down at FSB Bandit and one of the guys from the TOC came out to say we were requested to make a dustoff. This was unusual but he didn't have any details. I cranked up and the gunner and I headed to the area. When I got there I sized up the situation.

There was no place to set down so I would have to hover down to the track, and place one skid on the track while they loaded the stretcher across our rear cabin floor. We relayed the plan to the guys on the ground while the gunner shoved all the ammo boxes against the rear bulkhead to make room.

Once they got the stretcher in place on top of the track, I began the hover down. This was not a straight shot down; I had to hover down until I was under the canopy but now on top of another tree. With the gunner giving me directions, I slid under the canopy and then down to the track. I was able to get the skid on the track and told the gunner to make sure the process was slow so I could adjust the controls as the weight changed. The process went smoothly but made me work at keeping the aircraft in place with the movement and weight change occurring. The gunner understood the importance of not making any sudden changes in this confined area, and he stayed out on the skid as we made the hover back out of the hole, continuing to give me readouts on clearances from the trees. Once out of the hole, we followed the Huey back to Bandit where we both landed and made the patient swap. Up until then, that was the most challenging flying I had done. A mission a few days later was almost a repeat of this dustoff. It was the same unit in the same area and the same scenario, but we had the procedure down. I never did find out how most of the guys that were injured turned out. When they were hurt bad enough to return to "The World," we seldom heard anything about them again.

We often flew Red Cross girls, called "Donut Dollies," when they went out to spend the day with the troops. We almost never got to see a "round-eyed" girl. Sometimes when we took the CO to see the wounded at the hospital, we would catch a glimpse of a round-eyed nurse. So these visits with the Donut Dollies meant a lot to the guys in the field.

When we flew them out in the Loach, we had one up front and one in the rear seat. It was tradition to land facing the FSB, which gave the guys on the ground a little show as the girl in front had to lift her leg (they always wore skirts) over the cyclic stick to exit the aircraft. This worked with the new girls but if they had been around a while, they were on to that trick and would say, "Turn it

In keeping with the 1st Aviation Brigade's nickname "Hawk," monthly informational materials put out by the brigade featured a "Hawk Honey." Here, Hawk Honey "Baby Rae" graces the cockpit of an OH-6A. (U.S. Army)

around."

On one occasion, when I was taking a couple of the girls out, we circled the tracks looking for the best landing spot and were surprised to see some very tan backs and legs and very white butts lying in the grass outside the perimeter. The short-time girls had found the unit and were conducting business. I was a bit embarrassed with American girls on board, but they had probably seen it before.

I was to pick up one gal and take her out to the field. She was one of them who had me "turn it around." She was pretty good looking and I enjoyed watching her as she strapped in. When we were ready to go, she asked if she could fly. I said, "Sure, when we get to altitude." She said she could take it off and I thought, "yeah, right." I said I would cover the controls and she could give it a try. I was all set for her to find out that you don't just get in a helicopter and fly it away. Well, she did. Her liftoff was smooth, transition to flight had the proper pedal inputs, and she handled the collective smoothly. I let her fly all the way to the FSB and make the approach to a hover, where I took it and completed the landing. She probably could have done that as well. She told me that every time she had the chance, she would fly and most of the pilots were accommodating. She was either a fast learner or she was able to talk pilots into good instruction. I always wondered if she pursued getting her license when she got home. She sure had a good start.

Our chaplain was a Catholic priest we called "The Singing Padre." He had a guitar and sang at the different gatherings; he was pretty good. He would ask to fly with me and do some hunting. We went on at least half a dozen such flights and never came up empty handed. He had grown up in a family that hunted a lot and he was pretty good with his M-16. There was a breed of Asian deer that full grown was about the size of a collie dog.

We could see them running when we flew over and spooked them. I would fly the padre out to the area and he would use the M-16 on single shot and get them on the run every time. We picked up the deer and brought them back to the FSB. He would give the deer to locals for food. Other game he shot was peacocks and one time we got a wild boar.

That boar was tough. The padre hit him several times and he kept running. He finally fell and we landed near the thrashing body. The gunner got out and put a .45 slug in its head and that did the trick. We loaded the pig on board and flew it back to the FSB. After the padre posed for photos with his prize, we once again gave it the locals, who treated it as quite a gift.

The 15th of October was perhaps the most exciting day I spent in Vietnam. We had been conducting a joint operation with an infantry unit, that sometimes followed the tracks through the jungle. We were flying when I got a call from our TOC that one of the infantry platoons was pinned down in a heavily wooded area, and we were to see what we could do. One of our APC troops had been asked to assist but it was a full day's travel from the area. When I arrived, I contacted the unit on its FM freq and got a soldier yelling into the radio, "Get us out of here!" He was almost unintelligible. I could hear others in the background also yelling the same. I had to calm the guy down and get him to stop yelling so I could understand him. Their platoon leader, a second lieutenant, had been on point and was shot and killed. Their platoon sergeant tried to rescue him and was shot in the process, but made it back to the platoon and needed immediate dustoff.

An enemy machine gun position had gotten both of them,

An OH-6A of the 101st Airborne Division's 3rd Brigade at FSB Airborne overlooking the A Shau Valley in 1969. The small Loach often was used to get into places otherwise inaccessible to larger helicopters. (Joe Gwizdak)

but was just out of range of their position. A dustoff was being summoned. I was the only helicopter there so I thought that I would see if I could get in to pick the guy up.

I had the guys on the ground pop a smoke so I could see them; this was triple canopy stuff and I could not pick them out, so I didn't know where the enemy was either. I asked them what direction the firing came from after I confirmed their yellow smoke. They gave me a direction and I lined up on the smoke so that I would come up on them as far away from the line of fire that I could. I stuck to the tree tops up to the smoke when they advised I was taking fire. We could make out tracers coming up through the trees but they were going over us. I dropped down into the tree tops and the tracers remained over our heads and did not get any closer. We got to where we could see the troops on the ground.

Our Huey arrived with the CO and I advised them to stay away from the line of fire. They located me and the tracers and determined that the angle of the machine gun prevented it from hitting us. They had a good fix on the machine gun position and called in an airstrike with napalm. I told the C & C ship that I would try to hover down to the ground and pick up the wounded man. This made my previous ventures hovering down into the canopy look like a piece of cake. This was live jungle, not having been defoliated. With the crew chief watching the back, I watched the front and we descended into the trees.

This was no straight-down shot; this needed a series of moves left and right, fore and aft to miss branches, but I was able to get down to about 10 feet off the ground. There was no way to go any lower without hitting major tree branches, the kind that take blades off.

When we were at the lowest point I could see the sergeant being tended to by a medic.

The rest of the guys were frantically motioning us to continue down. Then they were trying to jump up to the helicopter. If a couple of them got hold of the skids, we would crash right on top of what was left of the platoon. I hovered upward a bit to make their attempts impossible and determined that the sergeant would

have to be taken out by a jungle penetrator from a hoist-equipped Huey. Our Huey crew advised me that one was *en route* but first the airstrike would go in.

I was to hover over the friendlies while F-4 Phantoms dropped a mix of napalm and 250-pound bombs. I thought that it would be a better idea if we marked the area with smoke and then let the jets work out. Besides, I needed to get fuel. I marked the spot where the troops were and watched as the first napalm went in. I headed for the closest POL point, which was only a seven-minute flight. The crew chief topped us off and I was anxious to get back to the action; this was my show. I was the first on scene and had the best picture of the situation.

When I returned, the airstrike had just been completed and the medevac ship was on station and getting ready to go in and drop his jungle penetrator. Just as the Huey started letting out his hoist cable, he was raked by the machine gun. The Huey took several hits in the engine area and headed out. We watched as he made it about a quarter mile to a clearing. He was losing power, made a hard landing, spreading the skids but kept it upright; the blades did not flex down hard enough to hit the tail boom. I immediately landed next to the downed bird. The crew chief and gunner were out of the aircraft with their 60s and setting up positions between the tree line and the aircraft. The copilot was out the door with a fire extinguisher and heading for the smoking engine. My crew chief went to assist. This area would become the headquarters for the rest of the operation, which would not end until early the next morning when our tracks would finally arrive.

Our CO called for another dustoff and more airstrikes. Our area was deemed secure and we took off to mark ground troops for the next airstrike. Our artillery was not an option because of the close distance the troops were to the machine gun. Another set of Phantoms showed up and I once again marked the ground troops with smoke and moved out of the area to watch the show. The Phantom pilots were concerned with how close our guys were to where the fire was coming from. On the infantry's FM freq I could hear a calming voice talking to them. It was their CO who was now on the way.

Unfortunately, he got the same response I did; screaming and crying on the other end, saying, "Get us out of here," with the sound of the Phantoms' bombs in the background.

These guys had no leadership. Their platoon leader was dead and their platoon sergeant, who had been shot in the back, was in no condition to provide any direction. It had been over two hours since I first found these guys, there had been an airstrike, then a Huey was shot up, and now another airstrike was going in, and I was getting anxious to see some progress. I had taken a personal interest in this operation as if it were one of our aircrews down there.

The grunts' company commander landed next to the downed Huey and our CO landed to confer with him. I came up with the idea to take him in and have him drop the 10 feet to his troops. I mentioned this to our CO and told me to come into the makeshift command area to discuss it. We landed next to the now growing number of Hueys. When my CO mentioned my idea to the other, he immediately said, "Yes!" As they were coming toward me I was having second thoughts. The infantry CO was about 6' 3" and at least 250 pounds of what looked like solid muscle. He looked like OJ Simpson. Dropping a guy this size off a skid would be a wild ride once he let go. I was committed so I explained to him that he would have to smoothly get out on the skid and lower himself gently until he was hanging. I would give him the nod so I could be ready to react to the controls with the sudden change of weight and center of gravity (CG). He agreed and got on board. We hovered low over the trees and did the same hover pattern down to the 10-foot level. Once again, the guys on the ground tried to jump up to catch the skids until they saw their CO. What a happy bunch of guys; you could see the fear melt away when they saw him get out on the skid. He dropped his M-16, helmet and belt with sidearm.

This was a pretty good drop and he wanted to be as light as possible. He did as I asked and gently lowered himself until he was fully extended and hanging off the skid. I told my crew chief that I was going to give him the nod and to be ready for the adjustments I would quickly make.

I gave him the nod and he let go before I could make any control inputs; we shot up and to the left, taking some good sized branches out before I could get the aircraft under control. I got out of the branches and into a stable hover and looked down to see the guys taking cover from the falling debris. The infantry commander gave me a salute; he was on his own now.

We slowly made our way back out of the jungle. This time there were no tracers from the machine gun. I took this as a sign that the Phantoms had hit their target. I radioed our TOC that the commander was on the ground but I had hit large branches on the way out and was going to shut down in the open area to check the blades. The aircraft felt all right, there were no unusual vibrations but I wanted to see what the blades looked like. I couldn't imagine that there would be no damage. I landed and the crew chief was out and looking over the aircraft as soon as we touched down. I completed the two-minute cool-down and shut the aircraft down. Other than small pieces of wood stuck in the tip caps, the blades had only minor scrapes. We discussed the tree hit with the maintenance people at Di An and we agreed that if there was no visible damage to the blades, it was okay to fly.

When the pilot of the second dustoff Huey called in, I talked to him. He was loaded with questions about what kind of fire we got, from where, what kind of airstrike and what they used. I told him that I had dropped the infantry commander and had not drawn fire, but that I was too low for them to hit, and I was sure the last airstrike did the job. I was starting to get irritated. The platoon sergeant had been shot over three hours ago and needed to be pulled out of there. I told the dustoff PIC that after all the ordnance that had been dropped on that machine gun position, they had to be toast. He sounded like a guy that had been around for a while; he had to be in his mid-twenties and must have been "short," because I thought he was being over-cautious. He wanted another Cobra strike before he would go in. I thought, "Come on you chickenshit, get this guy out of there." The call went out for the Cobras to come back and work out again. I cranked so I could once again mark the area with smoke; this ate up another 45 minutes.

After the two Cobras emptied their loads of HE rockets and departed, that chickenshit dustoff pilot was ready to go to work. I contacted the ground commander and asked him to pop smoke so the dustoff could lower a litter basket to them. The commander said the patient was conscious and was looking forward to the ride out.

The dustoff Huey maneuvered into position well above the area I had flown in and out of and lowered the litter. The sergeant was loaded and strapped into the litter. Just as they began to hoist him, the Huey got raked by the same machine gun that had done all the damage. The pilot radioed that they were hit. He lowered his nose in an attempt to gain speed and get away. He still had 200 feet of cable attached and was dragging the sergeant through the trees. He had gone about a quarter mile before the crew chief could cut the hoist. The ship was now trailing smoke and losing power; the pilot announced that they were going down. Our Huey cranked immediately and I followed the smoking Huey. By the time I caught up with him, he was making a running landing in a wide spot on a cattle trail.

I was planning to go for fuel as soon as the dustoff was completed, and now my fuel was down to the point where I had to get fuel, now. Dustoff reported they were down okay with no injuries and asked me to find the guy they cut off the hoist. I told him our Huey was inbound to pick them up but I had to go for fuel and would call our other Loach to help with the search.

I was frustrated with the whole situation. This guy was no longer a chickenshit pilot and I felt bad about my earlier thoughts. He really had been around and had a lot more experience with these types of extractions than I did. Now we had a second dustoff down, a guy in a litter somewhere in the jungle and I had no fuel. We made the best time we could and topped off and were back on station just as the Phantoms reported in for an airstrike. Aircraft recoveries had to be made and a third dustoff was requested to stand by to pick up the lost patient, when we located him. Before I could search the dustoff's half-mile long line of flight, the Phantoms called in and I volunteered to hover over the ground troops to mark their position. They would line up on me and drop their napalm.

One of the most memorable experiences of my life was about to take place.

The first Phantom confirmed he had me in sight and would line up on me for the drop. I was watching the jet make his run head-on to me when I saw two very large napalm bombs release and come tumbling right at me; this was one of those "Life flashes before your eyes" moments. They seemed to tumble in slow motion. The

Although OH-6As commonly rescued wounded, only one is known to have been dedicated to the Dustoff mission, in view of its small size and agility. Number 67-16254 was used by the 326th Med Battalion of the 101st Airborne Division in 1969. After only 20 medical evacuation missions, it was added to the long list of Loaches lost, having been shot down on 17 August 1969. (U.S. Army photo)

Phantom pulled up over me but the napalm bombs were still coming directly for me. Just as I was going to attempt to fly out of their path I could see that they would pass over me, but not by much.

I made a pedal turn as they passed over and hit the jungle 50 yards away. When they hit and exploded I could feel the blast jostle the helicopter, but mostly we got a blast of very hot air; I noted that the TOT briefly went up about 20 degrees. The Phantoms had only napalm and made two runs each. There was a tremendous amount of fire and smoke where the machine gun had been. I found out the next day that these guys were not dug in deep, just a hand-dug dirt berm about two feet high. They had survived all the previous Phantom and Cobra attacks and somehow survived long enough to get two Hueys.

Now the main concern was to find the platoon sergeant. Our other Loach arrived on station and I had him follow me along the dustoff's flight path. By now the third dustoff was orbiting on station. Five minutes later the other Loach called to say he located the man and that the Huey could land to pick him up. The sergeant was lying on his back in the stretcher with a coil of cable draped across his chest and he was waving at us. He had been dragged through trees a half mile and yet sustained no additional injuries. He had landed between two large bomb craters. The Loach landed right next to him and the gunner was out talking to him. The report came back that he had a bullet lodged in his spine and he was paralyzed from the waist down. The pilot of the dustoff that had been forced to drop him in the jungle radioed to ask how the patient was; I could hear the genuine concern in his voice.

This was another life lesson; maybe the experienced guy knows what he's doing. Since we did most of our own dustoffs, we didn't work with these guys much. When this guy wouldn't just go in and snatch the sergeant, I thought little of him. By the end of the operation, I had a whole different opinion of these guys. They were very experienced in working in hot areas. It takes a lot of guts to hover for an extended period of time to hoist wounded out of the jungle.

I headed back to FSB Bandit, picked up some mail and headed back to Di An so maintenance could take a good look at the blades. All they did was wash off the green stains. By dark, both disabled dustoff aircraft and crew, along with the security squad, had been lifted out. The infantry commander brought needed leadership to the ground troops. The APCs set up a perimeter and the rest of the night was quiet. At daybreak, the tracks went to where the platoon leader's body lay. He had been stripped of all his personal items as well as maps and radio freq book. His body was not mutilated like our troops would sometimes do to them. Although the machine gun position had been hit with napalm, no signs of bodies were found; there wasn't even any brass left from shell casings. Charlie always cleaned up the brass if they could. It was not determined how big or who the force was that we were up against. Running most of the air operations that day and dropping the commander to his guys on the ground earned me a DFC. I was not aware of the award until it was pinned on me several months later. At the time, I was just doing what needed to be done to get our guys out of a bad situation.

Lost
by Kurt F. Schatz

Kurt Schatz did it all during his 1969-1970 Vietnam tour, flying Scouts (OH-6A), Lift (UH-1) and Guns (AH-1G) with B and C Troops of the 1st Cavalry Division's famed "First of the Ninth." He volunteered for C Troop because so many pilots had been lost. Not only was he awarded three Distinguished Flying Crosses within his first five months as a Scout, he received a direct commission from Warrant Officer to 1Lt. After retiring 24 years later as a Lieutenant Colonel, Schatz tells these tales about two of his many hair-raising experiences as "Cavalier One-Two," his call sign as a Scout pilot. The first he titles "Lost," which makes you think back in time, when you were a child, not knowing how to get home. You stand looking in all directions and nothing looks familiar. You are hopelessly lost and tears begin to flow down your cheeks.

It was during the invasion of Cambodia. The 1/9 Cav C Troop had been working just to the west of the famous Fish Hook. A lot of action had been seen and we were seeing things that we just could not believe – convoys of NVA trucks loaded with the enemy,

Cobras making strafing runs on them, looking just like one of those World War II movies of P-51 strafing runs on a Nazi convoy, massive supply dumps. We were watching a large group of UH-1s – there must have been at least 50 of them – sitting in a huge landing zone, waiting on the infantry to load up, when what seemed like thousands of mortar explosions began. Hueys were being blown up and grunts were flying through the air.

God knows we wanted to help but all we could do was make it home on what fuel we had left. We watched in disbelief as we continued on at altitude, listening to the mayday calls for help on guard. We informed our higher-up of the situation and continued on.

On the horizon we saw the helicopter's worst enemy, a wall of

Kurt Schatz, having become well-rounded in flying Army Scout, Lift and Gun missions with the 1st Squadron, 9th Cavalry, is seen here in 1969 at the controls of an OH-6A. (Kurt Schatz Collection)

Represented in this four-generation portrait of the Schatz family are 53 years of proud Army service. From left to right are Richard Schatz (E-5 1st Cavalry Division) holding son Bruce, Kurt (Retired Lt. Col. Master Aviator), and his father, Joseph, who retired a Major in Field Artillery. (Kurt Schatz Collection)

Loaches damaged beyond in-country capabilities were shipped to the Army Aeronautical Depot Maintenance Center at Corpus Christi, Texas. This badly damaged OH-6A at Phú Lợi wears an owl on its rotor pylon representing assignment to 1st Brigade of the 1st Infantry Division. (Terry Love)

clouds covering any possible escape from Cambodia. Like the grunts being blown away, there was little we could do. It was getting dark and our fuel was low. We were almost 2,000 feet high and knew that the rain storm would eat us up, so the Cobra team leader said, "Take it down. We are going low level under this stuff to get home."

We were still deep inside Cambodia as we penetrated the storm. The Cobra was way out in front and I couldn't keep up. He was showing me the way home and he disappeared into the storm. Frantically, I called, "I can't see you. I lost you." The Cobra came back, "Sorry little buddy. You're on your own. We have gone IFR

and are climbing to altitude." At that point my heart sank into the bottom of my stomach. I was lost. Rain was pouring into the cockpit so bad that the radios began to go out, one by one. I pulled back on the cyclic and brought it to a hover over the triple canopy jungle. I transmitted, "How do I get home?" The last transmission I was to hear again that night came back from the Cobra: "Fly due east and . . . ." The radios had gone out completely.

I started hovering in an easterly direction and the rain intensified even more. I could only see under the OH-6 by looking out the door opening as darkness approached. On and on in an easterly direction, never more than a walking pace, until the demon of darkness arrived. I had no other choice. I turned on the landing light, illuminating the jungle below.

For what seemed like an eternity, I continued in that easterly direction into the blackness.

Below my right skid a dirt road appeared. At least it was something to follow, and I did.

On into the darkness, our landing light signaling to all that I was a fair target. In the distance, a small light glimmered through the rain. I stopped, turned off the light and had a conference with the observer and crew chief: "Guys, we have to make a decision. That light is either friendly or enemy and as far as I know, we are still in Cambodia. We have two choices; run out of fuel on this road going back the way we came, or finding out who owns that light."

They could have shot us down, so my best guess is that they must be friendly. The consensus was to go to the light. I set the Loach down and got out my .38 pistol. The observer got out of the Loach with his chunker and placed himself in a position to provide cover. The crew chief got his sawed off M60 machine gun and all the ammo he could wrap around his shoulders, and disappeared into the darkness toward the light.

After what seemed like an eternity, he finally came back with the biggest smile I had ever seen in my life. "Sir, it's one of ours. It's a fire support base." Thank God, the child had found his way home.

The Nut

There I was, the little bird being led back by an AH-1G Cobra to an old C-130 strip outside of Fire Support Base Buttons, near Nui Ba Ra for refueling. In Cav language, we were a Pink Team and the little bird was used to scout out the enemy at tree-top level, or, in my mind now, it was like being a worm on a hook. No wonder so many of us Scout pilots and crew got killed or wounded.

I was at about 2,500 feet altitude, almost directly above the strip, when my engine-out light came on. The nose dipped way down and everything went crazy in the cockpit. I was scared to death wondering if I could get the thing down. I never felt very confident about autorotations, but at least I was above a nice long landing strip with our own Forward Area Refueling Point (FARP) and not over the jungle. Thank God.

I remember screaming over the radio to my Cobra, "Going down!" I began to pull back on the cyclic and looking at my airspeed, which was passing through 110 knots! I was in about a 60-degree dive just like in the movies of a plane being shot down. Nothing happened. The cyclic was stuck and I put both hands on it, braced myself, pushing hard against the rudder pedals and pulled as hard as I could. Nothing. Nothing. Nothing. I thought that this was it and my crew and I are dead meat.

I began telling my high bird every instrument read-out and that the cyclic was stuck. I told him I thought it was a one-way lock failure and reached the emergency fuel cut-off and closed it. I never stopped talking. I had seen so many others go in and not know what happened, and, by God, it wasn't going to happen to me. I wanted the world to know what was happening.

My airspeed pegged out along with my rotor tach. The bird went through blade stall and the nose came up, way up, almost straight up until the bird slowed to about 80 knots. The tips of the rotor blades actually made a bang so loud that the guys at the FARP looked up.

Then it started all over again; nose down and pegged the airspeed indicator and rotor tach.

I was able to move the cyclic left and right and turned back toward the air strip.

Larry Krause was my CE gunner in the back and had no seat or seat belt and he was busy tossing out the homemade 17-pound rocket warhead bombs, WPs, and ammo and all sorts of goodies. He locked his arms around the center pillar that came up between the two front seats and braced his feet into the corners of the cabin. My observer next to me had fainted. I locked his seat belt.

Blade stall again! This time I was at about 200 feet altitude. I was lined up with the runway but was in a dive again, headed for some trees just short of the strip. For the first time, I put my hand on the collective and began to pull to avoid the trees. This brought my nose up and began to bleed some air speed off.

The next thing I knew, BANG, and I mean hard. Broke the skids in half and pushed the struts up into the body of the bird. It bounced up in the air like a ball and flipped on its right side and began to slide down the runway. My right elbow was dragging on the ground and eating through my nomex. I pulled my elbow in and wedged it between the armor plate and my chest.

Can you believe it? I was still talking on the radio! The bird came to a stop and I said, "I'm OK," turned off the battery switch, stood up on the ground with my head sticking out of the left door. Krause was hitting the engine compartment with a large fire extinguisher that he carried, just in case.

The CO's bird was hovering off to the side, landed and several people came running towards our bird. The observer was still passed out. I don't remember how I got out or how the observer got out, but I do remember walking all around the helicopter looking for my cigarette lighter; this was smoke break time. Someone gave me a smoke and I looked at the rotor blades. They were bent like a piece of lasagna.

Everyone hopped into the CO's Huey and we went back to our base at Phuoc Vinh. The only person to get hurt was me and it was only a skinned elbow. I said the Lord's Prayer real seriously that night.

The bird was slung back to Phuoc Vinh and, low and behold, the cyclic worked. I felt humiliated and I knew everyone thought that I had screwed up. Captain Cecil Smith, the Loach SIP, gave me a look that burned right through me. The bird was sent down to Vung Tau and taken apart, and they found a nut had fallen into the fore and aft bellcrank. If I had pushed a little forward, it would have fallen out, they said. Yeah, right. In that dive, I don't think so.

Cecil gave me the nut and smiled at me. God, did I feel phenomenal. The nut had been smashed so bad from me pulling back on the cyclic, it looked like someone had taken a hammer to it. The engine quit because the fuel line came loose; we had to bleed it off that morning to get it started, and we just didn't get it tightened up quite enough. Shit happens.

The maintenance officer was in a fit; the data plate was missing and they had to have it down in Vung Tau. They gave me the third degree. "Me, steal a data plate? I didn't even know it would come off the dash."

I did finally find the data plate, tail number 405, but it was too late to give it back, and besides, I was sure they had forgotten about it, so I just kept it. The nut? I lost it over time, but I still have the data plate.

Unforgettable
by Larry A. Brown

When I asked Larry Brown to relate some of his scout experiences in Vietnam, he thanked me for allowing him to share. He added, "There are some things in your life you never forget and very seldom tell anyone about, for numerous reasons." After enlisting in 1969, Brown ended up in Germany where he became an M-113 APC driver. He requested transfer to Vietnam, arriving in March 1971. Being taller than most, he was assigned to an MP company, which needed manpower. Brown says, "I was 11 Bravo when I got there with no MP experience but I learned quick."

He volunteered for door gunner and was sent to Vinh Long, where he worked as a Huey crew chief/door gunner with A Troop, 7th Squadron, 1st Air Cavalry. That duty would end three months later when Brown threw a Vietnamese officer out of his helicopter in a hot LZ. He explained, "The guy was chickenshit to get out and the pilots were a little anxious for us to leave since Hueys and mortar rounds don't mix well. It was real hot. It was the second insertion into the rice paddy and Charlie knew we were coming. They were giving us hell. We were only a few feet high but the officer landed face first in water. He pulled his pistol to shoot me but my M60 convinced him to not be stupid." Although such incidents were common and his actions were justified, Brown was to be court-martialed.

He got a reprieve, however, when the scout platoon leader asked him to fly with his crew.

Brown says, "I had no choice really. It was a way for the CO to get me out of his hair. He wanted me out; the scout platoon leader said the CO also wanted to see me dead.

So I flew scouts. I have the tale to tell of a day in my life as a 19-year-old kid that changed me forever."

"Scramble, scramble" at the top of his lungs. That's what the guy was hollering. I don't remember who it was that heard the first "Mayday" on the radio but we knew the situation was very serious. All hell had broken loose as the first team's lead ship and his wing man were both leaving the area after sustaining heavy damage from ground fire.

The Cobra gunships were laying it on strong with everything from 20mm cannon fire to high-explosive rockets.

It seemed like an eternity between each footfall as I ran from my squatted position over the slit trench. I don't remember how I got my pants on at a full run but I did, and no sooner than I sat my ass on the rear compartment deck of the OH-6 than we lifted off.

Even a newbie knew when the RPMs weren't at a sufficient speed for liftoff. Ours were far from it so I knew we were in trouble. Lucky for us it was still early in the morning and the wind hadn't picked up; the air was heavy with the morning dew. Funny how things work that aren't supposed to, and now it seems impossible that it did work at all.

We were dragging our skids as we first hovered and then moved out onto the runway. It wasn't really a runway by normal standards but it served its purpose. It was steel PSP laid together and covered with sand and grass. We cleared the barbed wire by inches and did an immediate hard left turn as we gained altitude and speed. I was doing it all so fast, laying the band of 7.62mm ammo across the top of my M60; putting my chicken plate on and making sure I had everything in position for action. I was sitting on a sheet of half-inch thick piece of armored plating taken from the side of an old pilot's

Like many young soldiers, Larry Brown was anxious to serve in Vietnam and in rotary-wing aviation. This photo was taken prior to his 1971 aviation assignment in Vietnam. (Larry Brown Collection)

With the war behind him, Larry Brown, seen here in 2010, recalls vividly the details of his combat experiences. (Larry Brown Collection)

Booby traps plagued Aeroscouts in their low-level environment. This Loach fell victim to one such device in January 1970, but its crew escaped the crash and fire. The aircraft was S/N 67-16068 of Headquarters Company, 3rd Brigade, 101st Airborne Division at Camp Evans. (Joe Gwizdak)

seat. You protect what you have with what you can find. Even back then we were having to make do with what we had, like in today's fighting in Iraq.

The radio was alive with everyone wanting a sit-rep on the first team's condition, hits, injuries, etc. Seems like they were lucky, no one hurt, just the planes shot full of holes.

We were minutes away from what they had run into on the first flight of the day. We knew we were in for it. Charlie knew we were coming. The first team's Cobras were still giving them hell. Our team of "Snakes" was on its way too, coming in at 4,000 while we were inbound at tree top level.

As we approached we could see the smoke from our first team's contact with Charlie. Red smoke mixed with smoke from the Cobra's rocket hits and the fires started by them.

The wind was low so early in the morning so we knew where the contact had been made and where to start our search for bad guys.

A little about my "driver" and front seat observer before I get too carried away. Captain Russell McCoy was the Scout platoon leader and was one hell of a pilot. We had flown together as a team since my move to lead team's back seat a month or so before. He was known for his guts and as far as I was concerned, he could fly through the gates of hell and I would lock and load behind him any day. He was cool, calm, and so far I had never heard him get excited or raise the tone or volume of his voice, no matter what we were doing, and we had some stories to tell already. One gutsy guy, in my opinion.

My front seat observer was one of my best friends, if you can call someone a friend that you try not to get too close to. My feeling was not to get too close to anyone because that meant you might have a

problem if they got hurt. That was how I got into the scout platoon, I replaced one of the two guys that got killed when they went down with WO1 Allen Dyer in the U Minh Forest. Paul Hardin was a Californian getting ready to go home in four days. He had been a Huey crew chief and was clearing base when I asked him to fly front seat with me. We were short on personnel and were always looking for men to fly with us. Scouts were the crazy ones among the flight crews. Who in their right mind would go looking for trouble in a little chopper not big enough to carry a crew of three and much more? I had convinced Paul to fly by telling him it was a milk run, a little hop out of Dong Tam just down the Mekong River from our base at Vinh Long. He had brought his camera to get a few more pictures of Vietnam and the river. It was a real nice Canon 35mm he had with him for his entire tour.

Our first pass over the area where we found the smoke the heaviest showed us what the Cobras had been working over. Remains of a few hootches and bunkers were exposed in the mangrove trees. As we made a second pass we received small arms fire which I returned. We climbed, setting ourselves up for delivery of a two-pound bomb consisting of C-4 and a concussion grenade. I pulled the pin, set myself up in the position where I could shoot my '60 and throw the bomb. We made the pass, bomb out and guns blazing, front and back, wing man too. In the pass over to assess the damage, we saw a bunker we needed to take out. Another climb and wingover, another bomb to put out. Pulling the pin, I inched to the edge of the seat to throw the bomb. Actually it was more just letting it fall since McCoy was so good at lining me up with the doorway of the hootches and bunkers. With my M60 coming hot on our inbound pass, I could still hear the words in my helmet earphones, "Mayday,

The OH-6A, S/N 67-17793, shows the typical crew arrangement of A Troop, 1st Squadron, 7th Cavalry Scouts. Without the minigun installation, a crew of three flew Scout missions: pilot, crew chief/gunner and observer/gunner. The latitude of hand-operated M60 machine guns often was preferred, as were the extra eyes and ears of crewmen. The third crewman also proved vital in the event of a shoot-down. Usually, when three crewmen were aboard, the Scout pilot, who flew right seat, preferred that his crew chief be positioned behind him. The crew chief could then see what the pilot saw and the pilot could direct machine gun fire on the target, in right-hand turns. The window above the crew chief was painted over to reduce glare and vertigo from the rotor overhead. (Charlie Palek/VHPA)

Mayday, Apache One-Six going down. Fire-Fire Apache One-Six going down!" I rolled back into the ship just in time to see every light on the dash flashing red, not a good sign when you see trees coming at you and hitting the skids at the same time. When we hit the trees, the ship went through to the ground.

Mangroves don't really have much to support a ship but they do play hell with the rotor blades.

As the ship hit hard, it was also rocking sideways as the blades disintegrated in the branches. I was thrown out into the trees and slid down the side of a tree truck, scraping all the skin off the left side of my neck and throat. As I hit, my first thought was to duck the blades so I jumped back into the back seat from where I had just been ejected. I quickly got back out and by instinct rushed up to where I could reach the harness holding McCoy in the front seat. From the first day I got into the unit, I was told, "get the pilots out before you do anything." So here I was, going for the release on his straps. As he clambered out, he and I fell but very quickly got on our feet and ran. I had shot a glance to look for Paul but he had already made it out of his harness and was nowhere to be seen.

I turned and started after McCoy when I heard Paul screaming at me. He was coming through the rear of the ship, from left to right, as the ship, with the remains of rotor blades still turning, was pitching like a bucking bronco. I ran over and grabbed Paul's big six-foot-five ass by the top of his chicken plate and he too then fell on me. It was a miracle that we weren't killed because at that moment the damned ship pitched over to the left and died.

Now it was time to run. Paul and I cleared the few yards to where we found McCoy with his .38 cal. pistol pulled. It was right then that we determined that we didn't have weapons. We stood there for what seemed like an eternity but it was probably no more than seconds. Now what? Just as we were about to decide which way to run, our wing man, WO1 Stewart, flew over us. He made a quick turn and came into a hover directly over us. As I turned to look at the other two, McCoy made a gesture for me to jump for the skid. I raised my arms like you would to reach for something over your head and it was right then that my life flashed before my eyes. I was still clutching the damn bomb with the pin pulled.

They teach you from the day you first see a grenade that you can never put the pin back in. You must throw it. Only one problem, where do you throw a two-pound bomb in a mangrove swamp with tree branches all over you? It's like being in a thicket of bushes but it seemed like the thickest bunch of branches I had ever seen.

It's funny how your mind works sometimes. For about a week I had been planning to get down to the avionics shed to have them

El Loch-O was S/N 66-14388 of the 1st Cavalry Division's D Company, 227th Aviation Battalion. The unit's emblem, a green triangle with lightning bolt, is barely visible on the door post. The darkened window above the cabin was often heavily tinted or even painted over in order to diminish the glare that hampered the gunner's visibility. Armored seat panels provided some basic protection from small arms fire for the pilots, while the crew chief in back had to make do by placing armor panels, usually from "chicken plate" body armor, under his seat. A splotch of zinc chromate paint forward of the aircraft's nickname in this photograph indicates the place where a bullet hole had been patched. (Manly Barton)

Assigned to A/2/17 of the 101st Airborne Division in 1968, the OH-6A S/N 66-17795 went on to serve two other units in Vietnam; the Army National Guard of three states; the Homestead, Florida, Police Department; and still flies with the Army Aviation Heritage Foundation. During restoration, 10 patched bullet holes were found on the aircraft. (Curt Knapp)

repair my helmet's microphone brace. I had broken one of the wires from the plastic mike portion but had never taken my lazy ass down to them. Well, that laziness saved my life. I pulled my helmet off, pushed the wire through the hole where the pin should have been, and voila, I had done what they say you shouldn't do. Paul and I looked at each other. I crammed all two pounds of C-4 and grenade into the helmet and pitched it as far as I could as we both hit the mud. No boom.

Wow, things were turning around for us. McCoy had already jumped on the skid when I couldn't. Now it was my turn. With no coin to flip, Paul pushed me toward the skid as Stewart made another pass at us. I jumped, grabbed the skid and threw my leg over it.

Man, what an adrenaline rush. Where did I get the strength to do that wearing my chicken plate? I sure didn't know. I do know I panicked when I realized Stewart wasn't going back for Paul. I was screaming at him, terrified that we were leaving him to die. Stewart was pulling as much pitch as he could to get us out. It was him, his back seat, McCoy, me and his minigun and ammo. Overloaded, over the red-line, and moving as fast as he could to get rid of us.

We were now over the river, jumping off as fast as we could. I landed in about five feet of water, luckily, because I still had my chicken plate on. McCoy hit beside me and we both made for the edge. We were up to our waists when I saw the prettiest sight in the world, a Cobra, low level, coming at us over the trees with the big galoot Paul hanging upside down from the skid. It seems that one of the gun pilots, having seen what was happening, dove straight at the site where Paul was. Captain Gibbons flared as he came to a hover right over Paul. He did a 360-degree pedal turn and his front

seat laid waste to anything around them with whatever ordnance they had left; that included 20mm cannon, minigun and a 40mm thump gun. That's hell on earth. They then hovered down so Paul could grab hold of a skid and came out and headed for us. Paul fell into the water beside us and we all made it to the bank just as our C & C ship came down to pick us up. I swear the time we spent on the ground was hours, but I'm sure it all happened in less than 30 or 40 minutes at the most.

The flight back to base was quite emotional. We were planning our return to get even for the little disturbance but all that was stopped when we were instructed to get a post-crash physical. After the hospital we learned that they had sent another team out to retrieve my machine guns, pick up the remaining C-4 bombs, and destroy the radios; they also found Paul's camera. Seems like the bad guys had all gone, or the Cobras had worked them over and they lost their desire to tangle with a third bunch of Apaches.

Our CO got wind of all the fun going on. He went out to get in on the action and any chance of an easy medal. He tried to ferry a group of ARVNs across the river, some of them sitting on the skids of his Huey. Seems that a couple of them lost their grip and fell over a hundred feet into the river with full ruck sacks on their backs. You don't swim very well under those conditions. I don't think he got his DFC like he had hoped.

This happened on 6 September 1971, a Monday, Labor Day back home. It was exactly eight days later, on the 14th, that McCoy and I had another milk run across the river from our base at Vinh Long. Only this time, he left the playing field not in a Loach but in the C & C bird being medevac-ed to Can Tho after being shot in both legs. But that's another story.

Warrant Officer James B. Howard strikes a casual pose in 1969 during his Vietnam tour as a Scout pilot assigned to Headquarters and Headquarters Company of the 1st Cavalry Division's 1st Brigade. (James B. Howard Collection)

Spin-Crash-Burn
James B. "Pokey" Howard, Sr.

Aeroscout crewmen throughout this book extol the OH-6A's construction features that were designed to minimize post-crash fires. But the fact remained that the Loach carried high-octane jet fuel that could, under violent circumstances, escape and burn, often with horrifying results. James Howard would suffer the consequences of those narrow odds, and his trip home would take much longer and be much more difficult than the coveted "Freedom Bird" flight of other returning veterans. Howard flew Loaches of HHC, 1st Brigade, 1st Cavalry, called "Flying Circus" for nearly three months in 1969 until he was shot down and burned. Here, "Pokey" Howard relates his story, but first he describes to us what it was like working with his comrades of the Flying Circus, and he pays homage to those comrades who did not come home.

This is my attempt to describe the men who flew as scouts for the Flying Circus. Keep in mind that this unit operated in Vietnam for just over five years and a lot of changes occurred in the selection of pilots and crewmembers, how they flew, the type of equipment they used, etc. Although I gathered information from other scouts with different experiences, this is peppered with the essence of my perceptions from my short tenure with the scouts in 1969.

The Army used the 1st Brigade, 1st Cavalry Scouts in the same manner as they had for centuries. Our job was to gather information

Despite his long and arduous journey, James B. Howard considers himself fortunate to have come home. Success in life is reflected in the smiles of Jim and his wife, Bonnie. (James B. Howard Collection)

on the enemy's movements and positions, in addition to assisting ground troops whenever and wherever possible. We used advanced technology and weapons to cover a large area faster. The scouts provided valuable information to command centers about what was happening in the field, and we could, on a moment's notice, go out to check on a specific area. The ground troops liked working with the scouts for the "eye in the sky" assistance, as well as for the additional firepower they could bring to bear on the enemy. The Air Force also enjoyed working with the scouts, as they could accurately pinpoint targets and provide necessary damage assessment afterwards.

The scout pilots and gunners were a special breed. Some of the more courteous descriptions are "Mavericks" and "Watanabe Warriors." However, we were all young, usually between our late teens and early twenties and full of passion for what we were doing. Generally, by the age of 23, the concept of self preservation started to develop and the individual would begin to look for another assignment with a higher survival rate.

Acquaintances said that the scouts were full of themselves, but they had to be in order to do the job. Self confidence in their ability to carry out their job in the face of adversity was an absolute necessity. If either the pilot or gunner lacked a high level of self confidence, then he was likely to get himself or his partner killed. The pilots and gunners were all volunteers. Flying scouts was extremely hazardous, for they went out every day flying deep into the enemy's territory to expose themselves in an attempt to locate the highly mobile NVA.

The Flying Circus scouts flew in pairs, with each ship manned by a pilot and gunner. One ship was designated as the "Lead" and the other was generally referred to as the "Wingman." The lead ship's pilot had the primary responsibility for communications with contacts in the assigned area, such as the landing zone base TOC, the company or platoon leader in the field, and coordinating with inbound air and artillery strikes. The lead ship was generally the first to enter a potentially hot area and, as a result, was usually the first to start receiving fire, at which time it became the wingman's responsibility to lay down suppressive fire to cover their breakaway. The situation would then dictate how the scouts would respond, such as engaging in a direct firefight, guiding ground troops to the area, or bringing in the heavy stuff.

A typical day would begin with the scout pilots reporting to TOC for orders. The company commander would direct the scout team to go to LZ Grant and check in with their TOC for further directions and information. For example, they would be directed to go out to grid coordinates XT381844 and contact Bravo company commander. Upon arrival they would learn that one of his platoons reported evidence of movement through the area about a quarter of a klick to the southeast of their current position. The scouts would then fly out to that area and attempt to locate and engage the enemy. Flying around at treetop level were four pairs of eyes with a good birds-eye view looking for evidence of movement or occupation. Sometimes it was possible to catch the NVA or gook out in the open, but generally the enemy would seek cover upon hearing a chopper nearby. In that case the pilots and gunners might spot things such as trash, food, a bicycle lying on the ground, a weapon leaning against a tree, or a bunker, indicating enemy infestation.

The gunner would then fire his M60 in the general area to stir up some movement or a response. If the NVA had weapons, they would return fire. Otherwise, they would go deeper into hiding. Sometimes the scouts would be able to take care of the enemy.

Frequently, however, reinforcement was needed. If necessary, Bravo Company would come into the area to check out the extent of the underground bunker complexes. Other times, the scouts would call in artillery from LZ Grant, or contact the Air Force to request an air strike. At the end of a long, hard day out in the field, the scout team would then fly back to base camp and shut the choppers down for the evening.

The scout program was extremely dangerous and the percentage of pilots and gunners who completed their tour of Vietnam was low. While some individuals wised up and got out of the scouts, the others generally did not make it out alive or they were carried out on a stretcher. These men had no real desire or interest in becoming decorated heroes and were not trying to pursue glory. Deep down in their souls, they just wanted to be warriors, and they were. They fought and died as warriors. Their success against great odds and in accomplishing their mission depended upon pilot and gunner working together, and both ships' working as a team, covering and aiding each other.

So what kind of man would voluntarily place himself in harm's way day after day, as part of his job? Movies like *An Officer and a Gentleman* portray pilots as officers and civilized, educated, sensitive and well-mannered men. Well, in truth, the scout pilot was an officer, but more often than not, there was nothing gentlemanly about him. Although there are always exceptions, there was greater tendency for him to be an audacious individual who was trained to fly helicopters. Some scout pilots were known to be cocky, and sometimes were considered obnoxious sons-of-bitches, with a tendency to act as prima donnas. For example, some of us did not exhibit astute military manners such as saluting officers below the rank of colonel. Of course, some officers, especially majors, did not take kindly to such lack of discipline. Our unmilitary attitude and behavior was tolerated because we were performing a very difficult and stressful task, day after day, and it was difficult to get new volunteers for a job with such a high turnover rate.

A scout pilot did not have to be an ace at flying, but he had to be a good pilot with fast reflexes, and possess the "cojones" to do what was needed with that aircraft. The pilot frequently flew by the seat of his pants as his full attention was focused outside the ship, at treetop and at ground level. Scouts flew low level, which was approximately two to five feet above the trees at air speeds ranging between 60 and 100 knots. Whether the pilot was looking outside or working the radios, he knew instinctively what was happening with his aircraft. The scout pilot climbed into that helicopter and put it on just like you would put on a suit. That scout pilot knew the helicopter from the vibrations felt through the seat, the feel of the controls, and the sound of the engine. He flew with the skilled reflexes that were needed to complete a 180-degree turn to get back on target in less than 10 seconds, and to perform evasive maneuvers that were not built into the aircraft design.

The pilot' activity exemplified the modern term "multi-tasking." The scout pilot would, more often than he desired, find himself performing many activities. During the heat of engagement, he would fly the helicopter at treetop level while maintaining ongoing communications with his gunner, with the other ship, with primary contacts such as ground troops, the TOC and air support, and engage in a firefight or fly evasive maneuvers.

There were changes over the years, not only in helicopters and weapons, but in methods and techniques. There were variations

pulle
atten
pitch
Just a
I hit
dow
com
I hit
the r
if th
away

H
it wa
and l
out o
secor
door
got u
retro
inter
the t
seat.
by e
flam
the h
off in
a cou
takin
Som
l too
mucl
dark
me u
dodg
took
it.

I l
my w
wher
weire
there
distir
of m
a sev
throu
giant
to do
that l
fighti
to th
fired
you?'
firing
back

C
to pl
How
above

Aeroscouts often presented themselves as targets for enemy gunners, an insane practice meant to expose the enemy to orbiting Cobra gunships. "Trolling for fire" also greatly increased the likelihood that the Loach ended up in the base "boneyard." This battle damaged Loach, S/N 67-16626, at Củ Chi in 1969 wears the yellow triangle identifying A Troop, 1st Squadron, 9th Cavalry, 1st Cavalry Division. (Dennis Dennison)

in how the scout program was commanded and I am sure that there were situations where a lack of military discipline was not tolerated.

Some pilots were really great and others were just very good pilots; mediocre or poor pilots did not live long in the scout program. No matter the differences, we did our job with pride and we were greatly respected for what we accomplished.

Scout gunners came from all walks of life. Some had been trained as crew chiefs or door gunners for Hueys. But many gunners came in from the field. These grunts decided that there had to be an alternative to tramping through the jungle, not knowing if you were going to be taken out by a sniper, a booby trap, or by the stupidity of someone in your own company. As a scout, being shot at would be shortened to a few hours a day, versus around the clock. At the end of a work day, they could fly back to base and enjoy the comfort and safety of their own abode. They could enjoy a meal with their buddies, spend some time at a makeshift bar, play cards, or write a letter home. They could fly only when the weather was accommodating, which beat the heck out of sitting in the middle of

the jungle during the monsoon season.

Becoming a scout gunner did not require a lot of training or preparation, although knowledge and experience were valuable and increased survivability. Certain attributes were vital. One of the requirements was that a scout gunner not get airsick. This was really tough because he would be in an aircraft moving at rapid speeds close to the ground and making abrupt changes in speed, altitude and direction. This was especially true of the Loach as it was put through many maneuvers that were not in the SOP manuals, or that the manufacturer had built into its design.

Another desired quality was that the gunner be a good marksman with the M60 as he needed to hit stationary and moving targets from a moving aircraft. The gunner also needed sharp eyes and quick deductive reasoning to identify evidence of the enemy from an average distance of 100 feet and while flying at a speed of 60 to 100 knots. The gunner also needed nerves of steel because he usually spent most of his time half out of the aircraft. He extended his safety straps as far as possible in order to lean out and be able to look under the ship as well as to the front and back of it. And

Enemy gunfire again found its mark on Number 290 of C/1/9, forcing it down in 1971. Pilot Lieutenant Paul "Batman" Murtha escaped the wreckage, which was sling-loaded to Camp Bear Cat. This was one of a number of Loach shoot-downs that Murtha survived. (Author)

Huey: "How's it looking One-Five?"

Loach: "Roger, it looks like the door gunner's dead, I'm not sure, but it looks like he's pinned under the aircraft. Okay, it looks like we've still got some bad guys down here."

Gun: "Three-Eight's got muzzle flashes north of the wreck, get out of there One-Five, don't get yourself shot down too. Those muzzle flashes are real close to the Loach."

Loach: "I know, I can see them, I'm inbound."

Gun: "Okay, get the damn Huey out of there, there are people all over the place."

Huey: "Can't, Two-Four's out of the aircraft to get One-Nine."

Gun: "There's more fire coming out of there."

Loach: "I know, I'm inbound, no, I'm expended, which way out Three-Eight?"

Gun: "Right turn, go south One-Five"

Loach: "Okay, One-Five out to the south."

Huey: Okay Three-Eight, this is Two-Four, they're on the way

back now, okay, we've still got the gunner in the aircraft, we can't get him out, but he's dead."

Gun: "You sure he's dead Two-Four."

Huey: "I'm sure."

Gun: "Do you have the pilot Two-Four?"

Huey: "Yeah, he's shot in the shoulder, he's hurt pretty bad, don't know how bad, all we can see is the blood coming out the back of the shoulder."

Gun: "Okay, medevac standing by at Chi Lang, meet you back at Chi Lang."

The shoot-down took place early in the morning. We were about an hour's flight time from Can Tho. It took us the remainder of the day to round up some ARVN troops, ferry them in our own UH-1s back to the crash site, secure the area and dig the body of the crew chief out from under the right side of the aircraft. So this was Vietnamization!

It was a sad day.

Good Things and Bad Things
by Lad Vaughan

In March of 1969, WO1 Vaughan was assigned to Alpha Troop, 1st Squadron, 9th Cavalry, 1st Cavalry Division (Airmobile), known as "Apache Troop, First of the Ninth, or A/1/9." Apache Troop had three aviation platoons, one infantry platoon, detachments of LRRPs, Kit Carson scouts, and dog teams. The White Platoon was the OH-6A Scouts, the Red Platoon was the Cobras and gunships. The Blue Platoon was the "Lift" Hueys, whose pilots were called "Headhunters." Their mission was recon and aircraft recovery.

When deployed for recon, the three colors together were termed "Purple Teams." For aircraft recovery, the infantry soldiers, called "Blues," were deployed.

Vaughan points out:

In the 1/9 we never had Slicks. We were Lift. Not Slicks. Slicks are after-dinner pants residue. Lift is salvation. Ask a Blue, LRRP, Grunt, or shot-down pilot.

Here, Vaughan recounts some good things and some bad things:

All pilots that flew Scouts were special. Those who flew the OH-6A flew a special aircraft. For scouting, the OH-6A was the best. I've seen them shot to pieces and still fly.

I've seen them crash, roll into a ball, and everyone walked away. If you had to crash, choose the OH-6A. I have a combined flight time in the OH-6A of three hours. These were very interesting hours spent as an Oscar (observer); low, slow, and a magnet ass. As a new guy in troop I was to be ignored. New guys are not important, as they will soon be dead. And who needs to remember the name of some dead new guy. There are enough old guys to remember. And old guys are much more important than new guys.

My first ride was as an Oscar in a purple team. WO1 Donics was in troop about 10 weeks before I arrived. But he was an old guy. He flew OH-6A Scouts. He was a pretty good scout driver. He was a jerk to all new guys. He took me out in the AO and tried to scare me with his daring-do, spotting .50 cal. pits and pointing out the rotting wreckage of line-one scummers; turning on a dime and drawing fire. All very ballsy stuff. Three hours of that was enough for me. I was assigned to the lift platoon and happy to get out of that hover hell.

Donics eventually got his 600 hours in scouts, and rotated out of the White Platoon and into the weapons platoon. He was now safe from the many times he had almost bought it while flying scouts. On 15 May, while flying night perimeter over Tay Ninh, sitting safely in the front gunner's seat of a Cobra flown by 1st Lt. Albert L. Koon, William Caldwell Donics died, as did Lt. Koon. Some lucky-ass shot by some lucky-ass bad guy with a bloody .50 cal. shattered the canopy and severed the rotor mast. Fifteen hundred feet of straight-down flight time. In the words of Army Aviation understatement, "the approach was terminated below tarmac level." I believe Apache Three-Four, Mike Adkinson, went out to make the recovery. There was nothing to recover.

WO1 Harker got to Apache Troop two weeks before I arrived. I understand that he desired to fly in Lift, as a Headhunter, but did not get past his check ride. His reaction to that disappointment was to volunteer for Scouts. Harker was a thin, modest looking Mormon boy from Bountiful, Utah. His nickname was "Squeak." During that summer of 1969, Alpha Troop had the hottest AO of our three troops. The joke at Tay Ninh was to direct the artillery

Army helicopter pilot George "Lad" Vaughan poses at Tây Ninh with a Huey's precious load of cargo for the troops in 1969. (Lad Vaughan Collection)

Like many veterans, George "Lad" Vaughan put the war in perspective and went on to succeed in business. (Lad Vaughan Collection)

Nothing better illustrates the hazards of the Aeroscout's low level environment than this image of a Loach that was flown into a tree. The pilot was dodging enemy fire when a large branch crashed through the windshield and lodged between the pilot and observer. Neither was injured and the Loach was flown to safety. (U.S. Army)

50 meters from the burning Loach. On that day, the 9th of June, Jack Albert Harker, Jr. died. He had been out near Cambodia, flying as low bird in a purple team doing BDAs (Bomb Damage Assessments) after a B-52 Arc Light strike. Flying back to Tay Ninh, Squeak spotted something, and the team engaged. Squeak took hits, and the Loach was badly hurt. Once clear of the firefight he put down at LZ Barbara, on the north side of Nui Ba Dinh. He exited the aircraft to do a walk-around. When he got back to the right side of the aircraft, the shot-up skid collapsed and the rotor blades struck and killed him. He was nineteen-and-a-half years old, the youngest 1/9 pilot to be killed during the war. We all loved Squeak very much, and this loss did not qualify for "Don't mean nothin'" It meant a lot.

In 1993, Alpha Troop had a reunion. We located Jack Harker's mother and father, along with a younger brother, who looked just like Squeak, and we flew them to Louisville for the reunion. After a presentation by General Paul Funk, who commanded at Tay Ninh, tears flowed for Squeak. And that was a good thing.

WO1 Mefford came to Apache after I had made AC (Aircraft Commander) and became a Headhunter. As a now official old guy I was required to be a jerk to all new guys. I wasn't very good at being mean to new guys. But I did manage to hang the nickname "Worm" onto him. Worm stuck. I don't think he liked that nickname very much. No one cared what he liked or didn't like. He was a new guy. He was "The Worm."

As the name implies, Worm was a bookish sort of fellow. Not really one of the clique of jerkheads like me but he was always welcome to the madness we insisted was normal. He was easy to make fun of and we were cruel to him in an accepting way. His status as an old guy was yet to come. Worm volunteered for Scouts. I teamed with him many times and he was a good aviator. He was not too much a magnet ass, cared for his crew, and liked to kill communists. That is high praise.

On 29 June WO1 Harrell Samuel Mefford died. It was early in the afternoon on a bright and clear day. Another Scout driver, Robert Larson, and I had down time that day. We were sitting on the sandbags outside my hootch getting some sun. The hootch faced the active runway, Apache Pad. After flying the AO, Mefford and his high bird refueled at Tay Ninh main airfield and returned to Apache Pad. Larson and I watched as Worm made a fast, on the deck, approach to the pad. After clearing the berm, Worm flared the Loach to a stop. It was an impressive flare and done with skill. At the end of the flare we heard a big "Pop." The tail rotor had failed. With reduced power, the nose was in a left turning direction and Worm managed to make a controlled crash. The left skid collapsed, the bird skidded on its belly, and the blades clipped the ground. The observer unbuckled and moved around the nose to safety. The torque un-assed out the right rear to safety. Larson and I ran to the aircraft. Through the Plexiglas Worm gave us a thumbs-up, pulled off the fuel, shut down the turbine and turned off the battery. Professional in every way, he unbuckled, climbed out and walked through the still spinning rotor blades to a chorus of "Get down, get

Aeroscout observer Clyde "Birdman" Hughes poses with OH-6A S/N 67-16290 of C Troop, 1st Squadron, 9th Cavalry, or C/1/9. Yellow areas on the narrow door section separating doorways are patched bullet holes. (Walker Jones)

down!" The first strike was to his mid back. The second was to the back of his still helmeted head. In what seemed to be slow motion, Worm was propelled into a forward flip. He crashed down onto his back. Worm looked up at Bob Larson and me and said, "Can't breathe." He was soon dead.

WO1 Young was already an old guy when I got to troop. As was required, he was a jerk to all new guys and I never really got to know him. The story is that his father was seriously wounded as a jet jock and his brother was killed flying for Blue Max, a gunship unit. I don't know if that is true, however, it made for good legend and may have been the reason for his passion for killing communists. I teamed with him quite a few times and he was ruthless. Very good, but ruthless. He knew all the tricks that got a Scout driver greased and shot down; hovering over bunkers while the torque chucked home-made bombs through small openings; using the rotor wash to blow open the jungle canopy while he hunted a blood trail to the eventual death of some dumb kid from the North. He was the only guy I ever heard to be shot down by one round from a pistol. The story goes that he was walking a prisoner out to a clearing for pick-up by the Lift bird. The commie panicked, reached into his belt, pulled out a pistol and fired one shot. The puny 9 millimeter round went up into the belly and the engine quit. Before the bird landed on top of the bad guy, the torque had stitched him.

Sergeant Dine had come to the 1/9 from a 1st Cav grunt unit. He wanted out of the field and volunteered for safer duty in aviation. They assigned Dine to me as a door gunner in the Lift platoon.

Dine was a cerebral sort of fellow. We had many conversations about esoteric subjects like reincarnation, spiritualism and the sensuality of fear in combat. He had many close calls as a grunt and was getting "short." I told him that having him DEROS (Date Estimated Return from Overseas) was important to me and that I would not do the stupid things that get short guys killed. I looked forward to seeing him go home. He had put his time in the barrel and his exit to the world would be an affirmation to all in troop that there is life after madness. He was short, less than 50 days left in country. Shorter than short. He had to spit up to reach the bottom of his boots. And he was out of the bush.

A very fine man and a superior leader, Captain Kit Beaton, the Lift platoon leader, assigned me to a purple mission. He asked that I take WO1 James Fields up for an AC checkout. Fields was an excellent pilot and deserved the next Headhunter AC slot. Fields had flown as my right seat copilot many times and I liked his style. As a pilot he was bold and cautious, cunning and aggressive, murderous and fair. Riding in the right seat again would feel strange, but it was an honor to be picked by Captain Beaton to pass judgment on a fellow Headhunter.

Captain Bowen would fly the Red bird. WO1 Young would fly the White bird. The mission was an Arc Light BDA very near Cambodia. Captain Bowen had transferred into A Troop. He was a careerist looking for a command, and we had the most action at that time. Many of us viewed Bowen as an interloper and I was not thrilled to have him as my Red bird on this day. Flying with

Mark Forget, call sign "Apache One-Eight," at the controls of his Loach at Tây Ninh in 1969. A gunner occupies the seat next to Forget and Michael Prindeville the cabin area. All wear chicken plate body armor, and red smoke grenades hang at the ready near both gunners. Apache Troop was A Troop of 1/9. (Mark Forget Collection)

Young was always exciting, so I knew what to expect from him. But I wished I had another Red driver. Red drivers run the show and keep the team out of trouble. They rein in the Scout driver.

As I approached the unfamiliar right side of the aircraft, I asked the crew chief who the new gunner was and where was Dine. He shrugged and said something about another flight. Fields cranked and we got ready to leave. Bowen pulled pitch and headed out to the AO. The Loach followed down the road at a hover. Waving from the left seat was Sergeant Dine. My Dine. Now observer Sergeant Dine. 50 days short Dine. I was sick.

Since the Cobra and the OH-6A are much faster than the Huey, they reached the AO first and started to hunt. The aftermath of a B-52 strike in triple canopy is impressive; 250-foot trees with the girth of buildings snapped like shafts of pasta. From the air you can see heat, dust and desolation. Streams and rivers are rerouted. Yet, there can still be life.

The mission was well into the last half of my fuel when Young got the scent. Red led White over the same areas and White started getting kills. From my perch 3,500 feet above the action I sat looking for the Scout bird. The cloud cover was light, wispy and could be seen through. The Loach had white paint on the top of the rotor blades to make it easier to spot from the air. The chatter on the radio between White and Red ended with the fireball. WO1 Young, the torque I did not know, and Sergeant "short-time" Dine had been hit by an RPG and the bird exploded. Flying at 40 knots or so, the flaming wreckage of the OH-6A spread out amongst the carnage of the bombed jungle. Bowen made pass after pass shooting up the area. I don't think he had a target. There was no return fire. I grabbed the controls and called Red to see what he wanted me to

do. I was ready to fall out of the sky and do a pick-up of survivors. But I knew there were no survivors. There weren't. I didn't want to go down there. I would have. But I didn't have to. Relieved, I felt like a coward.

WO1 Larson remained very much alive. Larson was the stereotypical helicopter pilot of that time. A youthful, very handsome little guy with a big watch. I knew and flew with many terrific Loach pilots. He was at the top of my list. Larson was the kind of Scout driver who would find and execute the enemy rather than hunt and kill. While there is a need for both styles in war, there is a difference between those styles. One day we worked a purple team out of a place named LZ Carolyn. Carolyn sat blocking the Mustang Trail, which was the main feeder route from the Ho Chi Minh Trail in Cambodia leading south past Tay Ninh to Saigon. It was a miserable AO and Fire Base Carolyn was being hit all the time. There were dead NVA hanging in the wire half eaten by tigers and wild pigs. Snipers made the grunts crazy. Most of the supplies were kicked out of fast moving Hueys eager to leave the place. When we arrived on station a pair of F-4 Phantoms was attacking a Quad .50 cal. just outside the fire base. Tracer rounds would shoot up at the jets on their way in and follow them on the way out.

On this day Larson was not feeling well. Being a teetotaler, it meant he had been eating with the hootch maids again. He was sick to his stomach, loose in the bowels and was exhibiting flu-like symptoms associated with food poisoning. I thought it was very funny.

It was just another perfect day of flying in Asia. Gooks with Quad 50s, fully freaked out grunts on the ground, and my low bird filled with puke and excrement.

After some secondary explosions from the area of the .50 cal gun, Larson swooped in to check it out. He immediately took fire from small arms. His Oscar threw smoke on the target and the Cobra rolled in shooting rockets. The OH-6A went back in many times with the same result. Small arms fire, then smoke, then rockets, then puke and finally bowel movements. On what turned out to be Larson's last pass at the target, the Loach took hits. He called up to the Red bird saying that the Loach was shaking apart and he had to put it down. He flew the short distance to Carolyn and landed. After shutting down the aircraft he did his inspection. He found on the rotor head one of the drag braces holding the blade in position had been hit by a bullet. There was only about a quarter inch of metal holding the blade in place. He and his crew had been very close to slinging a blade. That is not a good thing.

Now settled on terra firma, his Nomex flight suit soiled at the rear and his shirt covered with the remains of an exotic meal, WO1 Robert P. Larson instructed his crew to unload the ordnance and other items for transport to my Huey. I landed, but remained fully run up in anticipation of a hasty departure. From the comfort of my clean helicopter, I watched the Oscar put the torque's ammo box and cache of lethal home-made explosives onto the ground. The box ignited a trip flare. In panic, the Oscar fled. Larson viewed the situation, waddled pant load and all over to the box and calmly threw the flare into a ditch. Later, back at Apache Pad, I commented on his bravery. He told me to screw off and said he was hoping that the bloody thing would explode. What a guy!

WO1 Mark Forget was a superb Scout pilot. He was a terrific Hearts and Cribbage player and very much a smart-ass. His scouting instincts were outstanding and his concern for his crews an inspiration. I flew many missions with Forget and considered him to be a lucky charm. Together, we went out and came home. At the end of the hunt that is all one really cares about.

On one occasion our troop area came under heavy rocket fire during the middle of the day. We expected it at night, but during the day it was unusual. Forget ran to one of the make-do bunkers that were constructed by each hootch. In his haste, he dove for the bunker opening. He misjudged the entrance by a few inches and knocked himself out.

When he awoke he had a serious gash on his head and had a Purple Heart citation entered into his record. Much to his embarrassment, we teased him endlessly about the nature of the award.

Mark Forget was to receive another Purple Heart. That event and the circumstances were not so humorous. In the same area where Young, the unknown torque, and Observer Dine had died, an RPG hit Forget's OH-6A. Crashing was inevitable and the Loach did its job. The tail boom separated from the fuselage, the skids and rotor blades flew off, and the aircraft rolled like a ball and did not catch fire. The crew, both Oscar and torque, were dead. Mark awoke outside the aircraft lying face down on top of a severed rotor blade.

The Cobra was working the tree lines but Forget said there was a dead silence in the jungle between its passes. He made several attempts to move. The first attempt brought the realization that his right foot was sticking up instead of down like the left foot. He passed out a few times during his struggle to get up and moving. During one of the silence periods

Aeroscout pilot Mark Forget hospitalized at Củ Chi following his shoot-down by an RPG in August 1969. Forget's crew chief and gunner did not survive the crash and he was able to avoid capture until he was rescued. (Lad Vaughan)

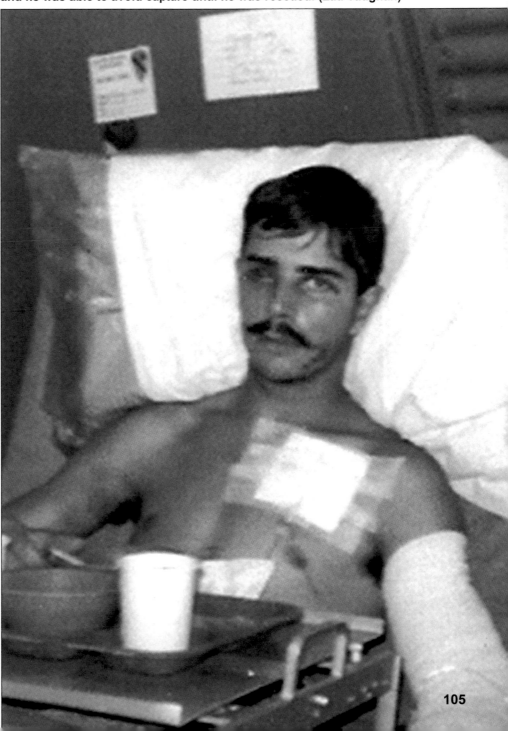

This OH-6A, S/N 65-12984 of 1/9 met its end in 1970. despite the survivability built into the Loach to minimize crew losses and injuries, it suffered one of the highest aircraft and crew loss rates of the war. (Walker Jones)

he could hear the NVA working towards his position. Chattering in gook, these folks were dodging the Cobra and coming to finish him off. Knowing he couldn't move to safety, he made for his sidearm. He was not going to be taken alive and maybe he could get a shot off at his enemy. His life was saved when he found that when he was pushing himself up to get his sidearm, he was actually pushing the compound fractured bones of his arm, like the tongs of a pitchfork, into the soft jungle floor. He could not get to his sidearm. Suicide was removed as an option. Mark was rescued. At the reunion at Ft. Knox I saw Mark Forget for the first time in 23 years. Sporting less hair and professional beard, he was still a wonderful smart-ass, and now a proper school administrator.

I left Alpha Troop. Kicked out would be a better description. Or better yet, kicked up. I was reassigned to Headquarters Troop and ended my tour flying support for B and C Troops, and performing the duties of Senior Instructor Pilot. It was a good thing.

I felt that the one blemish to Alpha Troop during my time as a Headhunter was the commanding officer prior to Captain Funk. In a previous tour with 1/9, he became a legendary Scout pilot in OH-13s. It is reported that on one occasion he was shot down and pursued by the enemy through a rubber plantation. The pursuit was a planned maneuver on his part in an effort to draw the enemy away from a crewmember left in the wrecked aircraft. He circled back and laid in ambush for the enemy. He killed two of the three pursuers when he sprang the ambush. And, out of ammunition, he chased

the third guy down and killed him barehanded. I don't doubt his bravery. But, as I was later to confirm, he was a drunken, sad bully of a man and a terrible officer.

To be honest, this CO thought I was the blemish in the troop. On the day that Harrell "The Worm" Mefford died on Apache Pad, he was to come late upon the scene. By that time Captain Beaton had taken charge of the situation and had Worm transported to the medical station via jeep. Beaton rode with Mefford and I was alone on the pad when the CO showed up to spout wrath. He screamed that he had $10 million worth of aircraft sitting on the flight line and how dare I put one of his troopers on a jeep. He was right, of course. Bouncing the one or two miles to the medical station on the back of a jeep could not have done Worm much good. But I never thought it was the reason for his death, either. Many years later, at the Ft. Knox reunion, while recalling the incident over a few hundred beers, Kit Beaton set me straight. He had put Mefford on the jeep. And Worm stopped breathing almost as soon as they had started off. For 23 years I truly believed what the CO had believed: that I had made that decision.

There are so many stories about the magnificence of the OH-6A and the pilots and crews that flew them. Now they come with no tail rotors, sexy noses and bubbles, and they aren't even made by Hughes anymore. But I can still hear that distinctive whine a mile or so away. And when I do, I recall my youth and remember my friends.

Capt. Bill Staffa and friend in Vietnam. Staffa logged more than 2,400 flight hours during two Vietnam tours; 700 of those hours were in Scouts. During most of his first tour, he was Section Leader of B Company (Aeroscouts), 123rd Aviation Battalion. (Bill Staffa Collection)

Misty
by Ed Gallagher

We are fortunate to listen to the veterans who speak so candidly of war, who speak from the heart and from the soul. Ed Gallagher takes us to a place we call, simply, "The Wall," where we can visit Vietnam veterans whose voices are stilled, but whose spirits live on forever.

The gray, wet sky is disappearing in the gloom of the oncoming evening. The cold breeze only intensifies the chill I feel as I top the grassy knoll, turn right and stare down the full length of the dimly lit Vietnam Veteran's Memorial.

The statue of the three Vietnam combat soldiers appears to my right. They almost seem to be moving as they shift in and out of the evening mist. Their skin is slick and wet as if from sweat, not rain, and their weapons reflect as in sunlight, not lamp-lit. The traffic noise of the city fades from my mind and is replaced by the steady thumping of rotor blades. I'm watching from the cockpit as they calmly approach my aircraft for yet another lift to yet another LZ. I turn my head and prepare to take off. The turbine whines, the dust starts to rise. As my eyes refocus, The Wall pulls me back to the present. I walk on and leave the three warriors to their eternal patrol.

I start down the slate stone walk that parallels The Wall as Section 12 West awaits me. The names of those I flew with and even the ones I grew up with are etched on this section. I've met here with them often. I touch one of their names and I see his face, hear his voice, feel the warmth of his smile. We're together at chow or playing cards in a hootch or he's laughing at one of my bad jokes. It's been 20 years but he's never gotten any older, nor will he. I move my hand and other youthful faces appear and accompany me in my journey. The smell of jungle, the noise of battle, the cold flashes of fear are there again with me, with us. It grows and intensifies as we continue our days, battle by battle, trading our youth for experiences. I drop my hand and slowly the world of now and today returns. They are gone and I feel very tired, worn, and alone.

As I start to walk up the incline to leave, I pass a man with his young son by his side. His hand is covering a name as he presses hard against The Wall. "Is that your best friend's name, daddy?" the boy asks. The father can't talk, he just nods his head. The boy takes his father's hand in his and asks, "Why did he die, daddy?" The man swings the boy up into his arms and holds him tightly as he says, "Saving me son, he was saving me."

Twenty-six years in uniform and I was never so proud of it as I was at that moment. For as long as men remember the legacy of truly unselfish acts of courage and sacrifice, of lives given willingly for the sake of others, then our heritage of freedoms shall be preserved. And for us who have borne this burden, we will have reason to go on.

Up on the grassy knoll, the colors of the well-lit flag seem bold as it floats on the dark night wind. And as I approach them, the warrior statues emerge from the mist. I stand and report to them that, tonight, all is well. As the mist closes in again, we warriors slowly fade into it.

At the Primary Helicopter Center at Fort Wolters, Texas, during the Vietnam war, fledgling U.S. Army aviators strapped into one of three basic training helicopters, the smallest of which was Hughes' TH-55A "Osage." Popularly known as the "Mattel Messerschmitt," the Osage began as the commercial Model 269 in 1956. In 1964 the Army took it as a trainer, ordering nearly 800 to meet the war's demand for helicopter pilots. Eventually, the school was turning out a record 600 Warrant Officer Candidate (WOC) pilots per month. The combined total of the three helicopter types peaked at more than 1,300 in 1969. Many helicopter pilots who survived the war made the Army a career. Others separated from the service but applied their excellent Army flight training to commercial aviation jobs. (U.S. Army)

Hiller's H-23 "Raven," which was based on the company's Model 360, joined the Army during the Korean war and served admirably in the air ambulance role. Improved models served as the Army's primary basic helicopter trainer until they were replaced by the TH-55A Osage. This Raven, S/N 61-3207, like most H-23Ds, was upgraded to OH-23G with a more powerful engine and a dual-control cockpit with seating for three. The H-23C introduced a "Goldfish Bowl" canopy to replace the original sloped canopy. Production of nearly 800 H-23Gs accounted for the largest number of Raven models. Army painting directives called for trainer aircraft to be painted International Orange, or to wear liberal amounts of the color. Nicknamed by pilot trainees "Killer Hiller," the OH-23G also made its mark in Vietnam's combat zones wearing olive drab, along with both fixed and crew-served weapons to help pioneer the Aeroscout mission. (Dick Van Allen)

Bell's "Sioux" served the Army since the late 1940s in a variety of models, two of which were used to train pilots: the standard H-13 and the TH-13T, based on Bell's Model 47. The Sioux is easily identified with its medevac role during the Korean war. This TH-13T was a dual-control instrument trainer and a common sight at Army bases. The OH-13S, the final Army variant, along with the OH-23G, pioneered Scout tactics in Vietnam until the arrival of the OH-6A. So delayed were Loach deliveries that more than 70 OH-13S had to be sent from European assignments to the war zone. Despite the wide range of roles in which the Model 47 served, and its popularity, the H-13 shined, first evacuating wounded soldiers during the Korean War, and later as Aeroscout platforms in Vietnam. (Stephen Miller)

The Pilot Pipeline

The U.S. Army's practice of first training pilots in fixed-wing aircraft before graduating them to helicopters would reverse as U.S. involvement in Vietnam escalated, causing a commensurate rise in the demand for helicopter pilots.

As more helicopters began to appear, sharing ramp space at Army posts with post-World War II airplanes, the bulk of flight training was shifted during the 1950s from Gary Air Force Base, Texas; and Fort Sill, Oklahoma; to Fort Wolters, Texas; and Fort Rucker, Alabama.

Those who aspired to wear the wings of an Army aviator fell into two categories:

Warrant Officer Candidate (WOC) and commissioned officer. Aviation warrant officers were born of the need for a large number of helicopter pilots for the Vietnam conflict.

The Army had decided that its pilots should be officers. But training officers as pilots would prove costly and far too lengthy in view of their required developmental track. The Army established promotional levels for warrant officers, who were specific to aviation. Warrant officers entered either a rotary-wing or fixed-wing training pipeline.

The WOC's first step into the world of Army aviation was Preflight, where they learned how to be an officer. During these first four weeks the WOCs didn't touch a helicopter.

They endured an Officer Candidate School (OCS)-like environment; harassment, classes, marching, inspections, cleaning, and more harassment. Officers, on the other hand, went directly to the Flight Line phase. Often referred to more earnestly than facetiously as "Real Live Officers," or "RLOs," they hailed from each branch of the Army: Infantry, Artillery, Armor, Signal, and Quartermaster.

After the first four weeks of learning how to do everything the Army way, WOCs, along with officers, with flight gear in hand and brimming with anticipation, strapped into training helicopters – TH-55As, OH-23s, or OH-13s – at Ft. Wolters' primary staging fields: Downing, Main, and Dempsey Heliports. The OH-13 was used for advanced flying, including tactical flying, cross country flights, and night flying. Instructional cadre comprised Army pilots and pilots employed by Southern Airways under government contract.

After having soloed and completed the 16-week Primary Training Course, it was on to Ft. Rucker for advanced training. There, it was instrument training in the Bell TH-13T, transition to the Huey, and the all-important tactics. Until 1972 all of the tactics instructors had served combat tours in Vietnam, imparting every bit of knowledge and experience in teaching the fledgling aviators to fly, fight, and survive.

So many helicopter pilots were needed to satisfy the American commitment in Vietnam that the number of pilot graduates jumped from 30 to more than 100, with classes graduating every few weeks. Evidence of this expansion occurred in 1966, when the Army's need for helicopter pilots surpassed the training capacity of its Ft. Wolters and Ft. Rucker schools, prompting establishment of

Wearing chicken plate torso armor, 1Lt. Joseph Eszes, Darkhorse platoon leader of C/16, in the driver's seat of his OH-6A in 1971. (James Sheetz)

The use of colorful emblems exploited by Army aviators in Vietnam was indicative of unit pride. Aeroscout observer PFC Peterson of C/16 in 1971 wears his troop's "Outcasts" emblem on his breast pocket patch and on his flight helmet. The red and white triangle above the Outcasts emblem identified the 13th Aviation Battalion. (James Sheetz)

an adjunct facility at Ft. Stewart, Georgia.

This was the Army's largest base east of the Mississippi River. Initially, only fixed-wing pilots were trained at Ft. Stewart. When the Army acquired nearby Hunter Airfield from the Air Force in 1967, the combination facility was re-named Hunter Army Airfield (AAF) and a helicopter training syllabus was added.

On graduation day the sky over Ft. Rucker was filled with helicopters flown by the students in a mass formation flyby. After "Mother Rucker," some pilots went to Cobra, Chinook, or medevac school; some went to Germany – most received orders for Vietnam.

Although armed with basic skills derived from expert tutelage, nothing could prepare the new guy for his arrival in Vietnam. This was where, given the Army's penchant for turning acronyms into slang, he became a "Wobbly One," taken from the Warrant Officer rank, a "Peter Pilot," or, more derisively, an FNG, or "Fuckin' New Guy." Once assigned to a unit, the new guy quickly learned the difference between stateside flying and flying in Vietnam. Under the guidance of seasoned pilots, he learned the countless critical items and how to take shortcuts safely, such as cutting down exposure time in an LZ and quick takeoffs. He was eventually given more responsibility and rose to the position of Aircraft Commander (AC). Not unusual after months of combat flying, shifts in his outlook and personality became apparent.

Most Aeroscout pilots in Vietnam were seasoned volunteers or on at least their second tour. Like pilots new to other aircraft, they flew with seasoned pilots until they could go it alone. Advanced instruction, refresher, or transition to another aircraft type in Vietnam took place at the Army's 5th Aviation Detachment at Vung Tau. Officially called the U.S. Army Republic of Vietnam (USARV) Training Team, the school was composed of four teams, one each for instruction in the UH-1, AH-1G, OH-58, and OH-6A. Team members were second-tour Instructor Pilots (IPs). Besides transition

John Garside (left) and Barry Sipple of C/1/9 in 1970 represent a typical Aeroscout crew. Garside holds a sidearm and his M60A machine gun, while Sipple holds an M-79 grenade launcher, typical tools of the trade. (Walker Jones)

training, the two-week school graduated instructor pilots (IPs) and standardization instructor pilots (SIPs).

The Observer

The term "Observer" seems an understatement when referring to this most indispensable member of an Aeroscout crew. Although during the 1960s the Army officially labeled the age-old aircraft crew position under its Military Occupation Specialty (MOS) classification system, an Aeroscout observer's function was far more expansive than merely observing. Aeroscout observers in Vietnam gave the mundane task new meaning and elevated its importance, in part, by becoming expert at "reading sign," much like their forebears of the Indian wars. Details such as camouflage, how grass was bent, and how much water had seeped into a footprint did not escape the observer. Such details, combined with knowing the enemy's habits, often painted a broader picture showing the size and type of an enemy force, and its direction of movement.

The observer's work in the low-level, high-threat environment required a keen sense of awareness, lightning-quick reflexes, and instinct beyond imagination. It was life on the edge in its purest form. When the crew arrangement dictated that the observer function as the crew chief, bestowed upon him was ownership of the aircraft – it became a personal matter. "My aircraft," he would say, which usually was verified by his name painted on the bird, or another nickname he had chosen. Aeroscout observers were nicknamed "Torques" or "Oscars," depending on unit, location, and time frame, with the latter name taken from the phonetic alphabet's word for the letter "O."

On the ground, the crew chief maintained the aircraft and the weapons. Often he was assisted by armorers, and mechanics skilled in powerplants, hydraulics, electrical systems, structural repair, and avionics. He inspected his bird thoroughly, fueled it, armed it, and

A 9th Cavalry observer, also called "Oscar" or "Torque," demonstrates use of the "free M60" from the OH-6A. Being part way out of the aircraft greatly improved the gunner's latitude and fields of fire. (Author's Collection)

Scout observer Michael Strobel demonstrates his position during low level operations in OH-6A 66-7783. The crudely painted yellow circle was the identifier for C Troop of the 1/9 Cav. (Nate Shaffer)

The observer's position of this C Troop, 16th Cavalry "Outcasts" Loach in 1971 is mission ready with an ample supply of M60 ammunition and incendiary and yellow smoke grenades. Body armor is stowed nearby and a flight helmet rests atop a box filled with homemade bombs comprising plastic explosive and concussion grenades. Use of the minigun ruled out the extra weight of a third crewman in the left front seat. Crewmen usually modified the M60A machine gun to reduce its weight, making it easier to wield in flight, and more mobile in the event of a shoot-down. Spare torso body armor "chicken plates" were a hot commodity among gunners, who placed them under their seats. The M60A is in stock infantry configuration, missing only the bipod. (James Sheetz)

maintained its green-covered flight and maintenance logs.

In the air, the observer performed double duty as the gunner. Although a stripped-down infantry type M60 hanging in the doorway was his stock in trade, he relied upon other weapons, including the M-16, its cousin the CAR-15, the M-79 grenade launcher, sidearms, hand grenades, and homemade bombs. Exotic weapons, usually of non-U.S. manufacture, often found their way aboard scout helicopters. Given the probability of ending up on the ground in hostile territory, crews depended upon such arsenals to increase their odds of survival. Aeroscout crewmen constantly faced the challenge of placing ordnance at different altitudes, speeds, and angles, often while being fired upon.

Prudent pilots wasted little time in teaching their Oscars how to fly the aircraft in the event they were wounded or killed. Enlisted crewmen logged countless hours of stick time, although unofficial, and their flying lessons often paid dividends in survival.

The Army considered the Scout observer's position important enough to establish its LOH Scout Observer course at Fort Eustis, Virginia. Scout units filled their observer ranks either with graduates of the course, who emerged with MOS 11D20, or with experienced volunteers from infantry or combat helicopter units. Aeroscout pilots were as confident in their crew chief/observers on the ground

as in the air. When the pilot arrived at the aircraft in the half-light of morning, he knew the crew chief had arrived there much earlier, undoubtedly pre-flighting the aircraft with a flashlight. And at day's end, after the pilot had turned the battery switch off and made his entries in the log book, the crew chief went to work inspecting the aircraft and performing maintenance.

Scout Steeds

Since the Korean war, observation helicopters have been a key element of Army Aviation. Five major types would serve, four of which filled the Aeroscout role in Vietnam; three of those also put in many years on training fields helping pilots earn their wings.

First to arrive was Bell's H-13 "Sioux," which became recognizable to the world as the bubble canopy, life-saving helicopter in the TV series *M*A*S*H*. The piston-powered H-13 was the first large-scale produced helicopter to join the Army, followed by Hiller's H-23 "Raven." Versions of both types distinguished themselves in the medical evacuation and utility roles during the Korean war. After the war, Sioux and Ravens served as trainers and were joined in 1958 by Hughes' TH-55A "Osage." Nearly 800 of the simple but rugged, two-place TH-55As would wear the Army's bright orange

Aeroscout crewman Specialist James Hand poses with a Loach of C Troop, 16th Cavalry of the 1st Infantry Division in 1971. Hand's bracelet, made from a helicopter tail rotor drive chain, was usually worn by crewmen who had been shot down. Here the protective cover of the M27 minigun system is removed and the replacement tail boom has yet to be painted. Prior to assignment to the Outcasts, this Loach, S/N 66-7849, had belonged to the 1st Brigade Aviation Section of the 1st Cavalry Division, the "Flying Circus." Aircraft were often reassigned and dispersed to fill unit shortages after being repaired in major maintenance facilities. Hand was not one of the two crewmen killed when number 849 exploded in a re-arm area in January 1972. (James Sheetz)

training scheme.

The Army's experimentation with arming scout helicopters during the 1950s foreshadowed their armed reconnaissance role in Vietnam. The most powerful version of the Sioux and Raven, the OH-13S and OH-23G, respectively, were among the first Army helicopters lashed to carrier decks for the voyage to Vietnam during the early 1960s.

The OH-13S couldn't carry what Army staff in Vietnam considered the scout mission load. Consequently, the Sioux was operated above its design gross weight, resulting in sluggish performance and shortened life of components. It didn't help that Sioux of the 1st Cavalry Division often were armed with eight rockets and a 7.62mm machine gun; Sioux of the 1st Infantry Division used two of the guns but no rockets.

Although the OH-23G didn't fare much better in Vietnam's high density altitude, it served a number of combat units. In the hands of skilled and dedicated crewmen, the Sioux and Raven did the job, pioneering the Aeroscout concept. Both types would earn their battle stars until their numbers dwindled during the early 1970s. A total of 93 Ravens and 147 Sioux helicopters were lost during the war.

Premier among the mounts of Aeroscouts in Vietnam was the Hughes OH-6A "Cayuse," known simply as the "Loach." After withstanding troubled beginnings and a wave of controversy, the turbine-powered Loach emerged to satisfy a 1958 study to find the ideal replacement for the Army's fleet of observation helicopters and the fixed-wing L-19 Bird Dog. The Cayuse proved to be everything the Army asked for, and more. Powered by a 250-horsepower turbine, with its basic weight barely exceeding 1,000 pounds, the Cayuse could cruise at 145 mph. High gross weights, crash survivability, and its nimbleness made it a favorite among pilots. Muscle for the Loach came in the form of a side-mounted XM-27 minigun system, which had an adjustable firing rate of 2,000 or

An early model, mini-gun-armed OH-6A, S/N 65-12975, of A Troop, 7th Squadron, 17th Cavalry stands alert at Ban Mê Thuột in Vietnam's Central Highlands in March 1968. The 17th Cav served as the eyes and ears of the 4th Infantry Division. (Robert N. Steinbrunn)

An infantry style M60A machine gun is suspended in the observer's doorway of this OH-13S of B/1/9 in 1966. An M-16 rifle rests on a center floor console and a makeshift container outside the cockpit holds white phosphorus grenades. Below a Confederate flag on the nose bubble is the name *Dixie Bell.* (Melvin Edwards)

Loaches not mounting the minigun carried a third crewman as observer/gunner in the rear cabin. This OH-6A, S/N 68-15990, nicknamed *Zit,* wears the markings of the 1st Cavalry Division's 1st Squadron, 9th Cavalry. A yellow circle on the doghouse identified C Troop. Army helicopters were usually operationally identified by the last three digits of their serial numbers, which often were painted white. Number 990 also wears One-Nine's crossed cavalry sabers. The fiberglass frame of the upper replacement window remains unpainted. Having the largest number of Loaches assigned, and having arrived early in the war, all of the 1st Cavalry Division's 1st Squadron, 9th Cavalry troops were instrumental in writing the book on Aeroscout tactics, often with tremendous loss. (Nate Shaffer Collection)

Crew chiefs maintained their aircraft when they were not flying. This crew chief attends an OH-6A at Củ Chi in 1969. Windshields required great care and polishing due to the abrasive sand and debris stirred by rotor-wash, especially in Vietnam's dry season. Vertical white lines at the outside edges of the cockpit glass are antennas that replaced external types on early production machines. This Loach served B Company, 25th Aviation Battalion of the 25th Infantry Division. The battalion's Scout element was called "Diamondheads," after the unit's base in Hawaii. Besides the Diamondhead emblem on the rotor pylon, or "doghouse," the 25th Infantry Division emblem appears on the aircraft's nose. As in other infantry divisions, Scout helicopters were also assigned to the 25th's Artillery Section for spotting and aerial observation. Several 25th Division aviation units, flying various helicopter types, developed innovative weapon systems. (George Reese, Jr.)

This OH-58A of D Troop, 1st Squadron, 10th Cavalry, or D/1/10, "Shamrock" of the 4th Infantry Division awaits a mission at An Khê in April 1971. Dubbed "The Golf Course" due to its sheer expanse, the An Khê base was the 1st Cavalry Division's major heliport upon arrival in Vietnam. During its Vietnam service, from 1966 to 1971, D/1/10 flew OH-232G, OH-6A, and, beginning in 1970, OH-58A Scout helicopters. One of eight Shamrock Scout Kiowas, S/N 69-16303 wears the unit's cavalry pennant on the forward rotor pylon and crossed sabers on its nose. Like the OH-6A that it augmented and later replaced, the Kiowa flew without doors for the Scout mission. More powerful engines earned the Kiowa wider acceptance as Aeroscout platforms. (Michael Belis)

Most OH-58As in Vietnam were shipped from new production to keep pace with OH-6A attrition. Typical in many Aeroscout units, both pilot and observer of this Kiowa of 3rd Squadron, 17th Cavalry are on the same side of the aircraft. (U.S. Army)

Huey gunships of the 240th AHC wore a distinctive nose panel bearing the gun platoon's motto "Death on Call" and the pilot's call sign, in this case "Mad Dog Three-Seven." (U.S. Army)

The first operational AH-1G Cobra unit in Vietnam was 1st Platoon of the 334th Armed helicopter Company, called "Playboys." The unit, which had evolved from three units, received its Cobras in late 1967 and began writing a new chapter in armed helicopter support. This Playboy Cobra, S/N 68-17037, refuels at Củ Chi's POL in 1970. POL stood for Petroleum, Oil and Lubricants, however, most were re-arming sites as well. (Gary Schmidt)

4,000 rounds per minute. Rocket launchers of the 2.75-inch variety were tried with some success.

The OH-6A New Equipment Training Team arrived in Vietnam in early 1967, and in October became operational with the first Loach-equipped combat unit, 7th Squadron, 17th Cavalry. Three air cavalry units were flying them by year's end. Since that number fell far short the quantity of Loach units the Army desired, additional OH-13S and OH-23Gs were sent to Vietnam. Aeroscouts paid a heavy price for their high-risk work in the low-level environment. Army records indicate that of 1,417 OH-6As produced, 842 were lost in Vietnam.

During a resurgence of the controversy that surrounded the Army LOH program, the OH-6A's replacement was spawned from an original competitor, the OH-58A "Kiowa," which was the militarized version of Bell's Model 206A "Jet Ranger." The OH-58A was given the same T63 engine used to power the lighter OH-6A. Also carried over from the Loach was the M27 minigun system. Although pilots gave the Kiowa high marks in some areas, its mission weight was twice that of the Loach and it was slower and less responsive, ruling out any chance of matching the OH-6A's speed and agility. Since such traits made a difference in surviving close encounters with the enemy, the Kiowa was deemed only marginally successful in the scout role. A total of 45 OH-58As were lost during the war, 28 of them to hostile fire.

Since, like the Cobra, the OH-6A and OH-58A were new aircraft pressed into service for the war, New Equipment Training Teams (NETTs) introduced them in theatre. NETTs comprised civilian tech reps and factory-trained, combat seasoned pilots with high flight hours to teach Vietnam-based units every aspect of the aircraft's operation and maintenance.

Snakes

The stable-mate of the OH-6A in Vietnam was the AH-1G Cobra gunship. It was the "Killer" element of the highly effective Hunter-Killer "Pink Team." The Vietnam war spawned the Cobra, which originally was designed as a pure helicopter gunship for armed reconnaissance, helicopter escort, and direct fire support. When teamed with the OH-6A Loach, the lethal snake proved a particular nemesis for enemy who dare fire at the low-level Loach.

Bell Helicopter Company officials had kept a watchful eye not only on the worsening situation in Vietnam, but on the Army's decade-long experimentation with armed helicopters. When it became obvious that Army leaders had set their sights on a pure gunship as a result of success with heavily armed Hueys, Bell officials intensified their in-house development of an advanced attack helicopter that made use of proven Huey components.

Labeled the AH-1G HueyCobra, the design featured a narrow fuselage that positioned the pilot behind and above the gunner. The 1,400-shaft horsepower-engine and rotor system borrowed from the UH-1C Huey model allowed the Cobra to cruise at 166 mph and dive at 220 mph. Able to carry a large weapons load and featuring protective systems, the sleek Cobra was built for war. Army helicopter pilots relished in the fact that they now had the ability to perform maneuvers previously limited to airplanes. Oh, how the Air Force bristled, sensing yet another Army infringement of their tactical domain.

Giving the Cobra a bite many times more lethal than its namesake

This early model AH-1G Cobra wears the markings of the 1st Aviation Brigade's A Troop, 7th Squadron, 1st Cavalry "Apache" Troop in 1969. Army helicopter units in Vietnam often respectfully based their names and markings on American Indian tribes and the original U.S. Cavalry. Common to Cobras in Vietnam was the time-honored shark mouth, with each AH-1G unit identified by its own style of mouth. This Cobra's mouth is not yet complete. Stub wing armament was 19-tube, 2.75-inch FFAR rocker launchers inboard, and seven-tube launchers outboard. Early blue-tinted canopies were replaced by clear glass to reduce the hazards of night operations. Air conditioning was added to counter the solar heat. Dual nose landing lights identify this Snake as an early production model. (Author's Collection)

were weapon systems carried in a chin turret and on stub wings. The most common under-wing ordnance was 2.75-inch Folding Fin Aerial Rockets (FFAR), 76 of which could be carried in four 19-tube launchers. Often, both rocket launchers and podded miniguns were carried.

Although rocket warhead contents varied, high explosive and flechette (steel anti-personnel darts called "nails") proved most effective. The podded M134 minigun had a firing rate of 2,000 or 4,000 rounds per minute. Early-production Cobras carried a single minigun in a chin turret, however, this became a dual weapon system accommodating two miniguns or two 40mm grenade launchers, with one of each preferred as the standard configuration. A 20mm Vulcan cannon, which was modified for the Cobra to give it standoff capability against .51-caliber anti-aircraft guns, was introduced to attack helicopter units in the combat theatre during late 1969. The Vulcan, which gave the Cobra devastating long-range and point-fire capability, was accurate at 2,000 meters and had an effective range for area fire at 3,000 meters.

The first Cobras arrived in Vietnam in late August 1967, and drew first blood one week later. The first combat unit to fly Cobras, the 334th Aerial Weapons Company "Playboys" at Bien Hoa, began writing the book on AH-1G tactics. As more Cobras were shipped

to Vietnam, they filled the ranks mainly of air cavalry troops, aerial weapons companies, assault helicopter companies, and aerial rocket artillery batteries. The Snake's high speed, agility, and narrow frontal profile made it a difficult target. Such traits allowed it to overfly targets. Cobras normally engaged targets at altitudes between 1,400 and 2,000 feet, with higher altitudes possible, depending on ordnance carried. Despite the AH-1G's popularity, some crews had reservations about its effectiveness in combat. Some Huey drivers-turned-Cobra pilots had learned to rely greatly upon the eyes, ears, versatility and firepower of door gunners. Even after amassing hours in the Cobra, some pilots remained partial to the cohesiveness with the "guys in the back." The Huey gunship versus Cobra argument would thrive throughout the war.

Nearly 40 units would fly the Cobra in Vietnam, although not all would fully replace Huey gunships. The eight assault helicopter companies that flew Cobras typically had four or six assigned, while most units carried between eight and 12 on their inventories.

The North Vietnamese Spring Offensive in 1972 set the stage for the first Cobra-versus- armor showdown. The Cobra would emerge the victor after four units proved the Snake's tank-busting capability. Cobra crews of F Battery, 79th Field Artillery of the 1st Cav's 3rd Brigade alone accounted for more than 20 armored vehicles. The

Since the majority of Loaches that served in Vietnam did not survive the war, it come as no surprise that research of OH-6As turns up more photos of crashed aircraft than flyable ones. This Apache Troop Loach of 7th Squadron, 1st Cavalry was added to the loss list in 1969. Aircraft this badly damaged were sling-recovered in areas made secure by ground troops, or they were destroyed by strike aircraft. Even when destruction seemed complete, the OH-6A's collapsible box structure beneath floor decks usually remained intact. It was common knowledge among Aeroscout crewmen, and reassuring, that even when parts flew off of a Loach in a crash, the basic structure would remain intact, hopefully, with crewmen still strapped in. (Charlie Palek)

During its five-year stint in Vietnam, D Troop (Air), 1st Squadron, 10th Cavalry, called "Shamrock," operated lift, scout, gun and rifle platoons supporting the 4th Infantry Division's armor element in II Corps. Cobras of D/1/10 were among the few that wore camouflage. Although shark mouths commonly were applied to Cobras, each unit used a distinct identifying style. This "Snake" is seen at An Khê in April 1971. (Michael Belis)

battle at An Loc, which pitched Cobras against massed anti-aircraft weapons, including heat-seeking missiles, brought about one of the few wartime alterations made to Cobras, which was the installation of heat-dissipating exhaust pipes. Of the total of 1,126 AH-1Gs produced, nearly 700 were in Vietnam at the war's peak.

Although the enemy knew that to fire at the Cobra meant certain death, a total of 279 AH-1Gs were lost at the hands of enemy gunners and to operational causes.

Aeroscout Tactics

As the Army developed tactical doctrine with helicopters during the 1960s, air cavalry units were formed. Embodying the airmobile concept, these units normally comprised an Aeroscout platoon flying observation helicopters, an Aeroweapons platoon flying helicopter gunships, and a Lift platoon flying Huey slicks for carrying quick-reaction infantry called an Aerorifle platoon. The Aeroscout element was deemed necessary to counter the enemy's hit and run tactics and his extreme reliance on concealment. Besides scouting ahead of ground troops, they searched for, and often engaged, the enemy in eye-to-eye combat.

Aviation units that arrived early in the Vietnam conflict flew the OH-13S and OH-23G observation helicopters. Although capable performers as front-line Army aircraft, they proved underpowered in Vietnam's high density altitude. The OH-6A's introduction to the war to satisfy scout helicopter requirements was spurred by interviews with OH-13S crews of the 1st Cavalry Division's 1st Squadron, 9th Cavalry and the 1st Squadron, 4th Cavalry of the 1st Infantry Division. Since it was originally intended that Aeroscouts

not engage the enemy, the OH-6A's speed and maneuverability were vital, yet scouts had to be capable of light defense and target-marking until help arrived; scouts usually flew within 50 miles of friendly troops.

But the ACTIV reported in November 1966 that the OH-6A would fare no better than the OH-13S in carrying what was deemed the essential load of scout helicopters. This included aircraft armor, a weapons package comprising two seven-tube, 2.75-inch rocket launchers, and a minigun system, along with the body armor, weapons, and survival gear of a pilot and observer. The OH-6A was unproven, however, very soon, skillful and courageous scout crews would put the Loach through its paces, regularly flying well over allowable gross weights and torque limits.

Without the benefit of years to develop the air cavalry concept, scout crews wrote the book in Vietnam. As the number of scout helicopters and crews grew, tactics were developed, varying according to geography and unit policy. Although various combinations of aircraft and scout crew arrangements were tried, two tactical concepts were adopted by most Aeroscout units: a White Team used a two-ship scout team, with a low bird and a high bird. While the low bird prowled in the enemy's domain, the high bird, called the "Trail" or "Wing," provided covering fire, navigation, and radio relay.

The other concept, called a Pink Team, had a scout low bird, with a gunship – or two or more – watching protectively overhead, ready to pounce when the low bird took fire. If a major force was encountered, the Blues could be inserted, or heavy firepower could be summoned. This took the form of Air Force, Navy or Marine tactical strike aircraft, along with artillery.

Depending upon unit policy, some scouts engaged the enemy,

Low-profile special agencies that were very much involved in the war found the OH-6A ideal for clandestine work. A small number of Loaches were acquired by the CIA for use by its air arm "Air America." A few were highly modified for quiet penetration to tap communication lines in North Vietnam. Aircrew training was conducted by seasoned Army Scout pilots, who ended up carrying out what was called the most secret operation of the war. Sporting a unique camouflage scheme familiar to that worn by U.S. Air Force aircraft in theatre, this Loach may have been assigned to an Army aviation unit whose aircraft and crew were parceled out for missions "across the fence." In the post-war era, one or two similarly painted Loaches were observed at stateside Army installations. (Rich Jalloway Collection)

A Loach crew of 1st Squadron, 9th Cavalry awaits rescue on their overturned aircraft after crashing into the Sông Bé River in 1970. Rescue of downed aircrew in all of Southeast Asia took the form of any aircraft that could get to the area and was available to help. Rescue forces often constituted an armada of aircraft as well as ground and waterborne resources from all services. Pilots who found themselves in trouble would transmit on the continually monitored "Guard Channel," which was reserved for emergencies. Usually, aircrew recovery took priority and was given maximum effort. Recovering the aircraft would be troublesome if there was a large enemy presence and some recoveries sparked major battles. If recovery was ruled out, the aircraft was destroyed. The hastily applied buzz number was in keeping with Army directives in the war's later years. (Walker Jones)

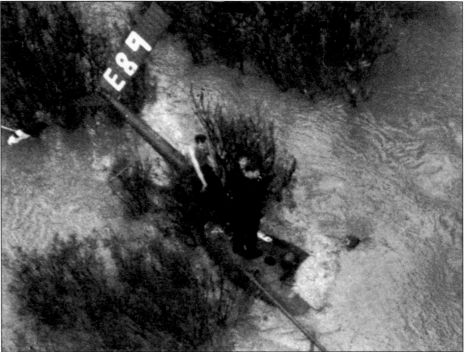

When "Outcast" Scout pilot Mike Guillot radioed his wing man that he had a problem after flying through a tree to avoid enemy fire, his wing man responded, "You don't have any skids!" Flying into the sun, Guillot struck the tree, which also knocked out the left side windshield. He and his observer landed safely atop a landing platform hastily built of sandbags. Much of the damage done to helicopters could be repaired by the unit, most of which had a maintenance platoon. Aircraft damaged beyond unit capabilities at their site, including OH-6A's that, literally, were rolled into a ball, were shipped to Corpus Christi, Texas, for depot level rebuilding. Often, crashed helicopters that were no longer recognizable emerged from Corpus Christi in mint condition. (Ellwood Soderlind/VHPA)

This view of an OH-6A of C/1/9 in 1970 shows the backside of the observer's position where homemade bombs and grenades were stored in containers placed upon armor plates. Grenades in the containers comprised 14 white phosphorous, 5 percussion, 20 fragmentation, 5 tear gas, and 15 incendiary. The ammunition box held 2,500 rounds of 7.62mm M60 rounds. (David Dzwigalski)

while some commanders remained steadfast in "observe only" policies. Whether a Loach carried a crew of two or three was solely dependent upon use of the minigun system. The system's loaded weight of 280 pounds restricted the crew to two: pilot and observer/gunner or observer/crew chief. The pilot usually flew right seat, with the gunner next to him in the copilot's seat, or behind him in the cabin. This put both sets of eyes and the gunner's weapon on the same side, as the pilot flew right circles. Often the minigun was omitted in favor of a third crewman who offered more latitude with an M60 machine gun, plus an extra set of eyes and ears. Often, the minigun was left off the Loach in northern regions, where mountainous terrain ruled out the gun's effectiveness. Regardless whether the minigun was used, scout crewmen went to war heavily armed.

The arrival of the Cobra brought about changes in scouting techniques since supporting Huey gunships had four pairs of eyes, door guns, and flew lower and slower, all of which factors gave the scout excellent cover. There was more interaction with the Hueys – the door gunners never lost sight of the scout helicopter, and Hueys were better suited to rescuing a downed scout crew. But all the players adjusted and got the job done.

Even the way that a scout pilot flew played an important part in the mission. What would normally be considered sloppy flying proved beneficial to the scout's survival. Former scout pilot John Briggs explained in the January 1969 issue of HAWK:

"The sloppier you are, sometimes the safer it is. Flying out of trim often makes it hard for Charlie to figure out which direction you're flying; then he can't lead you. Flying sideways, flying backwards, out of trim, lots of turns. They don't know where you're going next.

If they do, they'll probably shoot you down. About the only time they're going to get you is when you're hovering, flying straight, or passing directly over them."

Accordingly, scout pilots checked their speed – not too slow – not too fast. "The best speed," a pilot explained, "was one at which you could spot and recognize what you had to on the first pass, usually at 40 to 60 knots, flying just a few feet above obstacles."

Scout pilots knew the danger of retracing their steps or flying recognizable patterns in the enemy's back yard – the second time over the same route tempted fate – the third time guaranteed their being shot down.

The enemy, too, knew things. They knew that if they closed with U.S. troops – "Grabbing them by the belt buckle," was their term – the Americans couldn't use their beloved airpower. What the enemy didn't consider early in the game, but soon discovered, was that such "bear-hugging" normally didn't apply to Aeroscouts, who excelled at close-in work.

The Well-Armed Scout

Besides basic operating procedures adopted by Aeroscout units, defensive and offensive operations varied from one unit to another. Don Langlois explains:

"I served with two cav unit scout platoons during two tours in Vietnam. The first with D Troop, 3rd Squadron, 5th Cavalry, and the second with H Troop, 17th Cav. During my tour with D Troop, we developed the use of C-4 and TNT as part of our operations. The scouts did more than scout for the enemy. In D Troop, the body count was taken by the scouts. The War Wagons

Scout Platoon Leader of C Troop, 7th Squadron, 17th Cavalry, Carl King poses with the unit's rocket-armed OH-6A, S/N 66-7915, in 1968. Affixed to the Loach's right side, the four-tube system was designed by Rock Island Arsenal, but never approved for widespread use. While this system was officially sanctioned for combat trials, some unit-fabricated rocket launchers were not only frowned upon, but ordered removed when discovered. Sighting for ad-hoc weapons systems often was accomplished merely with a grease pencil mark on the windshield. Rockets were regarded as an area weapon and were not made more accurate until late in the war. Even then their use was limited to occasions when pin-point accuracy was not required. (Richard Hefferman)

In 1969, a two-tube rocket installation was experimentally fit to an OH-6A of D Troop, 3rd Squadron, 5th Cavalry. Loaches normally flew without doors, but here the pilot's door has been installed to shield him from rocket blast. As the most fired non-bullet ordnance of the war, the 2.75-inch Folding-Fin-Aerial Rocket (FFAR) was widely used in aviation. Developed in the 1940s as an air-to-air weapon, the rocket proved best suited as an area weapon for helicopters. The tube-launched, electrically-fired FFAR consisted mainly of a motor, warhead and fuse (either proximity or point-detonating), with High Explosive, or HE, being the most common warhead. Other period warheads included smoke marker, white phosphorous, anti-armor, fragmentation, and flechette – the last packed with more than 2,000 tiny steel darts. Flechette-armed rockets were commonly fired by Cobra helicopters at higher altitudes than Loaches normally flew. (Michael Galvin)

History records the Army's intense involvement with arming helicopters, prior to and during the Vietnam conflict. One of the many systems evaluated was the 40mm XM-8 grenade launcher, which occupied the M27 minigun position. Originally thought not to have seen combat in Vietnam, the XM-8 was tested in combat mounted to the OH-6A S/N 67-16312 of D Troop, 1st Squadron, 4th Cavalry "Quarter Cav" in 1969. The Loach suffered two shoot-downs in 1969, resulting in the deaths of three crewmen. U.S. Air Force special operations Huey helicopters would use a variant of the XM-8, although on a limited basis. Special Forces troops also found a ground tripod-mounted version of the weapon highly effective. (Roy Wiggs)

Use of the minigun system was based on unit preference. Not only did the system's weight restrict the crew to two, it left little room for a third crewman. This minigun-armed Loach, S/N 67-16326, served C/7/17 at Camp Holloway in early 1972. (Steve Shepard/VHPA)

did more than scout for the enemy; they made engagement a prime part of operations. With H Troop, it was an entirely different story. Destroying the enemy was less the function of the scouts, as "seek" was its main purpose. Gunships were more relied upon for inflicting damage on the enemy."

The Army had specified, as a condition of bid proposals during the scout helicopter competition, that manufacturers include in their design two armament kits that used the M60 machine gun. Tests of approved systems led to the emerging minigun on Hughes' winning entry, the OH-6A Cayuse. The M27 minigun system comprised the General Electric six-barrel, 7.62mm M134 Gatling-type weapon. The gun featured an adjustable firing rate: when the pilot depressed the cyclic trigger to the first detent, the gun fired 2,000 rounds per minute; fully depressing the trigger gave him 4,000 rounds per minute.

The gun and its 2,000-round ammunition box were mounted to the left side cabin of the OH-6A. Since the system's cockpit sighting device caused a delay in responding to enemy fire, and was considered dangerous in a crash, it was usually omitted in favor of a grease pencil mark on the windshield. The minigun elevated 10 degrees and depressed 24 degrees, but its fixed azimuth required that pilots use tail rotor pedals for lateral movement of the entire aircraft. The maximum effective range of the M27 was 1,000 meters. Scout units typically carried 2,500 rounds of ammunition and set the weapon to fire in three-second bursts to prevent damage to the barrels. James Howard offers this perspective on the minigun:

"Flying in on target during a firefight, the pilot depended upon several factors to get him through that run alive. Of course, he was dependent upon his flying skills, along with his gunner's ability to lay suppressive fire where needed, plus the other ship working with him to help him out of a tight situation. However, some pilots really favored the minigun.

"The gun not only had awesome destructive power, it had a psychological effect on the pilot, giving him confidence and creating the impression that, while it was firing, he was indestructible. The minigun made a wonderfully loud roaring noise and spit out a beautiful flame about a foot wide and two to three feet in length. Of course, the pilot's ability to aim the gun was limited, but with 80 rounds being fired every second, it was bound to hit something. In the pilot's mind, the NVA and the gooks were too busy diving for cover and did not have time to return fire. Another effect was that when the gun fired, the pilot could not hear when someone was shooting back, giving him a temporary, though unjustifiable, impression that he was safe."

Standard aboard every Loach that flew into harm's way was the M60 machine gun, operated by observers who occupied the copilot's and rear cabin positions. Long the standard U.S. infantry weapon, the M60 was gas-operated, air-cooled and fired 600 rounds per minute. Its effective range was 1,100 meters. Of two basic models of the machine gun, the infantry style M60A and the aviation type M60D, those carried by Loach gunners more closely resembled the infantry model. To lighten the weapon and provide gunners the extreme latitude necessary for covering their fields of fire, scout crews removed the weapon's butt plate, bipod, and sights. Sometimes the barrels were shortened, resulting in more noise and a tongue of flame, making the weapon even more fearsome. Recoil springs could be beefed up to increase the firing rate. These modifications also made the M60 easier to handle on the ground

A minigun modification in an OH-6A of B Company, 25th Aviation Battalion gave it awesome firepower. The battalion commander, Col. Kenneth P. Burton, gets a feel for the weapon. Nearby at Cù Chi was D Troop, 3rd Squadron, 4th Cavalry, which used a similar system in a Loach, suggesting that the units work together to develop the installation. (George Reese, Jr.)

The cockpit observer's position of this Loach of D/3/5 in 1969 shows tear gas and smoke grenades strung on wires, and a bag containing fragmentation and white phosphorous grenades. Visible also is a "short stick" that replaced the original cyclic control stick, enabling the observer to fly the aircraft. (Michael Galvin)

in the event of a shoot-down. Gunners fed their M60s belted ammunition from boxes or simply piled the ammunition at their feet. Sights were seldom used since gunners could more accurately place fire on targets by watching tracer rounds, which were placed every fifth link in the belt.

When observer/gunners occupied the copilot's seat, the cyclic stick was either shortened or removed, giving the gunner more latitude with his M60, which was fastened to the door frame with a strap. Should the observer need to fly the aircraft in an emergency, a length of pipe, or a stick, that fit into the cyclic base was stowed within easy reach.

Augmenting the M60 was a variety of personal weapons that included the standard issue Colt 5.56mm/.223 cal. M-16 fully automatic rifle, which was introduced to the Army in 1964 to replace the M-14. Its later cousin, the CAR-15 "Commando," was well suited to the confines of scout cockpits since it had a shorter barrel and a telescoping stock. Also standard was the issued six-shot Smith & Wesson M10 .38 caliber Special revolver with four-inch barrel; a two-inch barrel version was also available. Aircrew initially was issued the Colt M1911A1 .45 caliber automatic pistol. The switch was made to the .38 in 1966 when it was realized that, given the probability of a scout crew being downed, an injured crewman might not have the use of both hands to cock the .45. Other weapons of choice depended upon personal preference and availability. These included the 40mm M79 grenade launcher, shotguns, and more

exotic weapons, such as the dated M1A1 Thompson submachine gun and M3A1 Grease Gun, both .45 caliber. Personal weapons of more commercial variety also found their way onto scout helicopters. Such weapons were relatively easy to come by; if they couldn't be gained from captured weapon stocks, the black market did a thriving business, and special operations commandos usually had weapons for trade. Although the AK-47 was a reliable, powerful weapon, its novel use by aircrew was short-lived since it had a distinctive sound that was sure to draw friendly fire in a fight.

Grenades of all types were in abundance on scout helicopters, and usually were hooked by their safety pins on wires strung about the aircraft. These included fragmentation, concussion, tear gas, white phosphorous, colored smoke, and thermate. Although crewmen took special precaution with grenades, often packing them in body armor, scout helicopters frequently were lost as a result of incidents with onboard ordnance.

Noteworthy were powerful bombs that crewmen fashioned from various combinations of explosives and shrapnel to attack stubborn targets previously bombarded with grenades and then tear gas. These lethal concoctions usually combined C-4 plastic explosive, grenades, and shrapnel in the form of bullets, nails or other anti-personnel material.

Warheads of 2.75-inch rockets were also found to be effective components of homemade bombs. Sizes of the bombs ranged from two pounds to whopping 30-pound devices.

Joe Crockett occupied this work station when he flew as Aeroscout crew chief with D Troop, 1st Squadron, 4th Cavalry. Ammunition for the M60A machine gun typically was stored in and fed from a large wooden box on the deck. Smoke grenades were strung across the bulkhead separating the cockpit and cabin. (Joe Crockett Collection)

Scout gunners became proficient at dropping bombs on targets such as bunkers, vehicles, vessels, and even armored vehicles encountered late in the war. Aeroscouts found it much safer to make a single pass over a target to drop a super bomb, versus repeated, often ineffective, attacks with grenades.

Having such large amounts of high explosives aboard a small helicopter that regularly was fired upon only added to the high drama of the Aeroscout's perilous existence.

The Well Dressed Scout

Even before Army cavalry units first deployed to Vietnam, their members took on appearances that distinguished them from standard line units. And like their aircraft, weapons, and tactics, what cavalrymen wore to war would be based mainly upon changing tactical requirements and unit policy.

The cotton, olive drab uniform worn by the Army since the Korean war served not only as the work uniform, but as flight clothing. These starched "fatigues" quickly proved ill-suited to Vietnam's tropical climate. During late 1966 and early 1967, fatigues were replaced by a new jungle uniform; a camouflage version that was popular with ARPs sometimes was worn by scout crewmen. Although these "jungle fatigues" were more comfortable, their light weight offered little protection from burns, and the nylon woven into their fabric for strength melted in fires. More had to be done to reduce burn injuries from the high octane JP-4 that fueled helicopters.

Army labs came up with a fire-resistant, two-piece flight suit made of Nomex. The number of burn injuries declined after Nomex went into circulation in 1968. It too had drawbacks, however. Crewmen found the itchy material's inability to "breathe" well a small price to pay for its added protection. The Nomex shirt, like that of the jungle fatigues, was worn outside the trousers. Nomex flying gloves with calfskin palms were developed as part of the fire-resistant flight suit.

Unsurprisingly, Army "brass" had a lot to say about the selection of the flight suit, which fanned the embers of rivalry between various commands. Commanders of non-aviation units saw the flight suit as yet another element of what they perceived to be the undisciplined attitude that existed in aviation.

Non-flying headgear took the form of a baseball type cap, upon which aircrew had embroidered wings and rank insignia on the front, and their call sign and nickname on the back. Boonie hats, although less popular in aviation than in other fields, were worn by enlisted personnel. Although quite functional as tropical headgear, the floppy hats were frowned upon by many commanders who saw them as unmilitary and symbolic of the radicalism that pervaded the ranks. Boonie hats, like fatigue caps, were signed with embroidery, and their many loops often were festooned with hand grenade rings. Other adornments included miniature metal insignia and steel flechette darts.

Flight helmets came in two varieties: the APH-5, which had been in use since the 1950s, and the SPH-4, which replaced it in 1970. The latter offered more ballistic protection, more noise reduction, and featured a wire boom microphone, which was an improvement over the plastic mike of the APH-5. Both types featured a front cover that incorporated a pull-down sun visor. Rarely was the flight helmet of an Army helicopter aviator in Vietnam seen without

Carrying on the cavalry tradition of their forefathers, aircrew of D Troop, 3rd Squadron, 5th Cavalry in Vietnam don cavalry regalia, including Stetson hats, riding gloves, scarves, and belts. (George Rein/Don Callison)

some form of artwork, with some helmets serving as the canvas for elaborate, artistic themes.

Especially noteworthy among headgear worn by air cavalry units in Vietnam, and probably the most distinctive, was the Stetson hat. The name said it all – "Stetson" identified the established hat company and the hat itself. Reminiscent of the wide-brimmed hats worn by the original horse cavalry of the 1800s, Stetsons were introduced by the 3rd Squadron, 17th Cavalry shortly after it was formed at Ft. Benning in March 1964. When the squadron's parent command, the 11th Air Assault Division, became the 1st Cavalry Division (Airmobile) in 1965, 3/17 became 1/9, nicknamed "Real Cav," which took the Stetson to Vietnam. As additional cavalry units deployed, they too adopted the Stetson, which became standard officer headgear, although it was never officially approved. The hat was a source of pride and loyalty among cavalry units. They were trimmed with different color braids that signified rank, and they were adorned with metal rank and crossed-sabers unit insignia. Some air cavalry units added beaded, colored, or camouflaged bands; some added feathers. One scout cavalryman attached a fresh flower to his Stetson every day. Brims were worn curved upward, or flattened in more historically accurate fashion. The only known exception to black Stetsons were gray hats worn by Lighthorse D/3/5. So cherished were the cav hats that some officers took great risks to retrieve theirs from a crash, and most cav veterans still have theirs. The cav hat tradition continues in modern air cavalry units.

Affirming the air cavalry spirit was a wide variety of insignia that included unofficial unit patches, miniature metal "beer can" insignia, and scarves. Like the Stetson hat, cavalry scarves were a throwback to the horse cavalry. Most Army commanders ignored

that scarves were not officially approved in view of their positive effect on morale and unit pride. Scarves often were embroidered and their colors identified cavalry elements; ARPs wore blue scarves, while many aircrews wore yellow, which represented the armor branch. Most popular was the red and white scarf, the colors taken from the original cavalry guidon. As much functional as they were symbolic, scarves served as sweat bands and helped prevent neck chafing caused by body armor. Among the unique items worn by Aeroscouts were pins or scarves awarded to crewmen who survived a crash.

It was also customary in the Army aviation community for crash survivors to wear a bracelet fashioned from a Huey tail rotor drive chain.

Red and white Cavalry guidons, or unit flags, were officially approved and were formally passed between unit commanders at change-of-command ceremonies. Some units, such as D/3/5, embellished the cavalry image to the extent that sabers and riding gloves were worn during ceremonies.

Jungle boots were the standard footwear of U.S. soldiers in Vietnam, however, their softer construction did not offer much support in a crash, and their mesh nylon sides had a nasty habit of melting in fire and fusing painfully to skin. Aircrew went back to wearing leather combat boots, which became an Army requirement for flight crew.

Most important among the scout's wardrobe were items meant to better his chances of survival. Early in the war, helicopters were not equipped with armored seats, and aircrews wore bulky "flak jackets" designed for ground troops. Armor seats were soon installed and in 1966 the "chickenplate" appeared. Designed specifically for

Challenger, S/N 67-16524, was a "Skeeter" aircraft of B Company, 123rd Aviation Battalion seen here at Đức Phổ in 1970. The Loach's skid struts were painted black, yellow and white. (Robert Brackenhoff)

aircrews, chickenplate body armor consisted of a front and back armor panel. Pilots wore the front panel and gunners sometimes wore both. The front section of the vest that contained the armor panel featured a pocket for a survival radio, although it was seldom used.

Chickenplates were at a premium and aircrew took whatever means necessary to acquire additional panels to place in helicopter chin bubbles, to sit on (for obvious reasons), and to shield grenades and homemade bombs from ground fire.

Late in the war, a modified Air Force survival vest was issued to Army pilots. Contained in the many pockets of the nylon mesh vest were a variety of essential items that included the .38 caliber pistol, knives, compass, flare pen gun, strobe light, mirror, medical items, and various other items necessary to survive in the wilds. Crucial among the vest's contents was a URC-10 or RT-10 survival radio, which was preset to one emergency channel, and which had a range of 30 nautical miles.

A Spotter's guide to Aeroscouts

The long-standing tradition of using identifying emblems and markings, especially on aircraft, reached new heights during the Vietnam war. Aeroscouts, and Air Cavalry, as a whole, being an aggressive, high-spirited bunch, fully exploited the use of special identifiers, which reflected their pride and professionalism. Unique to the Air Cavalry community were colorful emblems, unit nicknames and call signs, cavalry dress, and aircraft markings.

The Army's elaborate system of wartime aircraft schemes and markings began at Ft. Benning, Georgia, with the formation of the 11th Air Assault Division in February 1963.

Among the mandates handed down from the Department of the Army was that division cadre generate new ideas and improve existing ones. Since marking of aircraft was one of the areas being explored, it was decided that special markings not only would make aircraft quickly identifiable to ground troops, but would bolster their relationship with air crews. Thus began a pattern of unit designators, which relied upon basic geometric shapes, especially the square, circle and triangle. The 1st Aviation Brigade in Vietnam and the 101st Airborne Division followed suit. The practice spread until identifiers appeared on nearly every Army aircraft that flew in Southeast Asia. Army aviation became so expansive in theatre that additional shapes were adopted, including inverted triangle, star, diamond, pentagon, vertical bands, arrow shapes and a cross; some were enhanced with numbers and graphics. Numbers, bands and emblems, which could represent any unit level, or multiples thereof, were applied at standardized locations on the aircraft. Many aircraft sported the time-honored emblems of their commands: crossed cannons represented artillery, while crossed yellow sabers and red and white shields and pennants were symbolic of cavalry commands. Eventually, a spotter's guide would be needed to identify the colorful and interesting array of identifiers.

One of the first steps in preparing Army aircraft for war was the 1965 directive that called for the glossy high-visibility scheme changed to a low-visibility livery. As lessons were learned, more markings of tactical necessity appeared later in the war. Aircraft that spent a good deal of time at low altitudes, the scout helicopter in particular, required markings that enabled crews of covering aircraft to keep them in sight. Accordingly, upper surfaces of rotor blades

In August 1969 Darkhorse loach pilot Chuck Davison was severely wounded when his OH-6A, S/N 68-17227, crashed almost on top of the North Vietnamese soldier who shot him. The badly damaged Loach was sling-loaded back to base, repaired and served C Troop, 16th Cavalry until 1972. Compared to other Darkhorse helicopters, Number 227 wore few markings, except for a cavalry pennant on the rotor pylon, or doghouse. This photo illustrates the OH-6A's tendency to remain intact even in severe crashes, although components such as tail booms, skid gear, and rotors came off the aircraft. In a crash, the OH-6A's tail boom and tail rotor were usually the first components to separate from the aircraft. Number 227's tail rotor drive shaft is visible inside the severed tail boom. (Hugh Mills)

OH-6A S/N 68-17365 wears the name *Electric Olive II* while assigned to C Troop, 16th Cavalry "Outcasts" of the 1st Infantry Division in February 1972. While with C/16, the Loach also wore the names *The Enforcer* and *Dark Death.* Stationed at Cần Thơ in 1972, The Outcasts were known for their colorful markings, including the popular shark mouth. More common to Cobra gunships, only two Scout units are known to have worn the toothy marking in Vietnam: C/16 and B Troop, 7th Squadron, 17th Cavalry. Loaches of C/16 often wore names above the rear cabin. Cavalry pennants, a reminder of the red and white guidons carried by U.S. horse cavalry units in the Indian Wars, were commonly worn by helicopters assigned to cavalry units in Vietnam. The pilots of this Loach are doing final instrument checks during run-up prior to departure. Instruments were generally not heavily relied upon in the AO, where pilots flew "outside the aircraft." (James Sheetz)

Aeroscout crewmen pose with *5th Dimension,* OH-6A S/N 68-17252 of C Troop, 1st Squadron, 9th Cavalry in Vietnam. Both crewmen hold grenades they are loading on the aircraft. After the war, Number 252 flew with the Army's "Silver Eagles" Flight Demonstration Team, the New York Army National Guard, the Riverside County, California Sheriff's Department, and, finally, ended up at the March Field Air Museum in the markings worn in the combat zone. Complete C/1/9 markings for the aircraft during the war included crossed cavalry sabers on the nose and engine doors, along with tail surfaces painted white. Those relatively few Loaches that survived the war went on to serve long careers in other organizations. (Nate Shaffer Collection)

This view of a White Team of A/7/1 illustrates the benefit of high visibility markings, such as white spines, orange tail sections and yellow rotor blade tips. Also common were stripes painted atop tail surfaces and upper surfaces of tail booms and rotor pylons painted white. (Bill Staffa)

received liberal applications of white paint, and the top surfaces of tail surfaces were painted orange. Some units painted the upper fuselage surfaces of Loaches white to make them more visible from above. In front-line units, often there wasn't time to change markings on aircraft that had been transferred, which created an interesting array of markings on some aircraft. Expectedly, for wartime, personal markings were in abundance, some of which not only were elaborate works of art, but covered a sizeable portion of the aircraft. To the delight of the historian, enthusiast, and modeler, it had become obvious that aircraft art in Vietnam eventually was limited only by the crewmembers' imagination, and, of course, unit policy.

Although familiar to the Cobra gunship, the sharkmouth, since it was closely associated with air cavalry, was worn by some Loaches. Older than Army aviation itself, the distinctive marking was written into legend by the American Volunteer Group's "Flying Tigers" of World War II. The leader of that group, then Col. Robert L. Scott, gave his blessings in 1966 to the 174th Assault Helicopter Company in Vietnam when they asked to adopt the marking for its gun platoon. Eventually, the majority of Cobra units in Vietnam, and two Scout units, adopted their own style of sharkmouth. The sharkmouth saw widespread use on all forms of equipment in Vietnam since it exploited the fears of the enemy, who called helicopters sporting the ferocious motif "Red-headed beasts."

Rescue

Because of the sanctity that Americans place on life, rescue became a byword of U.S. military air crews in Southeast Asia. In view of the hazardous nature of the Aeroscouts' work, and their sense of comradeship, that fact held especially true among their ranks. Some of these stories illustrate how every effort was expended to save downed crewmen. The enemy knew that tendency and exploited those efforts at every opportunity. Aeroscouts were keenly aware of the value the enemy placed on the capture or death of those who could wreak such havoc with the little helicopters. The favorable odds of being rescued did much for morale levels of Aeroscouts, especially since they knew the enemy had few POW camps in South Vietnam, and did not believe in the rules of the Geneva Convention.

Unfortunately, lessons from previous wars had not been learned and no rescue assets were in place at the onset of the Vietnam war. Rescue was, at best, an ad hoc affair, carried out by bloody trial and error. But as America waded deeper into the quagmire, the U.S. Air Force overhauled its Air Rescue Service (ARS) that had been established after World War II. A nuclear-war mindset, a global rescue concept, and budget constraints had forced the Air Rescue Service to lose most of its helicopters, despite the fact that helicopters had dominated the rescue experience in Korea. Although the ARS was the only U.S. military organization dedicated to rescue, its leaders had not planned for wartime missions in jungle and mountainous regions. Yet that was the awful scenario in which airmen operated when the Air Force had its hands full in Laos during the early 1960s. And combat pilots found no comfort in Washington's position that an air rescue force would only draw unwanted attention to U.S. military air operations in the then "Secret War."

Loaches lent themselves to ease of maintenance, including quick, simple removal of rotor blades. This convenience facilitated recovery of the aircraft in hostile territory and allowed at least one Loach to be flown out with only two of its four rotor blades. Here, Apache Aeroscout crewmen remove the blades of downed 66-17793 in preparation for its ride out below a Huey recovery aircraft. (Charlie Palek)

It would take the worsening situation in Vietnam, and much time and effort would have to be expended, before the helicopter again became the centerpiece of war. As the American presence in Vietnam grew and air operations intensified, existing helicopters were adapted and new turbine-powered types were acquired and pressed into service.

Meanwhile, all services shared the responsibility for rescue; unarmed Air Force helicopters designed for air base crash-rescue and fire-fighting penetrated enemy sanctuaries to rescue fliers, Navy plane-guard choppers launched from carriers, Marine Corps transport helicopters evacuated wounded, red crosses were painted on the first Army Hueys sent to Vietnam, and even CIA Air America helicopters rescued downed airmen. Eventually, a highly effective air rescue organization emerged within the U.S. Air Force, after having bolstered its forces, established doctrine, and deployed suitable aircraft.

Airmen who flew into harm's way had the morale-boosting solace of knowing that, should they go down, every effort would be

made to get them back. The enemy too was aware of such efforts and often used downed airmen as bait for the rescue forces they knew would come. A Mayday call summoned whatever resources were available within range, often before there was time to get an organized air rescue effort under way. It didn't matter from which service the rescuers came, only that they came. Often, trying to bring back air crew meant a massive effort, sometimes spanning days and involving lots of air and ground support. Regardless of the immensity of the rescue effort, no one ever questioned if the life of one man was worth it.

For the Aeroscout who found himself on the ground in enemy territory, his rescuer very likely was his wing man, or it could be the C & C Huey, or even the Cobra circling protectively overhead; it wasn't unusual for a downed crewmen to get a ride out clinging to the Cobra's open ammunition bay door. If a helicopter couldn't land, a rescue chopper with a cable hoist was summoned. Rescue helicopter crewmen who maintained a hover during a hoist operation shared the same degree of danger experienced by Aeroscouts in their low-

An OH-23G "Raven" rests atop a pad in South Vietnam. Units discovered that raised pads, constructed of pierced steel planking (PSP) and sandbags, reduced dust and debris during landing and takeoff, and kept the aircraft out of mud during monsoon season. (U.S. Army)

level environment. By 1967, the Army medical evacuation program, known as "Medevac" or "Dustoff," had evolved into an organized mission, with Dustoff crews forging their own proud history.

Although Aeroscouts commonly performed rescues, none was dedicated to the medevac mission. The rare exception was an OH-6A acquired in 1969 by the 326th Medical Battalion of the 101st Airborne Division. So many of the unit's Hueys were shot at while hoisting wounded in a hover that it was decided to try using a Loach. It was hoped that the OH-6A, with its small size, speed, and maneuverability, would fare better than a Huey in tight, dangerous areas. Despite the aircraft's capabilities and the skill and courage of its crew, on 17 August 1969, after only 20 missions, the only medevac Loach of the war was shot down and its crew killed.

Two Blades

The main rotor system that was needed to match the OH-6A's size, weight, and performance characteristics allowed use of the same blades used on the Hughes TH-55A Osage, already in production. Compared to the Osage's three blades, however, the Cayuse required four to handle blade loading and to minimize vibration. Quick-release lock pins allowed easy blade folding, making the aircraft transportable in large cargo aircraft.

It was the nature of military pilots to try things that were not covered in the manuals, and the Loach's amazing performance features only added to the temptation. So it was only a matter of time before someone tried to fly the aircraft with only two main rotor blades. In early 1970 the credit would go to Captain Tom "Preacher" Wiktorek of HHC, 1st Brigade, 1st Cavalry Division, called "Flying Circus." Wiktorek relates the details of his experiment:

"I was the maintenance officer, and after several Loach recoveries following shoot-downs and tree strikes, and flying a couple of scout missions myself, I wanted to know if our 'White Teams' could get

back if one of them had blades badly damaged in a still flyable aircraft.

"We went out to a small fire support base south-southwest of Nui Ba Dinh, where we always practiced autorotations into the rice paddy, which we weren't supposed to do. I took off two opposite blades, marked them, and had the crew guys sit there with fire extinguishers. I don't recall if I put the two large and one small pin back in their places. I had recorded the TOT, torque, etc. at hover prior to shutdown, and I was surprised there was no significant change with two blades at a hover. I do remember there was a little vibration as all the drag links situated when I started up, but it smoothed out quickly. I hovered, did a few pedal turns, flew a standard flight pattern at about 500 feet (all engine readings were normal), and landed and shut down and replaced the blades. I inspected the blades and hub and saw no obvious distortions or cracks. I was surprised that all the instrument readings were at or near normal during all the flight.

"That Loach flew regular missions after that, and I watched it and saw no irregularities. I wish I had kept a diary and had names and tail numbers. I do remember that a Hughes tech rep wanted me to repeat this flight for the reps in Saigon, but I refused; he promised to keep my identity a secret but I didn't want to get in trouble. He told me he won several bets with Bell reps when he got to the, 'Well, will yours fly if we take off two main rotor blades?' referring to Bell's OH-58."

When word of Wiktorek's achievement spread, the inevitable happened. A Loach crash-landed with a main rotor blade shattered by .50-cal. fire. Knowing that the enemy was closer than rescue forces, the crew quickly removed the useless blade and the one opposite. After dumping all excess weight, and with only half the rotor blades supposedly needed to fly, the pilot flew back to home base. The incident, its authenticity long held to conjecture, was confirmed by Hughes officials.

Scout Helicopter Units in Vietnam

Some artillery units in Vietnam had small contingents of scout helicopters, finding them useful for artillery spotting, reconnaissance and establishing links between remote sites. This OH-6A of 4th Infantry Division artillery is seen at Phù Cát AB in October 1970. (Norm Taylor)

The following are U.S. Army units in Vietnam known to have operated scout helicopters, in particular, the OH-6A Cayuse, better known as the Loach. The number of Loaches assigned, which ranged from one to 20, was based largely on the unit's function.

The sections and detachments of many units possessed small numbers of OH-6As, while front-line Aeroscout units were authorized 10, but usually averaged eight. Some large combat units were authorized as many as 18 Loaches. Many of these units operated OH-23G Raven and OH-13S Sioux Scout helicopters prior to the OH-6A's introduction. These units either ceased scout operations when the Loach appeared, or they used a mix of all three types until sufficient numbers of OH-6As were in country. A small number of units transitioned to the OH-58A Kiowa during the 1970s. Unit call signs and nicknames are given in chronological order of use.

OH-6A New Equipment Training Team (NETT)
U.S. Army Republic of Vietnam (USARV) Training Team
Command Airplane Company (CAC)
1st Brigade, Aviation Section, 1st Cavalry Division "Flying Circus"
1st Brigade, Aviation Section, 1st Infantry Division
1st Brigade, Aviation Section, 101st Airborne Division
1st Brigade, Aviation Section, 4th Infantry Division
1st Brigade, Aviation Section, 9th Infantry Division
1st Brigade, Aviation Section, 25th Infantry Division
1st Battalion, 92nd Artillery

1st Field Force, Vietnam
108th Artillery Group
11th Armored Cavalry Regiment, Air Cavalry Troop "White"
11th General Support (GS), 1st Cavalry Division
114th Assault Helicopter Company
116th Assault Helicopter Company
120th Aviation Company
121st Assault Helicopter Company
142nd Transportation Company
15th Maintenance Battalion, 1st Cavalry Division
15th Medical Battalion, 1st Cavalry Division
163rd Aviation Company (GS), 101st Airborne Division
165th Transportation Company
166th Transportation Detachment
173rd Airborne Brigade, Aviation Platoon ("Hot Stuff" OH-13S) "Inferno"
18th Engineering Brigade
196th Brigade, Aviation Detachment, 196th Infantry Division
198th Infantry Brigade
199th Brigade, Aviation Detachment, 199th Infantry Division
2nd Brigade, Aviation Section, 1st Cavalry Division
2nd Brigade, Aviation Section, 1st Infantry Division "Ghost Riders"
2nd Brigade, Aviation Section, 25th Infantry Division

2nd Brigade, Aviation Section, 4th Infantry Division

2nd Brigade, Aviation Section, 9th Aviation Battalion, 9th Infantry Division

2nd Battalion, 23rd Artillery Group

20th Engineering Brigade

20th Transportation Company

27th Maintenance Battalion, 1st Cavalry Division

201st Corps Aviation Company

25th Corps Aviation Company (Provisional), 212th Combat Aviation Battalion

25th Corps Aviation Company, 210th Combat Aviation Battalion "Red Carpet"

271st Assault Support Helicopter Company "Bartender"

3rd Brigade, Aviation Section, 1st Cavalry Division

3rd Brigade, Aviation Section, 1st Infantry Division

3rd Brigade, Aviation Section, 101st Airborne Division

3rd Brigade, Aviation Section, 4th Infantry Division

3rd Brigade, Aviation Section, 9th Infantry Division

3rd Brigade, Aviation Section, 25th Infantry Division/4th Infantry Division "Aloha Airlines"

3rd Brigade, Aviation Section, 82nd Airborne Division

3rd Squadron, 11th Armored Cavalry Regiment "Bandits"

3rd Military Police Battalion

303rd Transportation Company

307th Combat Aviation Battalion

326th Medical Battalion, 101st Airborne Division

330th Transportation Company

335th Aviation Company

355th Aviation Company

357th Transportation Company

388th Transportation Company

41st Artillery Group

45th Engineer Group

498th Medical Company

5th Aviation Detachment, 1st Aviation Brigade "Super Bee"

5th Transportation Battalion

5th Battalion, 22nd Artillery

5th Battalion, 27th Artillery

520th Transportation Battalion

54th Aviation Company

56th Transportation Company

58th Transportation Company

6th Battalion, 14th Artillery

604th Transportation Company

605th Transportation Company

608th Transportation Company

610th Transportation Company

611th Transportation Company

62nd Assault Helicopter Company

7th Support Battalion

7th Battalion, 15th Artillery

765th Transportation Battalion

79th Transportation Company

9th Air Cavalry Brigade (Provisional), 1st Cavalry Division

937th Engineering Group

A Company, 1st Aviation Battalion, 1st Infantry Division

A Troop, 1st Squadron, 9th Cavalry, 1st Cavalry Division "Peacemaker," "Apache," "White"

A Company, 9th Aviation Battalion, 9th Infantry Division "Jayhawk"

Company A, 101st Aviation Battalion, 13th Combat Aviation Battalion "Comanchero"

A Troop, 4th Squadron, 12th Cavalry, 1st Brigade, 5th Infantry Division

A Company, 123rd Aviation Battalion, 23rd Infantry Division

A Troop, 2nd Squadron, 17th Cavalry, 101st Airborne Division "Assault"

Company A, 229th Aviation Battalion, 1st Cavalry Division

A Troop, 3rd Squadron, 17th Cavalry, 1st Aviation Brigade "Silver Spur"

A Battery, 377th Artillery (Aviation), 101st Airborne Division "Gunner"

Company A, 4th Battalion, 4th Infantry Division

A Battery, 4th Battalion, 77th Field Artillery (Aerial Rocket), 101st Airborne Division

Troop A, 5th Transportation Battalion, 101st Airborne Division

A Troop, 7th Squadron, 1st Cavalry, 1st Aviation Brigade "Apache"

A Troop, 7th Squadron, 17th Cavalry, 1st Aviation Brigade "Bishop"

Air Cavalry Troop, 11th Armored Cavalry Regiment "White"

52nd Airlift Platoon, 52nd Aviation Battalion "Dragon"

B Company, 1st Aviation Battalion, 1st Infantry Division "Pony"

B Troop, 1st Squadron, 9th Cavalry, 1st Cavalry Division "Rough Rider," "Flashing Saber," "White"

B Company, 123rd Aviation Battalion, 23rd Infantry Division "Warlords," "Skeeter"

B Troop, 15th Transportation Company, 1st Cavalry Division

B Troop, 2nd Squadron, 17th Cavalry, 1st Aviation Brigade, 101st Airborne Division "Banshee"

B Company, 25th Aviation Battalion, 25th Infantry Division "Diamond Head"

B Troop, 3rd Squadron, 17th Cavalry, 1st Aviation Brigade "Stogie"

B Company, 4th Aviation Battalion, 4th Infantry Division "Gambler"

B Troop, 5th Transportation Company, 101st Airborne Division

B Troop, 7th Squadron, 1st Cavalry, 1st Aviation Brigade "Dutchmaster," Big Ugly"

B Troop, 7th Squadron, 17th Cavalry, 1st Aviation Brigade "Red," "Scalphunter"

B Company, 9th Aviation Battalion, 9th Infantry Division "Condor"

C Troop, 1st Squadron, 9th Cavalry, 1st Cavalry Division "Bold Avenger," "Brave Fighter," "Crimson Charger," "Phantom Raider," "Dashing Cavalier," "White"

C Troop, 15th Transportation Company, 1st Cavalry Division

C Troop, 16th Cavalry, 1st Infantry Division "Darkhorse," "Outcast"

C Troop, 2nd Squadron, 17th Cavalry, 101st Airborne Division "Condor"

C Company, 229th Aviation Battalion, 11th Aviation Group, 1st Cavalry Division

C Troop, 3rd Squadron, 17th Armored Cavalry Regiment

C Troop, 3rd Squadron, 17th Cavalry, 1st Aviation Brigade "Charlie Horse." "Kamikaze," "War Wagon"

C Troop, 7th Squadron, 1st Cavalry, 1st Aviation Brigade "Sandpiper," "Comanche"

C Troop, 7th Squadron, 17th Cavalry, 1st Aviation Brigade "Red," "Ruthless Rider"

D Troop, 1st Squadron, 1st Armored Division, 1st Cavalry Division "Saber"

D Troop, 1st Squadron, 1st Cavalry, 101st Airborne Division

D Troop, 1st Squadron, 10th Cavalry, 4th Infantry Division "Shamrock"

D Troop, 1st Squadron, 4th Cavalry, 1st Infantry Division "Outcast"

Company D, 158th Aviation Battalion, 101st Airborne Division

D Troop, 7th Squadron, 17th Cavalry "Saber" (ex D/3/5 and D/1/1)

D Troop, 2nd Armored Division, 1st Cavalry Division "Blackhawk"

D Company, 227th Aviation Battalion, 11th Aviation Group, 1st Cavalry Division

D Company, 229th Aviation Battalion, 11th Aviation Group, 1st Cavalry Division

D Troop, 3rd Squadron, 4th Cavalry, 25th Infantry Division "Centaur"

D Troop, 3rd Squadron, 5th Cavalry, 9th Aviation Battalion, 9th Infantry Division ("Spook" OH-23G) "War Wagon," "Kamikaze" (C/3/17 after 31 Jan. 1971)

Division Artillery, Aviation Detachment, 101st Airborne Division

Division Artillery, Aviation Section, 4th Infantry Division

Division Artillery, Aviation Section, 9th Infantry Division

Division Artillery, Aviation Section, 23rd Infantry Division

Division Artillery, Aviation Section, 25th Infantry Division

E Troop (Provisional), 1st Squadron, 9th Cavalry, 1st Cavalry Division "El Lobo," "White"

E Company, 725th Maintenance Battalion, 25th Infantry Division

E Battery, 82nd Artillery, 1st Cavalry Division "Woodpecker"

F Troop, 4th Cavalry, 12th Combat Aviation Group "Centaur"

F Troop, 8th Cavalry, 23rd Infantry Division (later 196th Infantry Brigade) "Red"

F Troop (Provisional), 1st Squadron, 9th Cavalry, 1st Cavalry Division "White"

F Troop, 9th Cavalry, 3rd Brigade, 1st Cavalry Division/H Troop, 16th Cavalry "Kill"

H Troop, 10th Cavalry, 17th Combat Aviation Group (ex F/8) "Red." "Rider"

H Troop, 16th Cavalry, 1st Cavalry Division, F/9 (ex B/1/9) "Saber"

H Troop, 17th Cavalry 11th Combat Aviation Group/Military Region II Acting Provisional
(ex B/7/17) "Scalphunter"

Headquarters & Headquarters Battery, 6th Battalion, 82nd Artillery

Headquarters & Headquarters Company, Aviation Detachment, 1st Brigade, 5th Infantry Division

Headquarters & Headquarters Company, 10th Combat Aviation Battalion

Headquarters & Headquarters Company, 2nd Brigade, 101st Airborne Division ("Tadpole" OH-23G)

Headquarters & Headquarters Company, 3rd Brigade, 101st Airborne Division

Headquarters & Headquarters Company, 11th Combat Aviation Group

Headquarters & Headquarters Company, 11th Light Infantry Brigade "Primo"

Headquarters & Headquarters Company, 12th Combat Aviation Group

Headquarters & Headquarters Company, 158th Aviation Battalion, 101st Airborne Division

Headquarters & Headquarters Company, 159th Aviation Battalion, 101st Airborne Division

Headquarters & Headquarters Company, 16th Combat Aviation Group

Headquarters & Headquarters Company, 1st Brigade, 1st Cavalry Division "Flying Circus"

Headquarters & Headquarters Company, 2nd Brigade, 1st Cavalry Division

Headquarters & Headquarters Company, 173rd Airborne Brigade "Inferno"

Headquarters & Headquarters Company, 227th Aviation Battalion, 1st Cavalry Division

Headquarters & Headquarters Company, 228th Aviation Battalion, 1st Cavalry Division

Headquarters & Headquarters Company, 229th Aviation Battalion, 1st Cavalry Division

Headquarters & Headquarters Company, 9th Aviation Battalion, 9th Infantry Division

Headquarters & Headquarters Company, 1st Combat Aviation Battalion

Headquarters & Headquarters Company, 212th Combat Aviation Battalion

Headquarters & Headquarters Company, 4th Aviation Battalion, 4th Infantry Division

Headquarters & Headquarters Detachment, 44th Engineer Group

Headquarters & Headquarters Troop, 1st Squadron, 1st Cavalry, 101st Airborne Division

Headquarters & Headquarters Troop, 1st Squadron, 9th Cavalry, 1st Cavalry Division "Long Knife"

Headquarters & Headquarters Troop, 11th Armored Cavalry Regiment

Headquarters & Headquarters Troop, 2nd Squadron, 17th Cavalry, 101st Airborne Division

Headquarters & Headquarters Troop, 3rd Squadron, 17th Cavalry, 101st Airborne Division

Headquarters & Headquarters Troop, 7th Squadron, 1st Cavalry, 1st Aviation Brigade

Headquarters & Headquarters Troop, 7th Squadron, 7th Cavalry, 1st Aviation Brigade

Headquarters, 173rd Airborne Brigade

Glossary

AC Aircraft Commander

ACR Air Cavalry Regiment

Across the fence cross-border operations into Cambodia and Laos

ACT Air Cavalry Troop

ACTIV Army Concept Team in Vietnam; a panel comprising military officers and civilian scientists that tested and evaluated equipment suitability for use in Vietnam

AFVN Armed Forces Vietnam radio station

AHC Assault Helicopter Company

AK AK-47 renowned 7.62mm Kalashnikov assault rifle

AO Area of Operations

APC Armored Personnel Carrier, usually the M-113

Arc Light code name for B-52 bombing missions

ARPs Cavalry Aerorifle Platoon infantry soldiers; also called "Blues"

ARS U.S. Air Force Air Rescue Service, which, in 1966, became the

ARRS for Aerospace Rescue and Recovery Service

ARVN Army Republic of Vietnam (South Vietnamese Army) pronounced "Arvin"

Autorotation a helicopter's ability to land safely with the engine out; the rotor system disengaged, allowing it to freewheel, thereby maintaining lift

BDA Bomb Damage Assessment; usually following a major airstrike

Bingo minimal fuel state sufficient to return to base

Blues Cavalry infantry troops of Aerorifle platoon; also called "ARPs"

C-4 Composition Four plastic explosive

CAG Combat Aviation Group

CAR-15 shortened version of M-16 rifle

Cav popular shortened version of Cavalry

C & C Command and Control; usually a UH-1D/H Huey helicopter carrying radio equipment and command officers to oversee a mission

CE Crew Engineer; more commonly called "Crew Chief"

Charlie slang for Viet Cong

Chicken Plate torso body armor, the chest protector insert of which was often used separately as armor plate

CO Commanding Officer of a unit

Collective helicopter pilot's control lever that controlled the amount of pitch in the main rotor blades; raising the lever increased pitch and subsequent lift; the collective was usually at the left of the pilot's seat and incorporated the throttle

CQ Charge of Quarters

CS tear gas; officially called "Riot Agent"

CTZ Corps Tactical Zone of which there were four geographically dividing Vietnam for military purposes; more commonly called "I Corps," "Two Corps," "Three Corps," " and "Four Corps"

CWO Chief Warrant Officer ranks two through four; usually termed "CW2," etc.

Cyclic control lever at front of helicopter pilot's seat, which controlled angle of main rotor disc and subsequent directional control

Dead Man Zone altitude between 100 and 3,000 feet at which it was especially hazardous to fly due to the range of small arms and anti-aircraft fire; considered the most hazardous was takeoff, when speeds were less than 60 knots and altitudes were less than 100 feet; the safety margin increased with speed and altitude

Density Altitude the combination of altitude, temperature, and humidity that adversely affected an aircraft's performance; Vietnam's high-density altitude severely taxed a helicopter's abilities

DEROS Date Eligible to Return from Overseas; commonly used in verb tense

DFC Distinguished Flying Cross

Di-di pronounced "dee-dee;" Vietnamese di-di mau meaning hurry

Dink slang for the enemy

DSC Distinguished Service Cross

Dustoff call sign used by Huey helicopters dedicated to evacuating casualties, often under perilous conditions; used interchangeably with "Medevac"

Eleven Bravo military occupational specialty designation 11B for infantryman; nicknamed "11 Bush" and "11 Bullet Stopper"

EM Enlisted Men of ranks up to sergeant

FAC Forward Air Controller; a small aircraft the pilot of which coordinated a mission and relayed radio traffic

FNG Fuckin' New Guy; often called a "Peter Pilot" among the pilot ranks

Frag fragmentation grenade; also used in verb tense

Freq radio frequency; also called "Push"

Front Seat the gunner/copilot's position of the AH-1G Cobra gunship; the gunner sat forward and slightly below the pilot in a tandem cockpit configuration

FSB Fire Support Base; also called "Fire Base" (FB); an artillery position, usually on high ground, that supported ground units in the area

Grunt widely used term for infantry soldier

Guard radio frequency reserved for emergency, which was monitored by all aircraft

Guns slang for any unit that flew helicopter gunships

Gunship a helicopter heavily armed for attack and direct support

HE High Explosive

Helo helicopter; a term more familiar to Navy personnel

Hootch an indigenous structure usually built of locally available material such as logs, bamboo, and palm thatch; sometimes used in reference to GI living quarters

Huey widely accepted nickname given the Bell UH-1 series helicopter, which, officially, was named the "Iroquois"

IFR Instrument Flight Rules that require a pilot to rely upon instruments to fly due to bad weather or darkness, as opposed to VFR

IP Instructor Pilot

JP-4 turbine engine jet fuel

KBA Kills By Air

KIA Killed In Action

Kit Carson Scout an enemy soldier who defected and served as a scout with U.S. ground troops; named after the legendary American frontiersman of the 1800s

Klick GI slang for kilometer; the metric system has long been is use by the U.S. military

Loach nickname for the Hughes OH-6A "Cayuse" helicopter, derived from LOH, for Light Observation Helicopter

LRRP pronounced "Lurp," Long Range Reconnaissance Patrol; a small team of highly trained and skilled infantrymen that probed enemy territory

LZ helicopter landing zone

MACV Military Assistance Command Vietnam, pronounced "Mac-Vee"

MASH Mobile Army Surgical Hospital

Mayday an internationally recognized distress call derived from the French m'aider, meaning "help me"

Medevac short for "Medical Evacuation;" used in conjunction with "Dustoff;" also used in verb tense

MIA Missing In Action

Mike also spelled "mic:" short for microphone; various positions of the mike switch permitted radio communication among crewmen, other aircraft, or ground units

Minigun common term for weapon systems incorporating the 7.62mm M134 multi-barrel machine gun based on the Gatling gun

MOS Military Occupational Specialty

Nails steel dart-like projectiles packed into a rocket warhead; used effectively as an anti-personnel weapon

NAS Naval Air Station

NCO also called "Noncom;" Non-Commissioned Officer ranks from Corporal to Command Sergeant Major; also called "Hard Stripe," inferring leadership responsibility as opposed to Specialist rank

NETT New Equipment Training Team

Nomex fire retardant flight clothing

NVA North Vietnamese Army; called "Sir Charles" to distinguish its more highly trained and organized soldiers from Viet Cong

Oscar slang for Aeroscout observer; also called "Torque"

PE aircraft periodic inspection and maintenance, scheduled according to amassed flight hours

PIC Pilot in Command

Pink Team observation helicopter and gunship paired as a Hunter-Killer team, derived from the mixing of their representative cavalry colors, white and red

PJ U.S. Air Force parajumper, later called "Pararescueman;" highly trained and skilled rescue specialist who was flight crew member aboard rescue aircraft

POL Petroleum, Oil, Lubricant; a fueling site that usually also served as an arming site

PSP Pierced Steel Planking; steel perforated interlocking panels that served as runways, taxiways, and aircraft parking areas

Pucker Factor unsavory slang term used to emphasize fear factor; alluded to tightening of sphincter muscle as a result of stress and anxiety

Purple Team a grouping of scout, lift, and gunship helicopters, derived from the mixing of their representative cavalry colors, white, blue, and red

Push slang for radio frequency

Red Team a grouping of gunship helicopters

Red-X a condition indicating that an aircraft is unflyable; a red X was entered in an aircraft's log book; sometimes used in verb tense

Revetment side walls designed to protect an aircraft in its parking space; constructed of various available materials that could withstand small arms fire, rockets, and mortars; construction materials included PSP, sandbags, sand-filled aircraft component shipping containers, and 55-gallon drums

RPG Rocket Propelled Grenade, often the Soviet-built RPG7

Short GI slang for having little time left of tour in country; any

number of days less than 100 resulted in the term "two-digit midget"

SIP Senior Instructor Pilot or Standardization Instructor Pilot

Sir Charles North Vietnamese Army

Sitrep Situation Report, usually given over the radio

Slick a UH-1D or UH-1H Huey helicopter used for troop transport and void of heavy weapon systems

Smoke a smoke grenade used for marking positions or targets, or for checking wind direction; colors were red, green, yellow, and purple

Snake the Bell AH-1G Cobra gunship

SOP Standard Operating Procedures

Spec Specialist rank at non-commissioned officer level, but without leadership responsibility; also called "Sp4," etc.

Superbomb homemade ordnance concocted by helicopter crewmen; usually combined C-4, a grenade and various types of shrapnel material such as nails; used against targets such as structures, vehicles, and bunkers

TACAN Tactical Air Navigation; a system that gives pilots information as to their range and bearing from a beacon

Tac Air tactical air support; usually Air Force, Navy, and Marine fighter bomber aircraft

Tech Rep shortened form of Technical Representatives, who were civilian employees of firms that built military equipment; often they were in Southeast Asia to consult, evaluate, and oversee their firm's hardware

The Trail Ho Chi Minh Trail, which was the enemy's major ground supply route from North Vietnam to units in the south; this was an extensive, heavily defended system of roads and trails, much of which wound through Laos in violation of that nation's neutrality

The Wall the Vietnam Memorial at Washington, D.C.

Ti-ti pronounced "tee-tee," Vietnamese meaning small amount

TOC Tactical Operations Center

Top the highest ranking NCO of a unit, usually holding the rank of First Sergeant or Command Sergeant Major

Torque Aeroscout observer; also called an "Oscar;" also refers to the level of mechanical stress placed upon a helicopter transmission and rotor system

TOT Turbine Outlet Temperature; an instrument panel gauge that indicated if an engine was running excessively hot

Thumper various versions of the 40mm grenade launcher weapon, so called due to its distinctive sound when fired; the most common types were the M79 infantry weapon and 40mm turret found on helicopter gunships; also called the "Chunker" and "Forty Mike-Mike"

USARV United States Army, Republic of Vietnam

VC Viet Cong, Vietnamese for "Vietnamese Communist;" also called "Charlie," "Victor Charlie," and "Mr. Charles;" often accurately referred to as "farmers by day and fighters by night"

VFR Visual Flight Rules; optimal daylight flying conditions with weather that allowed a pilot to use geographic references

VR Visual Reconnaissance

White Team a grouping of scout helicopters

Willie Pete white phosphorous round or grenade usually used for marking targets; also called "WP" or "Willie Peter"

WO Warrant Officer; first WO grade termed WO1 or "Wobbly One"

WOC Warrant Officer Candidate; U.S. Army pilot trainee

XO Executive Officer; second in command of a unit; normally the next lower position was the operations officer